10,001 WAYS TO LIVE LARGE ON A SMALL BUDGET

BY THE WRITERS OF WISE BREAD

#1 PERSONAL FINANCE BLOG

Skyhorse Publishing

Skyhorse Publishing books may be purchased in bulk at special discounts for sales promotion, corporate gifts, fund-raising, or educational purposes. Special editions can also be created to specifications. For details, contact the Special Sales Department, Skyhorse Publishing, 555 Eighth Avenue, Suite 903, New York, NY 10018 or info@skyhorsepublishing.com.

www.skyhorsepublishing.com

10 9 8 7 6 5 4 3 2

It is always the responsibility of the individual to assess his or her own capabilities (fitness, financial, and so on) before starting any activity. While every effort has been made to ensure the contents of this is as technically accurate as possible, neither the authors nor the publishers can accept responsibility for any injury or loss sustained as a result of the use of this material.

Library of Congress Cataloging-in-Publication Data

10,001 ways to live large on a small budget / by the writers of Wise Bread.
    p. cm.
 Includes bibliographical references and index.
 ISBN 978-1-60239-704-0 (alk. paper)
 1. Finance, Personal. I. Wise Bread (Firm) II. Title: Ten thousands one ways to live large on a small budget.
 HG179.A195 2009
 332.024--dc22

                                    2009002328

Printed in China

To our friends and family: Your love and support make us the richest people in town.

To the readers and contributors of Wise Bread: Your amazing stories of frugal ingenuity inspire us on a daily basis. This book is for you.

—

Contents

$$$$

Intro-
duction

Too many books on frugal living focus on the negative, throwing around words like sacrifice and responsibility as if there'd been a fire sale at the Boring Store.

We believe the key to financial wellness isn't a ramen-eating, vacation-skipping, fun-deprived life. In fact, we love to indulge in life's pleasures whenever we can—just as long as they fit into our budget. The best way to stick to a budget, especially in tough economic times, is to create a lifestyle that is as much fun as it is practical. Are you ready to live large within your means, no matter how small they may be?

This book will show you how. We are the writers of WiseBread. com—one of the most popular (and certainly the friendliest) personal finance communities online. We come from a rich array of backgrounds. Among our ranks are financial consultants, homemakers, journalists, career counselors, professors, and even professional hobos! Together, we will bring you the best tips based on our personal experiences, as well as savvy advice from other top financial gurus around the Web.

While many personal finance tips focus on a one-size-fits-all approach, we understand that no two people are exactly alike. We enjoy different hobbies, maintain unique relationships, and care for our finances in ways that are relevant to our own lives. With our rich diversity of tips for living large on a small budget, we are certain you can find what you need here, regardless of where you are in life. And if you crave more, you can get daily tips on WiseBread.com, or join the conversation in our community at WiseBread.com/forums.

Financial freedom is about making choices that are important to you, so you won't get a constant lecture from us of "Don't buy this" or "Keep your money at home." Your money is yours, and the decisions you make are yours, as well. We hope that by getting a hint or two from us, you can have more of it to enjoy!

PART ONE

Frugal Living

Frugal used to be a dirty word, reserved only for those who reused paper plates and refused to tip at restaurants.

Now that saving money is a trendy subject, gracing the front pages of nearly every major magazine and newspaper, frugality is finally catching on.

You won't catch us telling you how to painfully squeeze the last drop out of everything in life. We won't be suggesting that cheap is synonymous with thrifty. In fact, if you are living a truly frugal lifestyle, you'll only appear to be paying top dollar for the finer things in life, even as your wallet stays fat and happy.

We want to guide a new generation of money-conscious readers—one that oozes class, loves having fun, and knows that life is exactly what you make of it (and not how much you make).

We'll tackle food, entertainment, health, and education. And of course, we'll share the best ways to shop with what you have, not what you wish you had. By finding like-minded friends to share your frugal lifestyle, you won't be missing out on a thing. (Except maybe that high-balance credit card bill.)

FOOD & DRINK

If variety is the spice of life, then we should strive to create flavorful alternatives even on the smallest grocery budget. Finding the inspiration to prepare three or more meals a day can be difficult enough without the added task of trying to keep things affordable and authentic. That's why we've dedicated a large portion of this book to food, from its purchase and preparation to its presentation. Budding chefs and professionals alike can take something away from this collection of practical tips and tricks.

6 Simple Tips for Buying Great Affordable Wine

On a budget? Not wanting it to get in the way of a great wine and food pairing? Help is on the way. I was able to convince award-winning wine consultant Brad Haskel of London Lennies restaurant (LondonLennies.com) to share some of his inside industry knowledge.

Shopping for good wine without background knowledge can be intimidating. Everybody wants great flavor and good value, but where do you start? Wandering through the aisles of my friendly wine and spirits store with that "deer in the headlights" look has been my approach in the past. I don't recommend it, however, particularly in this economy. Dishing out for a special dinner or dessert wine when pennies are dear can feel like a major investment, and nobody wants to feel let down by an uninformed choice. Here are six simple recommendations from Brad.

1. Search out hidden gems

Look for wines from lesser-known regions like Argentina, Austria, Greece, South Africa, Israel, and Long Island. The world of wine is packed with terrific offerings that are sold at great prices. Some of the best values are not from the uber-trendy regions, but the countries and regions that focus on sustainability over commercial wine production. Undiscovered regions produce some of the world's best wines, inflated price tag not included.

2. Trick of the trade

Read the back label. Wine importers are often listed on the back labels of wine bottles, so seeking out the ones you trust is one simple trick that even the professionals use to make smart selections. Some of the more popular importers that offer great wines at bargain prices are Robert Kacher Selections, Winebow, Kermit Lynch, Michael Skurnik, Terry Theise, and Polaner.

3. Know your wine type

Do some research on your personal tastes. Do you like oaked or unoaked wines? Do you prefer full- or medium-bodied wines? Do you enjoy off-dry or dry wines? These simple indicators will help your sommelier and/or wine retailer identify great-value wines that will suit your tastes and your wallet.

4. Keep it in the family

For many great wine producers, wine making is the family business. Expertise and traditions are passed down for generations, so following a wine producer's "family tree," particularly for the new or special labels, is one way to find great-value wines that are created in a style you trust. Bill Arbios, winemaker for Lyeth Vineyards in Sonoma County, is an excellent example. After many years with Lyeth, Bill has branched out with his wife to create two smaller labels: Arbios and Praxis. His knowledge of the Sonoma region and his relationship with superior growers make it a likely bet that his new wines will be as good as his old, only sold for a fraction of the price.

5. Blind date

Host a blind tasting featuring wines from a single region. Lining up wines from a specific region, without regard to price, can be an eye-opening exercise. Oftentimes, high prices are more an indicator of a winery's real estate value than the quality of the wine it produces. It pays to explore the wide array of styles and producers that a region has to offer, rather than simply chasing the big names. You are more likely to find your perfect match. This would make a nice activity to do with more people—make a party out of it.

6. Grape gurus know best

Restaurants and retailers that specialize in boutique producers are your best resource for value wine suggestions. Boutique wineries offer some of the best value/quality ratios out there, but these wines are often limited and hard to find. Boutique-savvy wine retailers are never short on suggestions of new wines to try. Simply have a producer, style, or region that you like in mind and let the experts pair you with your perfect wine.

— **Myscha Theriault**

7 Things to Do With Inexpensive Wine

Want to add a little class to your meal? It doesn't have to cost a fortune to add a little wine to your recipes. Pick up some inexpensive Two Buck Chuck or boxed wine and you're well on your way to adding a little bit of elegance to your table without breaking the bank.

1. Mulled wine

I love strolling through the Christmas markets in Europe and drinking this stuff. It smells oh so fabulous and tastes yummy. Since it's mixed with so many other items, it's kind of expected that you won't use an expensive wine anyway. Either whites or reds can be used, and a simple Internet search can snag you a huge selection of affordable recipes.

2. Fruit salad glaze

Instead of using whipped topping or mixing up gelatin, whisk honey with white or red wine until it makes a bit of a glaze and add ground cinnamon to taste. Toss fresh chopped fruit like apples, grapes, or peaches with perhaps a few chopped walnuts and then coat with the glaze. This is a nice light after-meal treat with a fair amount of punch.

3. Sangria

As with mulled wine, using the cheap stuff is expected. You can make sangria with either red or white wine; add fruit juice and some sliced fruit. A sparkling sangria is also achievable by simply adding a bit of seltzer.

4. Marinades

I'm sure there are a ton of recipes out there for this, but a simple cheap one that I've gotten lots of compliments on uses just plain boxed white wine, honey, and rosemary. You can whisk this up to your own desired consistency. It's really great with chicken breasts.

5. Salad dressings

Whisking reduced red wine with olive oil, salt, pepper, and Dijon mustard makes an elegant salad dressing.

6. Spritzers

Mix wine with plain or flavored seltzer water to make a spritzer. This stuff is great because it has no calories, no sodium, and no aspartame.

7. Gourmet cooking on the cheap

Beef bourguignon, coq au vin, champagne and wine jellies, pot roast jazzer-upper . . . it's really up to you. The point is, there is absolutely no reason to spend major bucks on wine that's just going to end up in the cooking pot. — **Myscha Theriault**

12 Affordable Ingredients That Add Gourmet Flair to Any Meal

Does the ingredient list from that snazzy Food Network dish leave you feeling a bit underpaid and overwhelmed? Are you doubtful that your local grocer will ever carry per-simmons? Here is an expert list of a dozen common ingredients that will add some flair to your dish—for less than you'd expect.

1. Roasted garlic

I'm guilty of doctoring my garlic bread with that generic garlic salt from the dollar store. But Jeff Swedarsky, founder of DCMetroFoodTours.com, insists that you have to go fresh for the best flavor. Cut whole garlic cloves in half before oven roasting, and replace the stuff in the bottle completely. "It's a little more tame," says Jeff, "but it gives authentic gourmet flavor."

2. Greek yogurt

Jeff also suggests using this healthy alternative to sour cream. It has a richer, more complex taste, and it still looks fabulous as a topper.

3. Romaine, red leaf, and other "fancy" lettuces

Sure, the iceberg is usually what's on sale, but does that make it the best choice? Susan Palmquist, who blogs at The Budget Smart Girl's Guide to the Universe (BudgetSmartGirl.com), doesn't mind "spending an extra 20 cents for something like a romaine or red leaf. Think about what's going to be the star of the dish, what ingredient are you going to be tasting more than any other, and allocate more of your food dollar to that item. If the salad is just a side dish, the iceberg might work, but if the salad's going to be your main course, go with a lettuce with more texture, more bulk, and more flavor."

4. Kalamata olives

These are just delish. I like to eat them straight out of the container, but Michele Samuels, a public relations consultant, mom, and wife, has some even better ideas. She uses them to adorn salads, enhance a pasta sauce, dress up sandwiches, and garnish potato salads!

5. Capers

Seriously? I didn't even know what a caper was before I worked in a restaurant. After I learned of the odd little ingredient, however, I was hooked! Michele also loves the tiny flower buds, using them atop bagels and cream cheese and egg salads.

6. Dried beans

When you sacrifice convenience, you are often rewarded with flavor and savings! According to Anna Broadway, author of *Sexless in the City* (and a writer who spent nearly two years in Brooklyn eating on $50/week or less for food and transit), soaking and cooking them yourself will take extra time, but a 1 lb. bag of dried beans is a better buy. There is also a marked improvement in the flavor of the beans.

7. Sun-dried tomatoes

Many foodies claim that adding a few will bring impressive flavor to any dish. Blogger Stephen Bertasso dries his own, adding that the surplus of last season's fresh tomatoes are perfect as a dried ingredient in pastas, meats, and breads.

8. A ball of whole-milk mozzarella

This creamy alternative to prepackaged, already-shredded mozzarella comes recommended by Laura at EatingWellAnywhere.com. The higher fat content gives it a dreamy consistency and flavor.

9. Shallots

This was an overlooked ingredient at my home. Until I accidentally planted a batch in my garden, I was unaware of the flavor and texture these little guys can bring to an ordinary recipe. Chuck Wilkins, of Reston, Virginia, agrees. After reading Anthony Bourdain's *Kitchen Confidential,* Chuck began to live by shallots. "They are inexpensive and their flavor is so much lighter and more complex than ordinary onions."

10. Citrus zest

Nothing gives your dishes a zip like the zest of oranges, lemons, and limes. Jill Nussinow, The Veggie Queen (TheVeggieQueen.com), calls it the "bonus ingredient" because you also get to use the juice!

11. Toasted nuts

Just about any nut can add some crunch and depth to your recipes. Julie Languille, of DinnersInAFlash.com, favors toasted hazelnuts, pine nuts, and almonds. She suggests adding a few tablespoons to salad and pasta for an extra special treat!

12. Bulk dried spices

The little spice containers from your local grocer aren't the best deal you could be getting (and their freshness is questionable). Stu Lustman, an equipment and tech leasing broker, buys his favorite five or six dried spices in bulk to save money. They are perfect for rubs, but Stu also uses them in the same way as fresh herbs and spices. The trick? He pan-fries them slightly in a little oil to open up the flavor and adds them directly to his recipe.

This is by no means an exhaustive list of all the simple ingredients you can use to liven up your cooking, but it's a good place to start. Take a few and begin adding some lively and authentic flavor to your dishes. It won't cost you as much as you think!

— **Linsey Knerl**

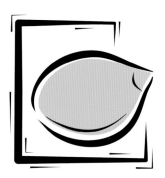

8 Tips for Bridging the Gap from Dining Out to Eating In

Though I never had any problems skimping on housing and transportation, my line was drawn on nourishment. It is a huge leap from eating out for many meals as a busy professional to cooking nearly every meal in an established household. Here are my strategies for bridging that gap.

1. Eat lunch out with these caveats: Get a vegetable plate or something reasonably healthful (entree with two veggies); don't get something that you can fix easily at home such as pizza or spaghetti.
2. Have a light dinner (salad, soup, and/or sandwich) on the days you eat your lunches out. Those are inexpensive to prepare at home and very easy to make. You'll save on your energy bill by cooking and washing dishes less.
3. Eat at home even if you don't cook at home. You'll develop the habit of taking the time to sit down sometime before 8:00 PM (hopefully) to enjoy a meal. And it's easier to split a large restaurant meal or Chinese takeout at home.
4. Snack before dinner. The snack won't ruin your dinner and it will help you have the energy to cook.
5. Buy high-quality prepared foods from retail caterers; you'll get a home-cooked meal at less than restaurant prices and reinforce the fun of eating at home.
6. Take a cooking class. I took classes at my community college and learned how to wash spinach and cook a roast. My instructor was the expert who could diagnose reasons for cooking failures and offer reasonably priced substitutions for unusual, budget-busting ingredients.
7. Try new recipes on the weekends or days you get home early. If a recipe takes a while (the prep time in cookbooks underestimates time by at least 50%), then you won't be starved come

dinnertime; start around 4:00 PM and you should be fine. At some point, you'll learn that spaghetti with meat sauce and a roast (buy an eye-of-round roast, put it in the Crock-Pot with cream of mushroom soup and/or dried onion soup mix, cook on low for 4–6 hours) takes far less time than you think.

8. Rename your creations: At my house, a burned entree might become blackened chicken.

— **Julie Rains**

7 Ways to Brown-Bag It with Style

Finding time to pack your lunch for work each day can feel pretty overwhelming. Trying to be creative about it can be even more frustrating. Following are ideas to help you get started, and stay psyched, about joining the brown-bag movement.

1. Large batch items

This can work well if you have several small containers to pack up ahead of time and toss in with your other lunch items. The smaller plastic containers or a small thermos from the thrift store are helpful items. Zingy pasta salad, chili, soup, quiche, fried rice, pizza, tabouleh, pancit or lo mein noodle dishes are some ideas for large batch items to round out your lunch repertoire.

2. Pre-pack some "grab and takes"

"Grab and takes" is the term we use in our house for those little extras that are easily eaten at your desk, on the run, or in the car. One of my favorites is the large packages of restaurant-style tortilla chips from the bulk warehouse stores. They are easy to break down into pint or snack-size resealable containers. They are also much sturdier than regular tortilla chips and hold up to some seriously sturdy dips. Popcorn, roasted almonds, homemade trail mix, pretzels (chocolate-coated

or otherwise), bargain store cheese and cracker combos by the case, dried fruit, raisin, and sunflower kernel mixture, and dried cereals are other ideas.

3. Finger foods

This strategy really goes a long way toward breaking up the monotony of the traditional bag lunch. Finger food is also great for those who don't have a long break for lunch and need to be nibbling on it in stages throughout the day. Consider hard-boiled eggs, cold chicken drumsticks, home made version "lunchables," pinwheel appetizer-style sandwiches (tortillas rolled up with your favorite filling spread and sliced into rounds works great for this), and self-cut string cheese snacks from bulk block mozzarella. Ham and cheese cubes you can snag with a toothpick are also great for cutting carbs as well as for schoolchildren who like to try something different.

4. Celebrate your sandwich

Let's face it. Tuna salad, while affordable, just really doesn't cut it long term. Neither does PB&J. I'm not saying there's anything wrong with those sandwich selections. But most people (including myself) will not stick with the "take my lunch to work" resolution if they get bored too quickly. If you grow your own basil, caprese sandwiches can be quite affordable. Another one is zatyr with olive oil as a spread, combined with mozzarella and roma tomatoes. A little curry powder in with your chicken salad can really help a lot, as can a pinch or two of horseradish. Alternative greens to lettuce (spinach, basil, radicchio, etc.) and homegrown sprouts can also help. A break from the traditional mayo for a spread can keep you motivated as well (think hummus or mashed avocado). Try a wrap, a roll, or a different grain entirely if you are bored with your regular white bread.

5. Dunkin' and dippin' combos

I'm partial to this, because I'm a dunker from way back. In addition to the age-old carrots and peanut butter, here are a few ideas you may not have thought of. Tortilla chips with salsa, guacamole, or ranch sauce. Celery with a multi-ingredient cream cheese spread (think smoked salmon or pineapple). Mini cocktail meatballs with sweet and sour dip. Pita-bread chips with hummus. There are many fun combos to keep your interest in brown bagging.

6. Romancing the stone

Make it sexy and you'll have a better chance of sticking with it. If some of the more elaborate ingredients are out of your budget reach, try keeping picnic supplies packed in your lunch bag (fabric napkin, sarong, good book). You can hit the park if there's one near your workplace. You could also try organizing a weekly or monthly potluck lunch at work, or a brown-bag buffet of simple sandwich items. Sign people up for ingredients like lunch meat, green peppers, sliced cheese, whatever. It's just important that everyone gets on board and commits to their assigned item.

7. Brown-bag theater

Make it a special event for coworkers who bring lunch. Decide on a time, and if there's a TV in the lunchroom, pick a show to follow. That'll give everyone a little extra motivation not to miss any fun by going out for lunch. Also, this could act as a support group, bringing a social aspect to a frugal lifestyle choice.

There's nothing wrong with adding a little spice to the brown-bag experience. It's one of the most powerful cash-carving strategies, and if shaking it up a little is what will help you stick with the habit, go for it.

— **Myscha Theriault**

How to Save a Bundle with Assembly Cooking

Bulk cooking, once-a-month cooking (OAMC), assembly cooking . . . whatever you call it, the concept remains the same: doing a certain amount of prep work in advance in order to enjoy the convenience of meals on the fly later. While many retail options exist for this technique, the financial and flexibility benefits of tackling it at home can be significant. This article covers the strategies and infrastructure you will need.

WHAT YOU NEED

As with bulk buying and freezer saving, once-a-month cooking (OAMC) or bulk assembly cooking requires a certain number of tools and infrastructure items. Here are a few that have enabled me to keep the bulk-cooking ball rolling.

Resealable freezer bags

The items you'll be preparing will need to be stored in various amounts, so have a range of sizes, from one gallon all the way down to pint and snack-sized.

Masking tape

Certain containers may not have a labeling space. Masking tape is an inexpensive solution.

Permanent marker

Personally, I'm a Sharpie fan from way back, but if you have another favorite brand, go with what you know. These give you an easy way to label and date whatever is in your small containers. The finer the tip, the more information you can fit on a small piece of masking tape.

Tupperware

I recommend having a variety of sizes, like the freezer bags. Depending on whether you are bulk-prepping pizza sauce or coq au vin, you will need a corresponding size of storage container. These are also way easier to wash out and reuse, enabling you to keep bag waste to a minimum.

Extra large airtight containers

This might seem like a repeat of the above item, but when it comes to some of the dry ingredient mixes, making one to five gallons at a time will really make it worth your time. If you are in extreme penny-pinching mode, your empty gallon mayo jugs or extra large pickle jars will store homemade baking mix and dry cream soup base just fine.

Time

You need to reserve a block of time to do the assembly cooking.

Canning jars

Cool home craft projects aside, these things are cheap and allow for quick, safe storage of hostess gifts, homemade jams, and various other things. Stock up. You'll be glad you did.

Metal baking pans with lids

These are best when making something to bring to a party. There are permanently reusable ones if the disposable option bothers you. Personally, I try to keep these to a minimum, but do allow myself a supply for events. They can go immediately into the oven, and I don't have to worry about remembering my pan if I take something to a friend's house.

Ice cube trays

This strategy is fantastic for easy once-a-month food prep. Baby food, curry pastes, pizza sauce, and home-made soup stocks are all easily frozen and thawed for use using the ice cube tray strategy. If you only want to buy a half dozen or so, freeze your selected stock, paste, or puree and then empty the cubes into a gallon freezer bag or reusable container.

Freezer(s)

Not all bulk-prep items require a freezer, but many do. If you've already embraced freezer savings as a personal finance strategy, then as-sembly cooking (at least the freezer variety) will be a quicker transition for you. If you have an upright, great! If not, and a chest freezer is what you've purchased, stay organized and disciplined about the freezer space.

CATEGORIES

While many resources focus on the freezer variety of batch cooking, there are other categories. Here are what I see as the four main areas, and ideas for putting them to use.

Dry mixes and spice blends

Whether you go with make-ahead bread mixes, DIY spice blends for meat rubs and baking, or like to make your own giant batches of dry ingredient mixes for baking mix, dry soup base, pizza crust, and more, many options are out there for saving money. If you are still saving for a large freezer, this is an excellent OAMC category to start out with.

Canning

Whether you choose recipes suited for the water-bath technique, do your own oven sealing for home-made glazed and roasted nuts, or experiment with more technically advanced pressure-canning recipes, this can save you major cash. It's also another way people without a freezer can participate with advance meal prep. Canning spaghetti sauce instead of freezing is a good example.

Dry ingredient kits

Whether you like the do-ahead kits for Asian coleslaw, small bags of texturized vegetable protein (TVP) and taco seasoning, brown-bag-grab-and-take lunch snacks, or make-your-own hamburger and tuna helper kits, dry ingredient make-aheads also don't need a freezer and can be stored in containers in a cupboard.

Freezer cooking

Casseroles, appetizers, certain desserts, fun restaurant knockoffs, and dinner entrees galore can all be prepared ahead of time for the freezer. Spend some time recipe researching. You'll be amazed at the phenomenal ideas out there.

SHORTCUTS AND STRATEGIES

Without a few tricks up your sleeve, once-a-month cooking can be far too daunting for the rookie frugalite. I think I am pretty hard-core, and before I gave myself permission to honor my own style and family scheduling needs, this process nearly did me in. I thought if I was going to embrace this concept, I had to do it the way all the hard-core once-a-month folks did it or it was somehow not valid. Hogwash. Get in there, figure out what works for you, and streamline it in a way that makes sense for you and your family. Here are a few ideas to help get you started.

A mix-and-match approach to storage

Different containers work better or worse for different things, and while I would love to be one of those eco-goddesses who can pull this system off with nothing but reused bread bags, it's just not realistic for me. Using a consistent yet varied selection of storage options helps me utilize the fruits of my bulk-cooking system.

Batch-size flexibility

While many people approach this from a perspective of family-sized meal storage, smaller portions are helpful for singles or families where scheduling may inhibit sit-down meals from time to time. Having a variety of stored batch sizes provides maximum flexibility.

Precision purchases of small appliances

While the right tools (or lack thereof) can make or break your OAMC experience, going nuts on the gadget front can really cut into the savings you are trying to achieve. Take the time to figure out your personal cooking style as well as what items you'll be making regularly. You'll be able to make much more informed decisions that way.

Assembly-line production

This is great for the packaging of your selected OAMC menus, but it can also work for the actual creation of the mixtures. Quiches and restaurant knockoff dips come to mind, as do several dry ingredient kit ideas. Give it a whirl.

The time factor

Taking two to three days a month to get the job done is a popular newbie approach. If you find you are one of the few people who can keep this up month after month without having a nervous breakdown, congratulations! Taking on too much in the beginning and ending up in tears at hour thirteen is no way to feel warm and fuzzy about assembly cooking. Believe me, I've tried it. Develop a system that works for you in order to be consistent.

Go flat

If you've been assembly-cooking at home for a while now, this may seem like sort of a no-brainer to you. But you'd be surprised at the number of people who whip up large batches of pasta sauce, only to bag it up and toss it on a freezer shelf. Ever try to pry a bag of spaghetti sauce from a shelf after it has frozen haphazardly around the various wire rungs? Not a good way to psych yourself up for a second round. If you are using the freezer bags for the bulk of your perishable freezer meals, fill each about three- quarters full, seal the bags, and then stack them flat. Once they are frozen, you can either keep them there and pull from the stack, or stack them vertically and grab individual

bags like you would folders from a medical shelf. Slick.

Sex it up

As with bulk buying, it helps to set yourself up for success. Include some gourmet entrees the first month, do some fun mozzarella stick appetizers, or try some DIY pull-apart cookie dough. Some of my favorites are eggplant parmesan and knockoff versions of dips and appetizers from various popular chain restaurants.

The container principle

Also great for successful small space living, this is a strategy for implementing assembly cooking into your repertoire of money-saving magic tricks. In the case of snack-sized bagged items or dry ingredient kits, putting all of the bags into a larger container or gallon-sized zipper bag is helpful. A similar concept could be applied to make-ahead bread mixes.

Themed prep sessions

This is basically where you do massive meal prepping based on an abundance of a particular item. For example, if potatoes go on sale, you could make mountains of mashed potatoes and save the scooped-out prebaked potato skins in freezer bags for a DIY appetizer later on. Snag a once-a-year sale on chicken breast? Go nuts with two or three bulk recipes that you can grab out of the freezer for dinner on the fly later on.

Flash freezing

This is particularly important for individual items you want to serve in a batch, but don't want sticking together in the freezer container. You'll need to set aside a free shelf at least temporarily. Space out the items on a cookie sheet and freeze rock-solid. Then transfer in family- or appetizer-size amounts to the appropriate storage item. A few ideas where this comes in handy include homemade chicken drumsticks, breaded veal portions, mozzarella sticks, and frozen breaded eggplant slices.

Start small and simplify

Breaking down large cans of cheese sauce and jalapenos into small containers of simple nacho dip, and doing bagged, flat-frozen, large-batch leftovers can go further than you think. One giant batch of spaghetti sauce can easily result in at least a dozen gallon-sized flat-frozen freezer bags. That translates to three months' worth of having one night off from dinner per week. If you take even one of those nights to whip up a few large batches of dry mixes, you'll really be on a roll.

— **Myscha Theriault**

4 Small Kitchen Gadgets that Equal Big Savings!

Here are four nifty appliances for the kitchen that can keep things cheap and simple at your home. Plus, learn how to get some of them for way below retail value.

....

1. The bread machine

....

I have always enjoyed making my own bread. Eventually, however, I really grew tired of kneading dough, waiting around for it to rise, and then using plenty of good oven juice to bake it. To get the same delicious results as a conventional oven, try a mid-range bread machine. For the absolute best savings:

Buy supplies in bulk. Get the largest flour bag and yeast package you can find. (Check your warehouse stores for deals.)

Package your mixes ahead of time. My mom and I had a marathon event of packaging up do-ahead baggies with all the dry ingredients. We even used up all of those dried potato flakes I had hanging around in some delicious potato bread recipes.

Plan bread making into your week. It takes no time at all to dump in the ingredients and push the button; you just have to plan for it. Most bread machines have a delay option to bake while you are at work. Use this to have a nice hot loaf waiting when you get home, and plan a meal around it!

Purchase tip: Bread makers are cluttering up secondhand stores and consignment shops across the country. Take one home for cheap, and search for the user's manual online. Snag one off eBay.com or check Craigslist.org. If you're determined to buy one new,

do some comparison shopping online to get the absolute best deal.

. . . .

2. The slow-cooker (Crock-Pot)

. . . .

Nearly everyone I know calls their slow-cooker a "Crock-Pot," even though that name is actually one of many brands that make them. Regardless of whether you go brand-name or not, the final product is a savory way to enjoy lower-quality meats and vegetables. Go ahead and buy that tough discounted roast from the meat department—no one will be the wiser. Tips that can help you maximize savings and give you additional ideas for using the cooker include:

Get some inspiration. I visit A Year of Crockpotting (CrockPot365. blogspot.com) regularly. The author is brutally honest about which recipes work, and the full-color photos will make you wish it didn't take 6–8 hours to reach that final product.

Plan, plan, plan. 4:30 PM is too late to decide you want to slow-cook some ribs. If you don't have it in mind at the beginning of your day, Crock-Pot cooking will not be an option for your dinner plans.

Think outside the box. Yes, you can cook just about everything in your slow-cooker, including dog food. Some home-decorating enthusiasts swear by the Crock-Pot method of stripping hardware, which involves letting painted metal hardware cook overnight in a bath of water and liquid laundry soap. (Just keep a separate cooker on hand for these non-food tasks.)

Purchase tip: When it comes to slow-cookers, most any brand will do. I have had great success from the small cookers sold at the Black Friday sales at popular retailers for under $4. They work well for side dishes and small cuts of meat. If you plan on buying secondhand, be on the lookout for chips in the crock, discoloration on the interior of the cooking surface, and frayed electrical cords. These are signs of future problems, so stay away! Flea markets and garage sales are great places to find older but functioning slow-cookers for a fraction of the new price. I own several!

....

3. The veggie / rice steamer
....

I had this sitting in my cupboard for years after our wedding. I just didn't know how handy it could be. Now that I've had a chance to really try this puppy out, we are inseparable! What's not to like? It cooks veggies, meats, and rice without any stirring or tending. It uses much less electricity than a stovetop, and for those of us who are a bit rice-impaired (translation: sticky-rice bandits), it's an easy way to impress guests. (Plus it's a really healthy way to eat.)

Forgo the bells and whistles. Rice and veggie steamers have come a long way. Too bad much of the "extras" are pointlessly expensive. I've never used the "flavor infuser" on my steamer. If the thing can steam veggies and cook rice, you're golden. Pay less by getting just what you'll be sure to need.

Follow the directions. This is a no-brainer that I'm surprised I couldn't figure out on my own. Only add water to the steam well. Be super careful when removing the lid. If you follow the basic instructions, you'll have awesome, tender veggies and extra-fluffy rice. (If you don't, you'll look like an idiot in front of your spouse and will be nursing a scalded wrist for a week.)

Use the recipe book. Each new steamer comes with a few recipes to get you started. Yes, they are simple, but they make an excellent jumping-off point for more daring meals.

Purchase tip: These also come up at used outlets fairly often. To be sure you really are getting a good deal, make sure the heating element works *before* you buy. (If this means you may have to add some water from the store sink and plug it in, do so.) Also, you will need to be sure you have the basic heating component, a drip pan, rice tray, veggie steamer basket, and a lid to do everything you will need it for. (My used one didn't have the drip pan, and I did fine—but I don't plan on cooking meat in it.)

. . . .

4. The chopper / processor

. . . .

Most of the time, I use the world's oldest food chopper (i.e., my knife). There are times where I really do go crazy with my tiny food processor, however. These are instances where a knife just wouldn't cut it, and it is worth the time cleaning components to get a good consistent chop going.

Making baby food. There's really no need to buy baby food if you have access to fresh or high-quality fruits, veggies, rice, and meat. A food chopper can get it to the right consistency in no time (and adding water can make it smoother). For excellent baby food tips, see the baby food preparation resources at Dr. Sears' Web site (AskDrSears.com).

Freezing for later. Looking to use up all of those tomatoes from your garden? How about whipping up some salsa, pasta sauce, or bruschetta topping? The food chopper can save so much time, and you'll be proud of all of the produce you can use up and eat later in the year.

Purchase Tip: This is a product that I prefer to buy small. Since I'm not mass-producing much these days,

I have found satisfaction with a cheapo, off-brand food processor from the same Black Friday deals that I get my mini slow-cookers from. Mine has lasted over four years, but if you want something bigger or name-brand, look for one with as few components as necessary. (Remember, you'll be taking it apart and cleaning it after each use!) — **Linsey Knerl**

7 Ways to Save Big Money with Ice Cube Trays

With all the new refrigerators coming with ice makers these days, ice cube trays can regularly be found at yard sales and thrift stores for quite literally, a dime a dozen. What does this mean for you? Big money, that's what!

Ice cube trays can be used to save you loads of time and money in the kitchen. Numerous liquids and sauces can be frozen in them, and then stored in gallon freezer bags for future use. Some ideas?

1. Tomato sauce or paste

You can usually find the large cans of tomato sauce or paste at warehouse stores for around the two-dollar range. This is much less expensive than the small cans from the grocery store. Freezing the leftover sauce saves you from having a half empty can of paste or sauce sitting in your fridge going to waste. Toss the frozen paste in with your soup broth, or add a few sauce cubes in the frying pan for taco night.

2. Leftover coffee

Frozen coffee cubes work great to make your own gourmet frozen coffee drinks. I like to have some coffee in a pitcher in the fridge as well. That way, when I add the liquid element to the frozen cubes in the blender it doesn't dilute the strength of the beverage.

3. Soup stock

Whether you freeze beef, chicken, or vegetable stock in the ice trays, it'll make your life easier when preparing recipes that only call for a small amount of stock.

4. Leftover gravy

This makes a great base for pot pies, or as a substitute soup broth item.

5. Applesauce

Since this stuff also comes cheap in the large jars at warehouse stores, the frozen cubes are great for those who bake often and want to control fat content.

6. Fresh herbs

If you have some fresh herbs from the produce section that are about to go bad, chop them up and put them in the cube sections with a bit of water. The frozen cubes are great to add to soups. This is also a way to preserve extra items from your herb garden at the end of the season.

7. Purees and baby food

If you make your own versions of these, it's a great way to have access to only the smaller amounts, which is what you usually need with these items.

STORAGE AND USAGE TIPS

To stay organized with this system and avoid freezer burn from open storage, pop out each set of frozen product and transfer to a specific gallon-sized freezer bag. In the past, I've routinely had gallon bags of tomato sauce cubes, herb cubes, and cubes of chicken stock in the freezer at the same time.

Each regular-sized cube holds two tablespoons of liquid. This means that 2 cubes equals ¼ cup, 4 cubes equals ½ cup, etc. This comes in really handy when recipes call for a specific amount of liquid for a recipe.

Putting the effort into this is worth the time. A gallon freezer bag of cubes lasts a reasonably long time, depending on how often you use the product, and provides an enormous savings of time as well as money. Also, considering all you need to do is ladle the liquid into the trays and freeze, it's not a great deal of time to begin with.

— **Myscha Theriault**

8 Natural Ways to Make Water More Flavorful

Many packaged drinks are quite expensive and the cheapest drink out there is water. The main reason that people don't drink water is that it is tasteless and not very "fun" to drink. On the other hand, water is definitely more healthy than soda, so now there is an entire category of packaged drinks that is basically bottled water with added coloring, vitamins, and flavor. Instead of buying these drinks, there are many things you can add to water at home to make it more exciting to drink.

. . . .

1. Salt

. . . .

I am sure you have heard of the term "electrolytes" in the marketing for energy drinks. Electrolytes are actually just ions that can be found in common table salt. Adding a little bit of salt to water helps your body absorb the liquid more quickly. As long as you don't go overboard with the salt, the water should be very quenching.

It is great for workouts since the body loses salt through sweat.

. . . .

2. Ginger

If you like spices, ginger is a great way to add a "zing" to your water. If it is added to boiling water it is also a great way to clear your throat and sinuses during a cold.

. . . .

3. Citrus

My Filipino husband's family members often freeze a small tropical citrus fruit called kalamansi in ice cube trays and then put the ice cubes in water for flavor. The same can be done with other citrus fruits, and the water produced would be infused with vitamin C.

. . . .

4. Herbs

Mint, lemongrass, and parsley are great for adding aroma and a hint of green to your water. If you want to release the flavor you can crush the plants a little bit before putting them into your water.

. . . .

5. Cucumber

I saw this at a spa I went to in Hawaii. A water dispenser was half filled up with cucumber slices, and the water dispensed tasted very refreshing and smelled a bit like cucumber.

. . . .

6. Wine

One of my favorite additions to water is plum wine or umeshu. Umeshu is a Japanese liqueur made from the ume fruit (also known as "Japanese apricot" or "Chinese plum"). Because umeshu is very sweet, I drink it with a lot of water. The distinct sweet flavor still comes through when there is one part umeshu in ten parts water. You can do the same with other syrupy liqueurs.

. . . .

7. Berries

Blueberries and strawberries have distinct flavors that could be soaked up by water. All you have to do is cut or crush a few of the berries into your water.

8. Vinegar

Adding vinegar to water is similar to adding citrus. You will get sour water that has vitamin C. When I was a kid I liked adding apple cider vinegar to water before drinking it.

Of course any of these things could also be added to soda water if you want to make your own lightly flavored soda. The possibilities are really endless since you can mix and match the ingredients any way you want. — **Xin Lu**

10 Ways to Create a Gourmet Kitchen on a Shoestring

Having a well-stocked, stylish gourmet kitchen does not have to cost a mint. In fact, implementing just a few of the following ideas can save you thousands of dollars, and make your kitchen look fantastic. Here are 10 ways to create a gourmet kitchen but still stay on budget.

1. Display your cooking ingredients

These have a great deal of color, texture and aroma, which makes for loads of visual drama in the kitchen decor department. A large jar of tri-color peppercorns with a nice grinder is an affordable choice. Garlic ropes, chili pepper garlands, and large bottles of infused oils and specialty vinegars are other consumable decor items that make a nice visual statement. Use space like the soffit over your cupboards. A great way to work this in with style is with clear glass containers. Extra large glass canisters available at restaurant supply and discount department stores are great for holding things you might normally put in white food storage buckets. Since the soffit is more of a decorative area, giant containers of things like dried chili peppers, chana dal, and turtle beans can serve both form and function in this case.

2. DIY kitchen islands

There are tons of fun, affordable ways to make your own island and add to the functionality and style of your kitchen. Get a cool old farm table with a nice patina and a long waist-height dresser with locking castor wheels attached to the legs. Add a couple of towel bars on each side, and you are good to go. Use an antique, top-opening soda cooler with an added stainless steel top. Kitchen islands can be phenomenally expensive to purchase from a design center. A little imagination can save you tons of cash.

3. Bulk spices

There are some incredible deals out there on large-quantity spice purchases. Since spices are often a main holdup to trying new menu items at home, indulging in a well-stocked spice pantry is a smart move for the would-be at-home gourmet.

4. Tools on the cheap

Along with slotted spoons, mixing bowls, and garlic presses, I include pots and pans in this category. One super place I've found to get decent professional-quality stainless-steel items is Ikea. Strolling antiques markets is another fun way to have an afternoon out and find old kitchen gadgets for cheap. You'll also find some with fabulous character and patina this way.

5. Industrial shelving

Industrial shelving is a prime kitchen-decorating candidate, particularly for single city-dwelling folks who are short on tools. The newer stainless steel versions come with not only the add-on wine and glass racks, but pullout drawers and add-on shelf options.

6. The corner pantry

While fantastic for large-quantity food storage, they are also handy for awkward-to-store appliances and holiday/party-serving dishes. If you can't build in a custom one due to renting or financial concerns, go with a long curtain from a rod or tension cable or a carved wooden divider screen. The items will be stylishly hidden, and imagine just being able to walk in and grab what you need off an easy-to-access industrial shelf. No more fighting with stuff in hard-to-reach cabinet corners.

7. Fewer small kitchen appliances

I recommend choosing these things judiciously. The last thing you need is to give up valuable storage space to gadgets you never use. Electric hand mixers, a good blender and if possible a widemouthed food processor are a few standard appliance staples. From there, choose only those appliances that will make a huge contribution to your life and cooking styles.

8. Fresh herbs

Buying these from the market often leads to waste, since you can't use it all, and they don't keep well. But these can make a tremendous difference to the flavor of your meals. Having a few pots of your favorite herbs will lower the cost and add to the look and feel of your kitchen environment. Even one really lush healthy plant featuring one of your favorite herbs can make a big decorative statement, such as a potted bay leaf tree or extra large rosemary bush.

9. DIY hanging pot racks

This is another item that can blow your entire budget at design stores. But multitudes of options are available for the DIY folks out there. Re-bar with chain and S-hooks, wagon wheels, antique garden ladders, and old gate sections are just a few. Get creative and have fun with it.

10. Open shelving

You can use this above the counter-tops as a carryover from the rolling industrial shelves idea. Just put them as far apart as you want for custom storage that meets your needs. If you are starting a kitchen from scratch, it's a way to scrub those expensive cabinets and save money for more important things like wine and brushed-steel appliances. Another place to go with open shelving can be below the countertops. Curtains in front are a popular way to hide stored items.
— **Myscha Theriault**

21 Great Uses for Beer

I love beer. From a warm, nutty pint of English bitter, to an ice-cold Belgian lager, I'm all over it. But you don't just have to drink beer straight from the bottle or jar (although that's the best way to use it). If you're feeling experimental, here are 21 (the legal drinking age in most states) different uses for beer, other than just pouring it down your throat.

1. Put it in your chili

One of the best ways to add flavor and a little extra liquid to a chili is with a nice bottle of beer. Use the darker beers, as they have more flavor and add more punch.

2. Make bread

My wife's grandma is from Germany and she swears by a good loaf of beer bread.

INGREDIENTS

1 12 oz. can of beer
2 1/2 cups self-rising flour
1/2 cup all-purpose flour
1/4 cup brown sugar
1 teaspoon baking powder
1/2 teaspoon salt
1/2 teaspoon onion powder
3/4 teaspoon Italian seasoning
1/4 cup butter or margarine, melted

DIRECTIONS

1. Preheat oven to 375 degrees F (190 degrees C).
2. Lightly grease a 9x5-inch baking pan.
3. In a bowl, mix the dry ingredients.
4. Add the beer and sugar, mix well, place in pan.
5. Top with melted butter.
6. Bake 45 to 55 minutes. Cool on a wire rack.

3. Kill slugs

Worms are a gardener's best friend, but slugs are not. Salt is a great way to dry up these slimy pests, but that means you have to find them first. Instead, entice them with a little beer, which slugs love. Simply pour a little into some empty jars and place them in the soil, with the rims of the jars at ground level. The slugs will drop in for a drink, but they can't get back out. And what a way to go; certainly better than the salt-shriveling death.

4. Take a beer bath

It's said that Cleopatra used to bathe in milk. Pah, that's for lightweights. P. Diddy went one better and filled bathtubs full of expensive champagne at a birthday party. I say, go with the middle ground. Drain a few kegs into the tub and let the invigorating bubbles cleanse the skin and exfoliate. The yeasts and other ingredients are great skin-softeners. Then take a long shower.

5. Cure your lawn of brown spots

I talked to a gardener who assured me that the acids in the beer help kill off bugs and the other ingredients promote green growth.

6. Ease a stomachache

The carbonation in the beer can help ease your nasty tummy rumbles. Of course, this is not a good one for children, or people with an ulcer or other serious stomach illness.

7. Remove stains

Something nasty on your carpet? Maybe a red wine stain? Well, a light beer will help pull that stain out. Sometimes a little club soda first will also help. Then use a regular carpet steam cleaner after to lift out the liquid and the smell.

8. Make a killer meat-tenderizing marinade

I have used soda in the past to help soften a steak before putting it on the grill, but that was too sweet for me. Now, I use a good beer or lager, and sometimes a stout if I'm feeling the need for some hearty flavor. The beer will really help soften the meat, add a distinctive taste, and it's way better than those chemical tenderizers.

9. Revive wooden furniture

Got a few opened, half-empty beers from a party? Well, flat beer makes a great wood reviver. Just dampen a microfiber cloth with your flat beer, then rub gently into your furniture. It will give it a polish and bring back some color.

10. Highlight your hair

Give your lovely locks that sun-kissed glow. Soak your hair in beer and then lay in the sun. It will pull out terrific highlights and make you smell deliciously hoppy! (Alternately, wash the beer out if you'd rather smell like a normal person.) Beer is also a handy hair conditioner.

11. Polish gold jewelry

Don't bother buying expensive store-bought cleaners. Drop your rings and other trinkets into a dish of beer, then remove and polish to a beautiful sheen using a dry cloth.

....

12. Attract bees

I really don't like bees and wasps, especially at barbecues and get-togethers in the park or backyard. So, an hour before the event is due to kick off, place some small containers of beer around the perimeter of the yard. The sugar and smell will attract the bees and keep them away from your party.

....

13. Beer batter

I'm English; I love my fish 'n' chips. Replace the liquid in your favorite battered fish recipe with beer to make a memorable dish.

- 1 12 oz. bottle of beer
- 1 cup all-purpose flour
- 2 tablespoons paprika
- 2 teaspoons salt
- 2 teaspoons ground black pepper
- 1 egg, beaten

....

14. Heal

As some of you may know, beer is a diuretic. And therefore, it can be used to help pass a kidney stone. It cannot, however, be used like other diuretics—to treat liver cirrhosis (for obvious reasons).

....

15. Liven up some bland shrimp or lobster

Well, Okay, lobster usually isn't that bland. But shrimp can certainly lack "oomph" on occasion, and flat beer can help. Simply boil it up with some spices, like turmeric, Cajun seasoning, a bay leaf, salt, pepper, and a touch of cayenne pepper. Then, add your raw shrimp and cook for around 5 minutes (15 for lobster). Serve with rice and steamed vegetables.

....

16. Make beersicles

Get yourself a popsicle maker from your local grocery store and instead of adding fruit juice, add a selection of different beers. An Indian pale ale, a lager, a bitter, a stout, and so on. You'll have a set of tasty adult treats for a hot summer day. You can also make smaller versions using an ice cube tray and toothpicks.

....

17. Start a conversation

By carefully spilling a little beer on the attractive person next to you, male or female, you give yourself an opening to apologize, buy them a new drink, and start a charming conversation. Just a nudge, though; if you drench them they'll be ticked off and you'll be considered a prize moron.

18. Soak your feet

If you've had a hard day at work, a cold beer isn't just good for your spirits. Those tired, aching feet can be revived by a beer foot bath. Please, don't be tempted to drink the contents afterward.

19. Turn ordinary rice into something very special

Next time you cook up a pot of long-grain rice, perhaps jasmine or basmati, cook the rice up in beer. Something with a lot of flavor will work well, like a brown ale or stout. The rice will absorb the beer and have a lovely flavor. Better still, it will look brown in hue, making people think you're eating healthy!

20. Wash your pillowcases

This may be an old wives' tale, but apparently the nutty smell of hops helps you fall asleep. If you're an insomniac, try washing a pillow-case in beer and you may just get to the Land of Nod sooner than you think.

21. Give yourself movie-star looks

Simply buy many bottles of beer for the person you want to date and ensure they drink it all. By the time they've finished, they'll think you have the looks of a million-dollar Hollywood star. (Warning: Beer-goggle effect will wear off quickly.) — **Paul Michael**

10 Simple Meals in 10 Minutes or Less

It's all well and good to save money on meal prep, but for those working outside the home or juggling various other projects, saving time can be just as critical. Here are 10 simple meal ideas you can prepare in 10 minutes or less.

. . . .

1. Tacos

For healthy, fun eating that brings together multiple food groups, tacos are tough to beat. They're also incredibly flexible, with versions available in chicken, beef, fish, and texturized vegetable protein (TVP).

. . . .

2. Fried rice

For this super-quick inexpensive meal, use pre-cooked rice from a prior assembly- cooking session, or a minute rice, then add almost anything you want. Whether you're using leftover pork ribs, sale ham, or even chopped chicken, fried rice is a great way to use up leftovers of all types. Don't forget the Soy Sauce.

. . . .

3. Soup on the fly

While many soups require longer prep times and slow simmering, there are a few ways to get a decent soup on the table in minutes. A restaurant knockoff version of pasta fagioli is one. Onions and celery cook quickly, carrots can be grated to greatly speed up the process, canned beans are already cooked, and most dried pastas

cook in six to eight minutes. Fresh pastas finish in even less time. Slice some leftover artisan bread, add some fun toppers, and you've got an elegant dinner on the table in no time.

. . . .

4. Gourmet sandwiches

Horseradish-infused tuna melt, oven-toasted ham and Swiss, a fresh basil caprese, spread with fun condiments and bargain banana peppers purchased in bulk . . . loads of options exist here for fun dinner food on the run. Add some homemade potato chips or mozzarella sticks and you've got a decently replicated café experience right at home.

. . . .

5. Dinner salads

There are lots of creative opportunities for salad: chicken caesar, sliced steak, spinach and strawberry with feta and sunflower kernels. The time-saver here is the low number of prep dishes to scrub and scour, and the reduced (or removed) cooking time depending on whether you choose to use precooked meat or grill it up fresh that night. Either way, this strategy puts a healthy, fast, and elegant meal on the table in a flash.

6. Stir-fry

Thinly sliced beef, shrimp, small chunks of chicken, and tofu cubes all cook quickly. Add to that the rapid cooking time of diagonally sliced vegetables, and stir-fry bumps nearly to the top of the list as far as time-saving dinners go.

7. The power of Crock-Pot

Obviously, the cooking time for meals in the slow-cooker drastically exceeds the 10-minute timeline. The benefit here is in the extremely reduced preparation time and flexibility. Not to mention having fewer dishes to clean afterward. It takes no time at all to toss in a pot roast along with some carrots, potatoes, and seasonings. Having a hearty dinner ready as soon as you walk through the door is decadent indeed. Many other simple, time-efficient recipes are out there for slow-cooker meal prep. A simple Internet search will yield a staggering amount of options.

8. Rip and dunk

These are simple, flexible, and depending on your choice of ingredients, extremely affordable. Hummus with a selection of flat bread and vegetables is one way to go. Brea-bowl dinners and fondue are others. This type of dinner option can be as rustic or as elegant as you like.

9. Breakfast for dinner

This is yet another area where you have a great deal of flexibility. Using homemade baking mix for on-the-go pancakes and waffles, or serving a hearty egg scramble with sausage and peppers are both quick options.

10. Affordable conveniences

Still cheaper than take-out or restaurant dining, having a few convenience items on hand for those evenings when your schedule is completely out of whack is a viable alternative. Frozen grocery store entrees, rotisserie chicken, even fish sticks and tater tots can get the kiddies fed and in bed on time, putting you back in control of a previously out-of-control day. The time saved can be used to regroup and get things back on track for the next morning. — **Myscha Theriault**

6 Simple Side Dishes that Will Save You Money

Need a little something to round out your standard dinner entrees? Not wanting to spend the equivalent of your monthly utility bill to do it? Here are six stylish sides to jazz things up affordably.

1. Two-tone oven roasted potatoes

This one requires a sweet potato or two along with your standard white potato. Chunk them each up separately, tossing with olive oil and your herb of choice (parsley works well). Put the sweet potato pieces in the oven first at around 375 degrees. They'll need a bit longer than the white potatoes (about 20 minutes). Then toss the remaining potato wedges in the same casserole dish or baking pan for another 20 to 30 minutes, depending on the size of the pieces you cut. This keeps things super cheap, but adds another color into the mix.

If the two-tone thing is too much work for you, consider going with the straight red Spanish potato wedges tossed with olive oil, rosemary, and a bit of sea salt. Keep the skins on for extra color, and you'll still have plenty of style.

2. Spaghetti squash

While squash in general is gorgeous and affordable, I find spaghetti squash to be particularly helpful with visual wow factor that involves very little work. Sure, you have to wait for it to bake up. But when it does, you just scrape it out of the skin with a dinner fork and it looks fantastic. No mashing, no julienning, no power-mixing with butter and milk. In fact, if you are trying to cut back on calories, you can skip the butter altogether and just go with a sprinkle of nutmeg. Great with roast chicken and another colorful side veggie.

3. Skinny beans

Otherwise known as haricot vert, these are the thinner European-style string beans popular in France. They are super simple to cook. No boiling and straining necessary here; these things cook through in less than five minutes in a frying pan. Hence, my love affair with these little strips of heaven.

Even when you go out of your way to jazz them up, they are still low on the work scale. Add in some quartered baby portabellas, almonds, shallots, or even a bacon and parmesan combo accent. Too much effort? Olive oil and pre-minced garlic will do just fine.

4. Spicy black beans

This is a trick I picked up from my favorite Mexican restaurant of all time, Cafe Noche in Conway, New Hampshire. For those of you who always wanted to know the secret to their popular spicy black beans side dish, it's this: hot pepper jelly. No, you didn't miss anything. That's truly it. You can go with a can or three of precooked ones, or cook up the dried version plain in the Crock-Pot. Either way, when they are done and drained, just add an appropriate amount of hot pepper jelly for that extra level of yum. Of course, to keep this afford-able you'll need access to an afford-able supply of really good pepper jelly. I recommend canning your own.

5. No-knead batter bread

For those who think this is not a stylish dinner side, I encourage you to take note next time you visit Olive Garden or Macaroni Grill. People blow through bread sticks and Italian bread like crazy. That be-ing said, most don't always have the time to do the full knead-and-rise scene. Recommended solution? Try including simple batter breads into your menu repertoire. If you go with a once-a-month dry-mix assembly plan, all of these can be put together with less stress than many casseroles. And, if you add in some meat and veggie leftovers from last night's din-ner, you can easily skate on the rest of the meal with a simple broth soup or bisque.

6. Three-ingredient salad

If salad is high on your list of dinner side preferences, your produce budget can become a serious issue. Consider keeping the base salad low-key with a simple spring mix, grape tomatoes, and sliced onions. This will give you a good base with dramatic color variations and very little cutting and chopping (I put my grape tomatoes in whole, which has the added benefit of sogginess prevention). Round it out as you see fit using your favorite add-ins that don't need to be used up right away, such as sunflower kernels, corn, or other crispies. Finish it off with an easy berry vinaigrette and you'll be rolling with nutrition and a punchy presentation. — **Myscha Theriault**

10 Things to Do with Bargain Beef

Steaks and roasts can often go on sale for less than the cost of lean hamburger. Ask the meat department to grind, slice, or chop it for you. They've always been happy to do it for me free of charge. Here are 10 ways to stretch the beef you bought for a bargain.

1. Teriyaki strips

This is most easily done with the larger, thicker steaks. If you slice them on a diagonal, it will leave you with a thin wide strip easily woven onto a wooden skewer. Soak it in your favorite teriyaki marinade (homemade or otherwise) and grill it for dinner along with some brown rice and a vegetable side. Bonus? They cook in a flash!

2. Kabobs

I really like making these with beef as well as chicken. Some of my favorite vegetables to include are green and red peppers, onions, and mushrooms. One great thing about grilled kabobs for dinner is having the meat and vegetable portion of the meal taken care of ahead of time. I only have to start the rice cooker when I get home from running errands.

3. Beef-fry

The key to a quick dinner prep with this stir-fry is to have the beef cut small enough to not take a whole lot longer than the vegetables. You can certainly add a sauce if you want, but I like the simple flavors of the ingredients in a bit of olive oil and a little low-sodium soy sauce.

4. Stew

Use whatever you have on hand as a penny-pinching strategy or implement your favorite family recipe. I've done this with browned ground beef or steak tips. Personally, I like a tomato-based broth for my beef soups and stews, but do what works best for you.

5. Stroganoff

This can also be done with either chopped beef pieces or ground beef. Some people may not consider this a penny-pinching idea due to the use of sour cream in the recipe. However, if you want to do something a little more elaborate for dinner without dishing out major bucks, this may be a moderate solution that fits your situation.

6. Steak and cheese quesadillas

Tortillas, cheese, leftover steak pieces, and salsa. It doesn't get much easier than this. If flipping the entire round version sends you into dimensions of ticked-off you never knew existed, try only filling half of a single tortilla and folding the other half over the top. This way you only have half the size to flip and one of the sides is closed, making it easier not to spill the contents on the frying pan.

7. Sloppy Joes

You pretty much need ground beef for these. Not the fanciest dinner idea in town, but certainly fun to eat with some veggie sticks or a salad side.

8. Pizza topping

Whether you want to go with the traditional hamburger pizza, or try steak pieces with BBQ sauce, this is a great way to stretch beef into a fun meal that will feed several people.

9. Spaghetti sauce

Again, ground beef will be necessary here. Try making a large batch and freezing it into meal-sized portions suitable for the number of people in your family. That way, you can dump some in the Crock-Pot once a week and have dinner nearly ready when you get home. Just boil the pasta!

10. French dip sandwiches

These are the kind you see on the menu of a lot of family-style restaurants. Basically, it's a warm toasted sliced-beef sandwich with a side of French onion soup to dip into. A cheese-steak sandwich would be equally doable. — **Myscha Theriault**

5 Easy Steps to Making Your Own Pickles

I'm a dill pickle addict. Once that seal has been popped on my jar of Claussen dills, I usually take care of that jar within 24 hours. Pickles aren't cheap, however, so I went for a DIY alternative that tastes pretty darn good (and you won't need any canning abilities to make these homemade pickles).

Pickle making isn't sexy, and it won't get you any special perks beyond the joys of eating your own pickles. But it's cheap, quick, and gives you a sense of accomplishment that you won't get from throwing an overpriced jar into your grocery cart. Here's a recipe that that will take care of your pickle cravings with little money and even less time:

. . . .
1. Grab your cukes
. . . .

Pickle connoisseurs will try to tell you that you can't use the overgrown ones to make pickles. You can; it just won't be quite the same. If you don't mind eating pickled seeds (I happen to love them), there is no reason you can't use up some of those giant, longer-than-your-arm cucumbers in your pickling recipe. If you don't like the mushy insides, you can always cut the cukes in half lengthwise and scrape out the seedy pulp with a spoon. No hard feelings. (Note: Be sure to wash the cukes and scrub them well or rinse them in a veggie wash—you will be leaving the skins on for flavor and texture.)

. . . .
2. Cut them
. . . .

This isn't rocket science. You can slice them in any manner you choose. (I prefer short, stubby pickles for snacking, but you can slice them thin or in hamburger-sized slices, as well.) If the cucumbers are small enough, you can leave them whole (but pickling time will be longer).

. . . .
3. Prepare your brine
. . . .

Simply boil 3 cups water (bottled is preferred), 1/8 cup kosher or sea (not iodized) salt, and 1 tablespoon white vinegar. Once it has come to a full boil, remove from heat and allow it to cool to room temperature (you don't want to boil your cucumbers).

4. Add your seasonings

While the liquid is boiling, you can begin packing the jar as full of sliced cucumbers as you can fit (with room at the top). Then add your seasonings, which include 1/4 cup chopped fresh dill (you can use less, if desired), ¼ tsp mustard seed, 1/2 tsp black pepper (whole peppercorns work well), and finely chopped garlic cloves (five or more, depending on how strong you want them). I also add a teaspoon of red pepper flakes and will occasionally throw in a small jalapeno pepper for extra kick!

5. Fill and seal

Now that your brine has cooled, pour it over the pickles until the jar is full. Screw on your lid (if you're using a recycled spaghetti sauce jar) or your canning lid and ring (no need to pressure seal). Now just stick these guys in the fridge for a minimum of five days for awesome pickle flavor! They'll keep in the fridge for weeks (although they are usually gone within days). — **Linsey Knerl**

9 Ways to Save Big on Meat

Looking to make the most of your money-saving opportunities while cooking for the meat and potato lovers in your family? Find the cost of your favorite cuts is putting a rather large dent in your child's college fund? Read on. Help has arrived. Here's a list of ideas for meat money management.

1. Crumble away

This one mainly applies to ground meats, and the simplest way to go is with the one-pound frozen bullets. These provide additional flexibility, they don't freezer-burn as quickly, and their smaller size makes it easier to skip the breaking down required for other bulk purchases. Bonus? Aside from hamburger, they are usually what goes on sale anyway.

Thaw enough meat for a particular meal-prep session, and repackage any extra for another menu. (A good example of this would be scoring a handful or two of ground beef from the taco pan before adding seasonings and setting it aside for pizza night later in the week. On assembly-cooking days, I'll cook up more.) Use a biscuit cutter or the open end of a clean, empty soup can and continue to press the meat against the pan, cutting it into smaller pieces as you go. Most people stop at the large chunk stage, which doesn't take the savings to the level most folks are needing these days.

Keep going until your pieces of ground meat are more the size of large granules or imitation bacon bits. You'll then be free to explore using meat more as a flavor source rather than a mainstay. By embracing this, you'll be able to stretch your ground meats further than you may have considered possible.

2. To dice is nice

While you can certainly do this with any leftover roast meat when you've cooked a large batch for dinner, this is also a super-easy hack for precooked boneless meats you are able to snag for a good price. Dice the heck out of it from the very beginning, and put it into smaller packages for use in casseroles, soups, pasta salads, carbonara, and more.

In addition to precooked boneless hams, turkey hams, Spam, and large blocks of pressed ham loaf, consider pepperoni, precooked boneless turkey breast, or even snagging some breaded chicken breast strips from the deli counter to dice up at home for a DIY crispy chicken southwest salad with corn and black beans.

3. Accent ingredient

You can create a tasty meal that places meat at center stage without making it the main ingredient. Add a few pieces of sliced steak to make a dinner salad. You get the full aromatherapy factor if you grill it at home, and can then thinly slice it diagonally for the full color variation. Want some more drama? Add a grainy spice rub prior to grilling for extra flavor and texture on the steak slices. Grilling a single marinated chicken breast and using the same dinner salad menu is also another way to feed more than one person from a single piece of meat.

4. Coupons can apply

Grant you, for larger portions of fresh cuts, these are rare and usually require the purchase of another item. However, when it comes to canned and presliced meats, coupons abound. Combined with a buy-one-get-one-free offer on double coupon week, you can score big. Another great time to try is during the summer when hot dogs go on sale.

5. Get larger cuts

Get comfortable working with some of the larger meat items that go on sale regularly, such as picnic pork roasts, giant legs of ham or lamb, and the long center-cut pork loins.

The pork loins can be cut into smaller roasts, or sliced into lean boneless pork medallions to serve with a spicy peanut sauce or a fruit compote. As for some of the others, the simplest way I've found to go is tossing them into an electric roaster on the counter and tossing some basmati into the rice cooker. Throw together a quick Asian coleslaw for a side dish, and you've got a low-stress meal that provides loads of meat and rice leftovers for the freezer. (Think fried rice, casseroles, and soups galore.) Found a great deal on boneless leg of lamb? Hack it up for grilled meat and veggie kabobs, or make friends with the butcher and have it ground up as a replacement for hamburger.

6. Stockpile during seasonal sales

This does require freezer space, but can easily save 50% or more off your total meat bill. Combine this strategy with other ideas in this article, and you'll be living large while saving big. Look out for hot dogs during summer picnic season, turkeys during the winter holidays, and hams throughout various times of the year.

7. Shaved, not sliced

For those who want deli meat and nothing else, you can get more mileage from your meat money this way. If you buy meat from the counter regularly, just ask them to shave your meat for you rather than slice it. Hard-core savers can get a slicer and try it at home if they want, but busy folks who are just looking for some minor tweaks in their meat budget can do this with no extra stress, time, or up-front cost. Beef up your sandwiches with banana peppers, bargain bacon, hummus, and other goodies. Or splurge on a chef's salad since your pennies have been pinched ahead of time. Oven-toasted subs are a great way to go with this as well, as the minor roasting time releases more of the fats and flavor. You'll be using less meat, and won't even really notice that much. I promise.

8. Buy a side

A side of beef or lamb, that is. Again, this will require some freezer space.

If you are short on that, consider chipping in with a friend and sharing a side. You'll each get some of the cuts you would have gotten if you bought the full side, but you won't have to carve out as much freezer space or lay out as much cash up front. Bonus? Everything comes custom-cut the way you want it, and prepackaged.

....

9. The half-and-half approach
....

This requires mixing 50% meat with 50% texturized vegetable pro-tein (TVP), which I realize sounds like sacrilege to the true carnivore at heart. Consider, though, that if you already eat a fair amount of prepared meat products from the freezer aisle, you may be eating more of it than you think. A few places to work it in painlessly would be meatballs, chili, spaghetti sauce, and Sloppy Joes.

— Myscha Theriault

 TRAVEL

Money: You can't leave home without it. But are you aware of just how little you may actually need? With expert planning and a bold attitude, it's possible to see the world for much less than you'd expect. If you're looking for a quick weekend getaway, an adventure vacation in a foreign land, or any old place to crash while visiting your cousin, there's an affordable option out there for you. Find out how to get where you need to go and enjoy every budget-friendly minute of it!

14 Tips to Have a Frugal Vacation and Still Treat Yourself

How do you vacation frugally, yet not allow your budget to compromise your traveling experience?

On one hand, you're on vacation, so you don't exactly want to squeeze every penny until it screams. The very idea of going on vacation means treating yourself to a special experience, seeing new things, and meeting new people. If you refuse yourself that museum admission, or that meal at a restaurant you've been dying to try, or the tour you've dreamed of taking, then what is the point of even leaving home in the first place?

Then again, if you go to town and spare no expense while on vacation, you may compromise your finances, and come home to a mess that may not only take a long time to clean up, but may also cause you to think twice about going away again.

Here are a few tips to help you balance out that vacation to enjoy the things you want to do, while keeping your checkbook balanced.

EATING

Meals will make up one of the most expensive parts of your trip. If you are unable to cook for yourself in a hostel, you are relegated to eating largely at restaurants, which will in turn eat up your cash pretty quickly.

1. Go to that special restaurant, but for lunch, not dinner

Oftentimes, the menu items and portions are similar, but the price can be as little as half of what you would pay for dinner.

2. Scrimp on breakfast

At home, you probably have a fairly plain breakfast: toast, or cereal. But when you go to a restaurant for breakfast, you'll likely end up ordering the full meal deal, and not only roll away having eaten more than you are used to, but also having spent way more money than you needed to. Instead, pick up some groceries at the local store (ideally a grocery store, not a convenience store!). Most hotel rooms have a minibar fridge where you can store anything that requires refrigeration. Not only will you save time by eating something quick on your way out for the day, but you'll also save money.

3. Never eat breakfast at a hotel!

Unless it is included with accommodation (and we'll get to that pitfall in a minute), hotels usually charge exorbitantly for breakfast, knowing that it is easiest for you to start your day with a meal right on your doorstep. If you insist on eating a full breakfast at a restaurant, then take the time to find an inexpensive diner where the locals eat. You'll likely pay half the price.

4. Buy prepared foods at a grocery store

Many grocery stores have sandwiches (some of which are made to order), soups, salads, hot meals, and even sushi. Pick something up to go, and have a picnic while you are out and about. Or if it's dinnertime, take your meal back to the room and serve up your inexpensive meal by candlelight. Create your own ambiance, and you won't have to worry about tipping the server or being pushed out the door if you want to linger over the meal.

5. Beware of snack foods and concession stands

It seems that hot chocolate, roasted peanuts, or ice cream stands are strategically planted in front of every major tourist destination around the world. If you wouldn't get that snack or beverage at home, then don't do it on vacation. You'll probably pay too much for that ice cream cone anyway. If the kids won't let the ice cream idea go, then go to a local convenience or grocery store and buy a box of prepackaged ice cream cones or popsicles and pay less than half as much money.

ACCOMMODATIONS

This is the number-one expense you will incur while on vacation (unless you are flying). The range of prices depend not only on the establishment and amenities, but also the location and time of year. Choose carefully.

6. Beware of the free breakfast

Although it may be enticing and convenient to have a free breakfast, you are paying for it one way or another. And if the breakfast turns out to be stale muffins, weak coffee, and some fruit, you may be losing money hand over fist. Even if the breakfast is glorious, compare how much you are paying for accommodations with breakfast versus without. Would you eat a full breakfast like that either way? If so, how much are you willing to pay for it? If not, then why bother?

7. Location, location, location

It stands to reason that the hotels located in the middle of it all will charge a pretty penny for the convenience. By staying somewhere a little further out, you may get a better sense of the city and its people by taking public transportation, and/or by walking more (which never hurts when you're eating all those rich vacation meals).

8. Choose your amenities

Although a pool, spa, exercise room, wireless Internet, rooftop patio, and bathrobes may sound luxurious, will you use them? As much as I love seeing a bathrobe in my suite, I almost never use it. Why would I lollygag about in my room wearing a robe when I can go out and explore the place I came to visit? And as much as I'd like to sit in the sauna, I probably won't. Look for the more basic accommodations; you'll save lots of money.

RENTING A CAR

9. If you are visiting a city, don't bother renting a car

Lots of city dwellers don't have cars, so try living like they do. Take public transportation, and walk lots.

10. If you must, go with a compact option

With the cost of fuel skyrocketing, the luxury sedans we like to get upgraded to will end up costing dearly. Do your pocketbook and the environment a favor: Keep it small, and don't drive it unless you need to.

TOURS

Sure, you need to be frugal, but don't sacrifice the things you really want to see for the expense of seeing them. If you want to see the Great Barrier Reef but balk at the price of the scuba-diving trip, then consider a snorkeling trip instead. Or, book the boat trip from a further-out and lesser-known port. If you come and go without seeing it because of the cost, you'll be kicking yourself all the way home.

11. Make a group list

Each person in the family should choose one thing they really want to do on the vacation. Put it all on a list, and discuss the options and costs. This is a great way for the whole family to participate in the trip-planning process, and for children to become aware of the financial balance and compromise required not only on vacation but throughout life. If everybody gets a chance to pick one special thing to do, then they will assume ownership of the trip and enjoy it all the more.

SOUVENIRS

Here's another way to break the budget, to be sure.

12. Avoid souvenir shops altogether

The best way to avoid going overboard with souvenirs (or to disappoint the kids by insisting they can't have anything they see) is to avoid the souvenir shops altogether. Many of the goods in such shops are mass-produced, overpriced, and not authentic.

Instead, try choosing one or two things you want to take home with you that will remind you of your trip and be a special memento. Or, like your tour choices above, get everybody in the family to pick one thing they want as their own personal souvenir from the trip. Everybody can research the destination prior to going to find the trip memento that characterizes the trip best for them, and will be all the more pleased with the end result.

For example, my souvenirs from Australia are a black opal and personally handcrafted didgeridoo. From South Africa, I have a mask and piece of blue tanzanite. From Thailand, a silk shirt and photograph of a monk praying. These are all things I can enjoy in my home, or use practically and have fond memories of every time I use it.

BUDGET

The best way to avoid sticker shock when you return is to budget the trip to begin with. There are a number of ways you can stick to your guns while on the road.

13. Leave credit cards at home

By bringing traveler's checks and spending only those, you know exactly what you'll have left over when you get home. No nasty surprises. When the checks are running low mid-trip, then you'll figure out where to scrimp if you need to.

14. Set daily meal cost limits

Accommodation, flights, and tours are often fixed prices and you know before you even leave home how much you'll be spending. But meals can throw the budget out the window if you're not careful. By setting a daily limit for how much you can spend on food, you can keep this variable expense under control too. If one day you go out for that special (and more expensive) lunch, then you'll have to make do with a smaller breakfast and budget dinner to make the day's budget balance.

A BALANCED VACATION

Like so many things in life, your vacation is about balance. You're on vacation, so treat yourself to the simple pleasures in life you have worked hard and saved up for. You want to return home energized, refreshed, and with lots of happy memories. Don't waste time scrimping and saving on every little thing. But don't throw caution to the wind and return home to a series of surprising bills, statement shock, and uncontrollable debt. Make sure your vacation is pleasurable, from the initial planning stages to the lifetime of memories afterward.

— **Nora Dunn**

3 Easy Steps to Finding Great Airfare Deals

Finding the cheapest ticket can be a confusing process. However, by understanding the system and the motivations behind pricing, you can develop a strategy to consistently find a good deal.

....

1. No search engine is better than any other

....

The first thing you must accept is that no fare search engine is the single best. All fare search engines in the United States, including the one in a travel agent's office, scan the same database using identical search algorithms. You can actually access this system directly, for free, from the company that designed it, using their Fare Shopping Engine (matrix. itasoftware.com/cvg/dispatch). While you cannot buy tickets at this site, it will help when comparing the fares across multiple agents and engines by giving you the probable best price as a benchmark for comparison.

2. When you fly is the most important factor

Flying off season, overnight, during the week (usually Tuesday or Wednesday), with a companion, to and from less popular or more inconvenient airports, and including more transfers in the itinerary, are all factors that commonly reduce a ticket's price.

Keep in mind that airlines can change their domestic fares up to three times a day. They usually do this at approximately 10:00AM, 12:30PM, and 8:00PM eastern standard time, and once on the weekend at 5:00PM. International fares can change once a day. It takes the search engines a few hours to respond to these changes.

A trend-based search engine is the best way to get a sense of when it's cheap to fly. Farecast (farecast. live.com) and Farecompare.com search historical records of fares to give price trends for your itinerary. AirFareWatchDog.com is a great site that will e-mail sales and alerts for a specific airport or route. While limited in scope, these services can help determine when the best time to buy a ticket might be.

If your itinerary is flexible, you have the luxury to choose the time and day that provides the cheapest ticket. If your schedule is more rigid, it is advisable to book your ticket either around a month in advance, or immediately before the flight, for the best price. While there is an availability gamble involved, the price usually reaches its lowest point in the last 24 hours before the flight.

3. Take matters into your own hands

Once you have a good sense of the fares that are turning up in the database, contact the airline directly to ask if they can do any better. Be sure to ask if they have any special deals applicable to your specific route, as airlines will often give huge discounts to fliers willing to make an airport transfer, or use minor hubs.

An example of this is Air India, which gives huge discounts on the less popular trans-Atlantic leg of their flights to India. As another example, I used to consistently save $100–$200 flying to Europe by phoning the British Airways ticketing office and telling them I was willing to make the Heathrow to Gatwick transfer. Sadly, this deal is no more, but that does not mean that there are not others like it waiting to be found.

Finally, most regional airlines do not use the national database of the larger airlines. As a result, using only Internet search engines might miss some great deals on connecting flights. There is nothing stopping you from calling these airlines directly and piecing your itinerary together yourself. — **David DeFranza**

16 Ways to Go Light and Low-Budget

With all the talk of airlines starting to charge for the very first bag you check, "one-bag" travel (or the pursuit of it) is going to become a larger priority for many. This is easier to achieve on some trips than others. Indicators are the length, diversity, and independence level of the trip. For your average three- to seven-day adventure however, affordable "one-bag" travel is definitely doable.

1. Limit the footwear

If you're going to a specific region and planning on mainly a sightseeing mission, one pair of sensible adventure shoes can get the job done. KEEN sandals for both men and women are good picks. They are available in either washable leather or various colors of nylon webbing. And while it might not be my favorite fashion statement, you can squeeze a pair of socks under them on a chilly day.

If you have multiple agendas or obligations on your journey, downsizing to a single pair of shoes can be a real challenge. Sticking to just two pairs, however, is achievable with a little forethought. And, if you make sure one set is as flat and flexible as possible, they shouldn't cut into your space allotment too much.

2. Go miniature where possible

This won't work for everything, but many items are perfectly functional in miniature form. Head lamps and nail clippers are a couple that come to mind. Sea to Summit's travel clothesline is one of my personal high-performance favorites.

3. Follow the container principle

Having small and like items in separate containers or organizer bags keeps you from feeling like you are reaching into a chaotic bag of doom every time you need to find a particular item. In addition to being a huge fan of the personal organizers for toiletries from L.L. Bean, I also like Ziplocs, Space Bags, and packing cubes.

4. Go as thin as possible on layers

Bringing several lighter layers enables you to have more wardrobe options, be cool or warm as needed, and not take up too much space in your bag like a bulky sweater might. Besides, if you really want one of those, you can buy one made from a local artisan on the trip. It makes a functional souvenir and you'll be helping out the local economy. We picked up a couple in Peru and shipped them home during the trip once we switched climates.

5. Consider minimalism

I'm not saying to deprive yourself to the level where you won't have a good time, but it is possible to pack everything you need and still save on space and number of items. Bring multiuse items, even if they're not your favorites. For example, I prefer liquid foundation, but the pressed powder is more compact, lighter, and there's no risk of leaks. Bring solid shampoo and conditioning bars rather than big bottles, and choose alternative reusable feminine products.

6. Pick a color scheme

Selecting items of clothing that have the most versatility for maximum mix and match opportunities is crucial. A color scheme will ensure that any top can go with any bottom you brought.

7. Wear as much as possible on travel day

Think leggings under travel pants, tank top or swimsuit under a dress, T-shirt under longer-sleeved shirt, etc. It's usually chilly on the plane, so an extra layer or two won't be super uncomfortable. Clothing with large and/or many pockets can be useful when trying to avoid needing an extra piece of luggage.

8. Quick-dry is king

This also fits in with the thinner is better philosophy listed above. The quicker items dry after sink or shower washing, the sooner you'll be able to wear them again or pack them and hit the road without risking that mildew smell that's hard to get rid of.

9. Multipurpose

There are men's swim trunks that are lined and look more like travel shorts.

Women's swimsuits make a great underwear substitute, and bandanas, in addition to having multiple uses around the house, are a great travel item.

....

10. Digitize, digitize, digitize

....

Take photos of your travel documents and send them to yourself via e-mail. If anything unfortunate happens to the actual documents, you might save a lot of time, hassle, and money by having that information readily available.

....

11. Do it yourself

....

This can apply to making gear, doing laundry in the shower, booking your own reservations, cooking on the fly, taking loads of photos as your alternative souvenir collection, and more. It also applies to things you can do before and after your trip to save money for travel on a regular basis.

....

12. Carve out the cash

....

This is possible in all areas of travel. Some ideas will be more appealing to you, others not so much. But the fact is, money *can* be saved, and independent long-term travel is far more affordable than most people think. In fact, we found we spent less money on the road having a blast than we did living outside of Tucson and clipping coupons. Pack a brown-bag type of picnic, incorporate a few hammock-sleeping campground evenings, or BYO sleep-sack hostels along the way in between the other guesthouse or B&B stops. Just bring along a travel padlock or two for standard travel security issues.

....

13. Slow down

....

Seriously, just slow down. Just like letting off your car's accelerator can save you gasoline, slowing down the pace on your trip can help pinch more than pennies. With travel as in business, time is money.

....

14. Location, location, location

....

This applies to more than just business. Certain regions are far more affordable than others. If you are just starting to explore travel as a hobby or life passion, do you have to see Europe first? I love it there too, but South America or Southeast Asia is way more affordable. Ditto with Indonesia versus Japan.

15. Bond with your car

Or if possible, a camper van. Many people try this as an alternative to RV trips. If you want to take the whole "fam damnily," the RV plan is certainly more affordable than high-end hotels, particularly for the long term.

16. Be as independent as possible

Sometimes travel agents can come in handy. But with the amount of online resources these days, they're less valuable and more expensive. Check out the online communities and get familiar with Lonely Planet. Do a quick Google search for reviews on hotels and restaurants. There's are loads of information to help you find affordable travel stops.

— **Myscha Theriault**

9 Great Ways to See the World for Free

Would you like to travel for free, even be paid a stipend, in exchange for contributing time to help a foreign community as a volunteer? Here are several options for free or very cheap travel through volunteering.

FREE LONG-TERM PROGRAMS

1. The Peace Corps

The Peace Corps (www.peacecorps.gov) is the classic all-expenses-paid volunteer option that first comes to an American's mind. They offer two-year appoints, mostly in Africa, Asia, and South America, as well as modest stipends. Popular among recent college graduates, the Peace Corps is actually open to people of all ages.

2. The United Nations

The United Nations (www.unv.org) volunteer program sends experienced professionals from almost any field to every region on earth. As a volunteer, all expenses, including airfares to and from your work site and any pre-appointment necessities like vaccines and visas, are covered. In addition, volunteers receive various grants and stipends that vary in amount depending on the project's local economy. Like most of the groups in this list, they are looking for people with extensive experience in their field. Like the Peace Corps, most appoints are for two years, though they claim to be increasing the number of six-month and year-long options.

3. Art Corps

Art Corps (www.artcorp.org) is a program specifically designed for professional artists. The program focuses on using art as a teaching tool, as well as a means of expression, for communities that face pressing social problems. Though the program does require that participants do some personal fund-raising, the cost of travel is otherwise fully covered, along with a small stipend. Most assignments last 11 months.

4. Voluntary Service Overseas

Voluntary Service Overseas (www. vso.org.uk) was recognized as the International Development Charity of the Year at the 2004 UK Charity Awards. They have placed over 30,000 volunteers, primarily in Africa, Asia, the Caribbean, and Eastern Europe. They provide a stipend in addition to covering all expenses. While most assignments last two years, there are some special projects for experienced professionals lasting between two weeks and six months.

FREE SHORTER-TERM PROGRAMS

5. Geekcorps.org

This volunteer program specializes in placing experts from the IT industry in communities with the goal of fostering digital independence. Geekcorps runs projects primarily in Mali, Ghana, and Lebanon. The program covers travel and living expenses in addition to providing a small stipend. Most of the placements are four months in duration, though options range from one to six months.

6. Winrock International

This nonprofit organization (www. winrock.org) works to build economic prosperity and civil empowerment while encouraging sustainable resource use and environmental protection. They have projects in many parts of South America, Asia, and Africa. They offer to cover all travel expenses, including a small per diem, and most assignments last two to three weeks, including travel time.

7. ACDI/VOCA

ACDI/VOCA (www.acdivoca.org) leads projects focused primarily on economic development. They are looking for experienced professionals with knowledge of business, banking and finance, marketing, agriculture, food processing, and community development, in addition to other project-specific areas. They administer projects all over the world and cover all project-related expenses. Typical assignments are between two and four weeks long.

8. The International Executive Service Corps

IESC (www.iesc.org) encourages the development of private business and industry with the goal of increasing prosperity and development around the world. They are looking for volunteers with a background in business or industry and operate in many locations. All travel expenses are covered by the program in addition to a small stipend. Assignments vary from one week to several months long.

9. The Financial Services Volunteer Corps

FSVC (www.fsvc.org) places business and finance professionals in developing and reforming economies to provide education and guidance. They cover all expenses and operate primarily in Eastern Europe, Africa, and Asia. Assignments typically last between one and two weeks.

ALMOST-FREE PROGRAMS

Willing Workers on Organic Farms (http://www.wwoofinternational.org) places volunteers on organic farms around the world. While working, your room and board at the farm is free, though volunteers are responsible for all expenses involved in getting to and from the site. Volunteers must pay a small annual membership fee to join the organization in the country they wish to work in order to access the database of farms. This is a great opportunity to learn about organic farming and spend a week or two doing some fun physical work.

Finally, there are a number of "work camps" worldwide that place teams of volunteers on a two- or three-week project. These can involve everything from farming to construction, education to art; every project is different. It costs about $300 for two or three weeks of room, board, and work. Not free, but not bad for two weeks of traveling. These projects are organized through clearinghouses, the most popular being Volunteers for Peace (www.vfp.org) and Service Civil International (www.sci-ivs.org). As a great deal, Volunteers

For Peace charges $500 for an entire family, regardless of the size.

Keep in mind that these trips will not be a week sitting on the beach. You will have to work, but even if you are doing something related to your everyday job, the location and unique challenges will make it seem fresh and new.

Besides a vacation, these opportunities provide an opportunity to learn a new language, take a leadership role, experience everyday life in a foreign country, and make some new friends and professional connections. With experiences like that, maybe it is smart to take a vacation during a recession. — **David DeFranza**

6 Savvy Ways to Travel around a City

Getting from one place to another presents a challenge in any city. For figuring out free and low-cost city transportation, nobody finds better deals than Sharon Rosenberg, the Frugal Duchess and author of the hot new book by the same name. Here's her list of insider suggestions for figuring out free and frugal transportation options in nearly any major city here in the U.S.

1. Free trip planners for mass metro transit

Many cities provide online trip planners for their visitors. Some even team up with Google Transit (www.google.com/transit) to allow people to plan trips within various major United States cities, and a few others around the world. Miami, for example, has this cool feature built in to their transit site which will allow you to view via your handheld mobile device the time of the next train's arrival, just in case you miss your connection. Or, you can print out some schedules ahead of time and keep them in page protectors to reference in case of delays.

2. Employer subsidized transit / parking passes

Big corporations often provide transportation subsidy programs for their employees. It's a huge financial help to you and an affordable job benefit for them to provide.

3. University shuttles

These are almost always free for the riding, and Sharon has recently used this service successfully for her entire family while out and about on her book tour. In her case, she was a guest of the university making a public appearance, but consider trying this out for yourself while touring a new metro area. Often these shuttles have regular routes to and from major tourist destinations and other transportation hubs.

4. Seasonal or monthly mass transit passes

Basically, this is bulk buying for on-the-move city folks. Super deals are available if you are not just in town as a tourist needing a day pass. Getting bulk passes for bus rides, train trips, and subways is a great way to get more bang for your buck.

5. Hotel shuttle service

Apparently, many hotels have shuttle service to various large tourist attractions as well. Got an entire family? Even a generous tip to the shuttle driver is way cheaper than bus tickets for a family with four children. The Frugal Duchess recently used this in a couple of different major cities and calculated that even the savings from traveling to one destination a day came out to around a $20 savings for her family. Doing a morning run, an afternoon activity, and heading out

for dinner? This can rack up major bucks in a hurry. I know the next time I'm trying out a new city, I'll be trying this tip out for sure.

6. Creative use of airport shuttles

Hotels aren't the only ones with shuttle services. Now, going from airport to airport, or catching a shuttle from your door to the departure terminal might not be free, but it is way cheaper than a cab. A true story Sharon told me about a woman she met during her book promotional travels: The city this woman was flying into had two airports. One had a much cheaper airfare to travel to than the other, but was further away via ground transport than the other, which would apparently have affected the cost. So she took the airport-to-airport shuttle (which was in this case free), and then snagged the drive-you-to-your-door shuttle from the closer airport. Another example Sharon shared was a situation where catching two airport shuttle vans in a row with an airport in between can often get you where you want to go cheaper than flying or driving yourself. Bonus? You get dropped directly at your door. How cool is that? — **Myscha Theriault**

How to Save Money by Taking a Vacation

A cruise to the Bahamas or a trip to that luxury spa isn't going to get you ahead financially. However, if you're looking to sock away a couple hundred bucks or more, some time off from work just might be the way to get you there—if you do it right.

According to the *Portland Business Journal*, Expedia's eighth annual Vacation Deprivation Survey shows that 31% of Americans will not use all of their allotted vacation days. With most workers averaging 14 days per year, they are giving that time back to their employers in cases of "use it or lose it." The majority of those not using their total vacation time cite work pressures as the main reason for forgoing time off.

A small percentage of employers will allow unused vacation time to be paid out at the end of the year as an hourly wage, but many don't play by this rule. It's these employees that might consider looking at unused vacation time from a different point of view—one that may allow them to actually save some money for a large purchase, unpaid bills, or savings. A paid vacation away from work, but within the comfort of your own home, can net you big bucks.

Let's take a look at what you may save on a typical five-day paid vacation. Assuming that you work a set number of hours or don't depend on overtime to supplement your income, you can avoid paying for:

Gas for the daily commute: $3–20
Parking and tolls: $1–4
Lunch out: $5–15
Wardrobe costs (dry cleaning, etc.): $4–15

These totals are an average, with some employees paying more and others far less. If you look at savings for an entire week, you could save between $65 and $270 on a five-day vacation, with no decrease in your income!

The time away from work may also reap some benefits that are a little more difficult to measure, including: an improvement in mental or physical health, enhancement of family relationships, and the communication of healthy boundaries to your boss and coworkers. Some may even find that it is a perfect opportunity to earn some extra cash beyond their vacation pay by doing odd jobs or participating in a temporary or contract position!

If you've been putting off those much-needed vacation days for fear of falling behind at work, consider the monetary gain of getting away for a bit. You worked hard for those days. Why not put them to work for you?

— **Linsey Knerl**

4 Secrets to Eating Cheaply while Traveling Abroad

I've been on the go a lot this last year, but no matter which city I was in, I still had to eat. I learned a few tricks to keep myself comfortably fed on the go, without breaking the bank.

1. Pack a lunch

I bet you looked at "pack a lunch" and laughed. How can you pack a lunch while living out of a suitcase or staying in a motel room? But there are grocery stores everywhere, from Cardiff, Wales, to Tel Aviv, Israel, and most places even have cheap little markets with fresh produce. Even if you'll only be around for a few days, toss a couple of staples in your backpack and skip restaurants altogether! As long as you don't pick anything that needs refrigerating, you're safe.

I had the opportunity to go to Spain with my grandparents when I was a kid. I had two years of introductory Spanish, but, between the three of us, that was it. My grandfather managed to find a bakery in every town we stopped in, and could usually find a farmer's market of some sort, too. We ate bread and apples, often with some cheese, and I don't think I ever got bored of it. It wasn't even an issue of frugality—we could just see more if we weren't stopping for a meal every couple of hours.

2. Make friends

I've managed to get myself invited along on cheap evenings out with the locals. Even though I hadn't been around long enough to learn which restaurants and bars were significantly cheaper, my local friends always knew the places to go. It's no good to just ask for recommendations, unfortunately. Most people will just point you toward the obvious tourist traps, especially if you don't speak the local lingo so well. I think a lot of them think that they're doing you a favor, making sure you can get a meal where someone speaks English.

It works in English-speaking countries, too. By hanging out with fellow college students on a trip to Oxford, I managed to get myself invited along to their version of the cafeteria on someone else's meal plan. Their food was much better than the typical American college's, too!

3. Order the soup

I was able to stretch my food budget in Ireland by ordering the soup, and I've been able to use the same technique in a lot of places. As long as you enjoy chowders and stews, you're set! Most restaurants will add in bread, and I've never been hungry after a good-sized bowl of soup and some bread.

I try not to ask what's in soup anymore, though. I was in Doolin, Ireland (population 500), and in dire need of some lunch. The cheapest thing on the menu was seafood chowder. I ate a huge bowl, and it was delicious. Afterward, I made the mistake of asking the ingredients. The waitress gave me an odd look; turns out that scraps of just about every item on the menu made it into the chowder.

4. Greasy is okay

If you walk as much as I do when you're traveling, you'll burn the calories from that greasy kabob off the cart. I realize it's not the healthiest thing in the world, but it works for a quick, cheap meal. As long as you don't restrict your diet to greasy street food, you'll survive. And I think a lot of those barely identifiable meals on a stick can be pretty tasty. In Jerusalem, I always make a point of visiting the nearest falafel and shawarma stands. My money goes far, and I get what may be my favorite meal in the world.

— **Thursday Bram**

 HEALTH & BEAUTY

You don't have to be a fashion diva to understand the importance of both feeling and looking good. However, when makeup, accessories, and a killer wardrobe bust the budget and leave you feeling remorseful, it's no longer about staying on top of trends—it's about sticking to your financial priorities. Learn how to look fresh and stay within your means in this next chapter. With all of our tips on staying healthy and looking good, you can show the world that smart spending is officially in style!

15 Ways to Make Your Clothes Last Longer

With everyone trying to stretch their dollars further these days, it makes sense to take care of the things we have rather than buy replacements. This goes for clothing as much as anything else we own and use on a daily basis.

As a reformed clotheshorse, I struggle to prevent myself from shopping for new duds on a daily basis. Here are 15 tips I've used to help preserve my wardrobe.

. . . .

1. Know thyself

. . . .

The first step in maintaining a wardrobe is to be aware of your cleaning limits and your clothing habits.

If you can't afford to dry-clean clothing, don't buy dry-clean-only clothes. If you despise ironing and avoid it with all your might, don't build your wardrobe around French-cuff shirts or blouses that need starching. You'll only regret it later when you can't be bothered with the cost or hassle of upkeep, and you'll either have to get rid of the clothes, or wear them wrinkled.

If you have a habit of spilling coffee down your front, there's no shame in wearing lots of chocolate brown, charcoal gray, and navy blue. Dark colors hide a multitude of clumsy moments.

Make sure that you don't fold clothes that need to be hung and don't hang clothes that need to be folded. Sweaters stretch on the hanger and dress shirts don't do well folded, unless you are an expertly masterful folder of some kind.

. . . .

2. Dress for the task at hand

. . . .

It can be tempting to simply get messy chores done while wearing whatever it is we wore at work, but that's a fast way to ruin work clothes. There's a reason why moms frequently make a distinction between their kids' "play clothes" and "school clothes." If tackling a potentially dirty project, don't do it in a dress shirt and slacks. It's much less expensive to leave a stain on an old sweater (to keep the other stains company) than to dry-clean it off your blouse. Also, wear an apron while cooking. I've ruined many a lovely dress over a pot of simmering bolognese.

....

3. Stop laundering so often

....

Washing an item of clothing is the fastest way to help the fibers break down. The fewer times you have to wash an item of clothing, the longer it will last. And realistically, as long as you weren't sweating up a storm, you can get a few wears out of a dress shirt before needing to throw it into the wash.

Create a system that allows you to remember which items of clothing have been worn (if you are too lazy to rehang lightly worn clothing, it's okay to drape it over surfaces like your dresser or a chair, just as long as it doesn't drop on the floor). The following items can also help you wear a shirt or a pair of pants more than once before washing:

Tide to Go Pen

These little pens cost less than $5, last for a long time, and will save your blouse when you manage to drop a dollop of marinara down the front. Coworkers and friends are always wowed by how quickly this trick works to remove stains from fabric. I use a Shout stick stain remover as well, on large stains, but the Tide pen allows you to use the stain treatment without having to wash the clothing item immediately thereafter.

Lint Roller

Sometimes a pair of black slacks doesn't really need to be washed—it just needs the cat hair removed from around the cuffs. My white dog really loves to jump on my lap whenever I'm wearing dark colors (it's like he *knows*), and it's not that he's dirty—he just sheds like it's going out of style. I have lint rollers in every room of my house, and they keep my slacks looking professional. I also keep one at the office to pick up stray hair and fluff that inevitably lands on my back and shoulders during long days spent scratching my head.

Deodorant

Your shirts will smell better and stand up to multiple wearings if you yourself don't stink.

....

4. Keep all those buttons

....

Every time you buy a new piece of clothing that comes with spare buttons, immediately put the buttons in a jar or box reserved entirely for buttons and spare thread. It's easy to lose track of these important surplus buttons, and it's one of the fastest ways for a cardigan to become useless.

. . . .

5. Wash in cold water

People who wash their clothing in cold water will notice a drop in their energy bills very quickly. In addition, many fabrics (especially nylon and elastics) hold up better when subjected to less heat. Cold-water detergents are designed to remove dirt without the help of hot water, but even normal detergent will work well. Also, even though I try my hardest to be a stickler for the environment, a good capful of bleach will do amazing things for your whites—it's almost like having new clothing.

. . . .

6. Wash inside out

Clothes with texture (jeans) or designs and adornments can last longer if washed inside out. With jeans, you'll find that holes around the knees where the fabric is worn thinner appear less quickly (unless you wanted the holes). You'll see less cracks and fading on your T-shirts, too.

. . . .

7. Obey the laws of color

At the end of a long day, with loads and loads of laundry facing you, it can be tempting to just throw the reds in with the blues, but try to keep like colors washed with like colors. Reds and blues fade easily, and everyone knows how one red sock can turn a whole load of whites a light shade of rose. Try your best to keep dissimilar colors apart in the laundry.

. . . .

8. Zip up before washing

Unzipped zipper edges on pants and hoodies are often very rough, and if left unzipped during the washing and drying cycles, they'll chew up the rest of your clothing in no time! Make sure that all zippers are zipped to the top before tossing them in the wash. And while you're at it, fasten the bras, too, to prevent hooks from catching on delicate knits or sweaters.

. . . .

9. Be gentle with underwear

Don't tumble-dry your over-the-shoulder-boulder-holders. Bras and underwear made of fabrics and fabric blends (especially nylon) besides cotton don't do well in the heat of a dryer. Hang or drape them to air-dry instead. And those little mesh bags that your mother used to nag you to use when washing delicate brassieres? They really do help to keep bra straps from wrapping around other clothing while in the wash.

10. Slip into something new

Consider wearing some of the more traditional underclothes that have fallen out of fashion as of late—slips, body shapers, and undershirts will both help your clothing drape better over your body, and also protect clothing from sweat stains and friction that can cause wear and tear. I recently spent $70 on a body slimmer by Spanx (I used to buy the cheaper ones called Assets), and not only do I look slimmer, but the darn thing actually helps improve my posture. Also, it keeps my wobbly thighs firmly encased in fabric, which means that the insides of my pants don't wear as quickly because my thighs don't rub against them as much.

You obviously don't have to spend nearly as much for a cotton undershirt or a silk slip, but these things keep clothing away from your skin, and it doesn't matter if they get stained, since no one else is going to see them. Undershirts, slips, and camisoles can help your clothing last longer.

11. Notice your surroundings

Those Aeron chairs, while comfortable, really rub the seat of your pants the wrong way. If you are noticing increased wear on your clothing, look around to see what part of your work or home environment could be contributing to it. The edge of your desk might be wearing down your shirt cuffs. Look for small ways to improve your position so that your clothing isn't taking a beating while you are working.

12. Clean/polish shoes

Polishing may seem a bit tedious, but frequently wiping down your shoes with a barely damp cloth will prevent dirt from settling into cracks permanently, and will keep leather from getting too dry (which causes cracking).

13. Don't drive in dress shoes

I've ruined many a pair of dress pumps by doing nothing more than driving; the back of the heel rubs against my car's floor mats, and before long, my black shoes are spotting fuzzy gray patches on the back where the carpet did its work. I'm not high-class enough to wear driving moccasins, so I just wear sandals or Crocs in the car and put my shoes on once I arrive at the office.

14. Patch early, patch often

Blue jeans are usually the first items of clothing to develop little holes in them. You can patch clothing by buying fabric patches and applying with heat-activated adhesive, by sewing a cute patch over a tiny hole, or just stitching it up with a little needle and thread.

15. Reinforce hems

Even cheap clothing can last a long time if you reinforce the hems with a simple stitch on a normal sewing machine. Skirts, pants, even underwear will wear longer and better when the hems are less flimsy. You don't have to be a talented seamstress to hem a pair of pants; anyone can do it with a little practice. In addition, once a shirt's wrists are looking ragged or your slacks are starting to wear at the hem, you can always take them in a bit. Hemlines rise and fall every season, but you can probably safely remove a half-inch from your favorite jeans without anyone noticing. This keeps hems nicer and overall appearance neater. — **Andrea Dickson**

10 Ways to Fake it till You Make it

Needing to look the part, even if you'd rather not be bothered? Having to save some scones while still playing the game? I hear you. And sitting on the sidelines isn't always an option— particularly when your network is directly related to your net worth. Here are a few suggestions to help you survive on the corporate playing field and still bank some bucks.

1. Sex up your travel mug

By losing the plastic freebies with the snap-on lids and going for a sleek brushed-steel, insulated model, you'll turn BYO coffee from frumpy to fashionable. Bonus? Your coffee will stay hotter much longer. With $8–$10 (much less if you find it on a clearance rack), you've just upped your style factor by several notches.

2. Lose the watch

Anyone who has had to spend time on the heavy hitters' business circuit knows that a great watch is just as important as a phenomenal pair of shoes. And it had better be one phenomenal watch. While in this country Rolex is sort of known as the gold standard, there are other parts of the world where walking in with a Rolex is equivalent to having purchased your business accessories at a bargain basement department store. What's a billionaire in the making to do? Lose it altogether. These days a watch is just a style accessory. It's much cheaper to glam up your cell phone or Blackberry and get the same recognition.

3. Stylish bottled water

Green is in, and having an eco-friendly water bottle will make you look chic and in the know. Take a look at Nalgene for BPA-free plastic, Klean Kanteens for stainless steel, and Sigg for aluminum.

4. Skip the perfume

The good stuff is insanely expensive. Consider skipping it altogether and just going natural. If you really feel a scent is necessary, try making your own. If custom-blending the perfect personal scent is a little more than you want to attempt, a DIY shower spray is more than doable. You'll still smell great and spend less.

5. Reheel and repair

While you can easily skip the watch, there's no way around the shoes. Find a high-quality pair, even if they are gently used, and take them to a shoe shop where they are good at jazzing up an older pair of quality leather shoes. If that grosses you out, save up until you can get a good set at an outlet store or on clearance. Pick a style that's versatile and don't wear them out unnecessarily. Save them for those meetings where you know you need to make a statement. Keep them repaired and shined, and you've got an investment purchase you can get years of service from.

6. Travel

Think you can't afford to travel for long periods of time to highly coveted destinations? Consider a long-term house-sitting job in London or Paris, or a long-term trip in an exotic location like Africa or Southeast Asia via the hostel or English-language teaching circuit. And nothing gets you in the door faster than a shared knowledge of a location, region, or world-renouned heritage site. And if you're there long term, you'll have plenty of opportunity to take advantage of the free admission days. Take lots of pictures and have them playing in a digital desk frame during your next investor meeting. Travel experiences provide a common ground for discussion. And if Mr. Big Shot can only manage to make it to London once or twice a season for a weekend at a time, and you spend every winter there and can recommend some great little café next to a fabulous museum, who do you think he's going to call the next time he's in town?

. . . .

7. Celebrate the power of basic black

. . . .

Whether it's the right dress or suit, or a fresh coat of touch-up paint on that pile of thrift store frames, black is classic, oh-so-Euro, and one of the most inexpensive paint treatments out there. Got a couple of freebie floor lamps that have seen way better days? Spray them with a coat of primer and add either matte or textured black spray paint. Then shop for some stylish discount shades and you've got a remake on the cheap.

. . . .

8. Com is king

. . . .

This is literally our family motto, and has served both of us well professionally. You need to be able to

have communication with contacts regardless of any temporary set of circumstances. You can solve your own problems more quickly and nobody will really know how much you've been thrown for a loop if you still have communications established. Being out of the loop for too long is a huge professional risk. So is changing your phone number and e-mail too often. Even if you are transitioning to the role of stay-at-home parent, you can still keep up with business contacts and start an online gig or two to keep in the game.

. . . .

9. Coffee versus drinks

. . . .

If dishing out a bar bill of several hundred dollars to court a client isn't in your budget, consider treating them to coffee at a well-known stylish establishment. Just because these shops aren't the most frugal for your daily budget doesn't mean they can't be a frugal choice when trying to climb the corporate ladder.

. . . .

10. Streamlined is sexy

. . . .

Consider some of the photo shoots from the popular design magazine, *Dwell.* They feature uncluttered, low-on-hype space. Keeping it simple allows for the most efficient use

of your time and money, and leaves loads of opportunities for extra projects, meetings, or getting it done on the golf course, so to speak.
— **Myscha Theriault**

10 Beauty Products You Can Make at Home

Tired of hearing health and beauty product recipes you need a chemistry textbook to decipher? Here are 10 simple ideas that anyone can try at home. No 28-step, 15-ingredient face masks here. Simple. Quick. Workable.

For the most part, these ideas are pretty unisex. So guys, feel free to indulge too. The only thing you'll need in addition to the ingredients is a few different types of empty containers such as spray bottles, squeezable squirt bottles, and empty jars with screw-on caps.

1. Spray conditioning treatment

All you need is a fine mist spray bottle. Put a small squirt of your favorite

hair conditioner in the bottom. Fill the rest with water. Close the bottle. Shake like crazy. Spray on wet hair and comb through. It's also a great detangler for kids. That is literally all there is to it.

All spray bottles are not created equal. I bumped up to a larger one so I would not have to remix as often. Check to make sure it's a spray coming out, not a stream.

Also, play around with the amount of conditioner that works for you. What works great for one person may leave another person's hair oily. This is easily solved with either extra water or extra product.

2. Homemade scented hand sanitizer or aftershave gel

Equal parts of rubbing alcohol and aloe vera gel with a few drops of your favorite scented oil. Seriously, that's it. My husband also likes to add sandalwood oil to this mixture and uses it as an aftershave gel.

We like the pump-action containers left over from liquid hand soap. You might like the smaller squirt bottles; whatever works for you. I put one by every sink in the house, and next to the keyboard. We've gotten in the habit of having a small bottle in each vehicle as well.

3. Body ointment for those extra-dry spots

This is dirt cheap and works really well. Buy the cheapest generic brand of vegetable shortening you can find. Melt it slowly in a mini Crock-Pot or double boiler. Pour into a small, heat-resistant airtight container and add a few drops of essential oil. (I like using peppermint oil in this ointment because it has a soothing yet zingy feel when you use the balm.) Close the container and allow to resolidify.

Use as a night balm on lips, elbows, heels, and knees. This ointment is dirt cheap, works really well, and has no unidentified ingredients.

4. After-shower body oil

You can skip the regular stuff with all the petroleum additives and just use olive or soy oil with your favorite scented oil. Olive oil blends work great. Women in the Mediterranean have been using olive oil on their skin for a very long time.

5. Salt and sugar scrubs

I usually make salt scrubs. They feel the same to me, and bulk salt costs a fair amount less, which enables me to enjoy even more of this stuff! Pick a great essential oil scent or a fun combo like orange and cinnamon or grapefruit and sage. Put a few drops of the scented stuff into a larger amount of soy oil, which is available in bulk at warehouse stores for pretty cheap. Mix in either salt or sugar until you have the desired consistency. Scoop into airtight containers and set aside for use. What is great about these scrubs is that you can exfoliate and get a moisture seal at the same time.

6. Make your shampoo a multipurpose item

Here are some additional things I use shampoo for: shower gel, facial cleanser, light stain remover, substitute sudsing item in homemade spray cleaners, and as a laundering agent for hand-washable delicates.

7. Everlasting hair spray

Okay, it doesn't last forever this way, but it lasts much longer. The only trick is you need the pump-bottle kind, not the aerosol. You can transfer this to another empty pump hair-spray bottle, or wait until yours is half empty. Ready? Mix it half and half with water. Yup. That's it. It works just fine when diluted by up to 50%.

If you enjoy the salon brands of hair spray (and what woman could blame you?), this will really help you maximize your product investment.

8. Astringent

Maybe all of you women out there have had better luck than I've had finding a brand of astringent that is effective enough to do the job, and yet gentle enough to not completely dry out your skin. Since that's never happened for me, I use this version.

All you need is two parts witch hazel to one part distilled water and a few drops of tea tree oil. I suppose you could skip the tea tree oil, but it works well for this, is refreshing, and allows you to adjust the recipe for those times when your skin is more oily than others. I put this in a small travel-sized squirt bottle from the pharmacy section of my favorite bargain department store, and use it with a cotton ball.

9. Hair-clarifying treatment

To give yourself a hair-clarifying treatment, mix a tiny bit of baking soda with your shampoo in the palm of your hand. It doesn't take much. Do this at least once a week to keep the buildup off your hair and promote volume.

If you've never tried this, or it's been a while since you have, use lots of baking soda all through your hair before you shampoo. You'll need to deep-condition afterward for sure, but it's a good way to get the gook off. If you really want to not have to bother with the mixing part, you can put a tad in a separate bottle of shampoo and mark it as clarifying shampoo to use once a week or so.

A tip: Too much of the baking soda can cause a bit of drying. Start light and work your way up.

10. Scented body spray

Put two parts rubbing alcohol to one part water, and a few drops of your favorite scented oil in a spray bottle. If you'd like a little more luxury, add a bit of olive or soy oil for moisture to rub in.

Some tips on scented oils

If money is really tight for you, or you have sensitive skin, feel free to skip the scented oils. We used bits of our weekly and monthly savings to slowly accumulate a collection of various essential oils. My favorite kind is the generic brand that many health-food stores carry. They are the most afford-able brand I've found, and they have a killer selection of scents.

My husband and I really enjoy having these homemade products on hand. Having several scents to choose from really makes us feel like we're living large and getting a custom product every time we make stuff for baths and massages. Even some of the more expensive scents like san-dalwood last a really long time. So in the end, you are getting more spa, beauty, and bath products than you ever would otherwise. Which leaves you more money for other important bubble-bath necessities . . . like wine!

— **Myscha Theriault**

6 Ways to Get Your Toiletries for Cheap, or Even Free!

With my budget straining at the in-crease in the cost of milk, I can't always justify buying my favorite shampoo, the best razor, or that luxurious body wash I crave. I have found ways to ease the pain, and while not always predict-able, they work! If you don't mind get-ting a bit creative with your methods, you can pay much less (even nothing) for your bath and body treats, too!

1. Guest services

When I was a girl, my aunt came home from a convention in Vegas and dumped a gallon bag of designer minisoaps and tiny shampoo bottles into my lap. At the time, I thought she was loony. Who would use these hotel spiffs for everyday grooming? Years later, my husband be-gan working a "road-warrior" job that left us with too many of the tiny treats. We continued to save them in a small plastic bucket in our bathroom closet. They came in handy when guests or rel-atives visited, and when the budget got a bit tight, we would hold off on buying full-size products until the bucket had been emptied. We could go weeks on what he had acquired in a year. (Before you complain that it's greedy to take the hotel soaps, if you don't use them, many places will throw them out any-way, as a hygienic measure.)

2. Free samples

Joke all you want about those of us who sign up for every free sample you can get online. With the ample supply of one-time-use samples I've received, I have been able to enjoy some of my favorite brands at times when access to them would be scarce. (With each birth of a child, for example, I would pack the samples into my baby bag for my first shower at the hospital. After three or four days of hospital care, having the tiny packets of my favorite body wash in my institutionalized beauty routine seemed like heaven.)

Other fun uses for them? Send them with kids going to summer camp, tuck them into a car kit for unexpected road trips, or add them to that "hotel mini" collection mentioned above. You can set up Technorati (Technorati.com) tags to scout out anything labeled "freebies" for even more good leads. (To cut down on waste, I would personally avoid signing up for items I would be certain not to use. It is clutter, and it costs the companies money to mail. Let's be responsible here.)

3. Shop till you drop

This tip takes much more work, but can net you some great deals on your top brands. Many seasoned savers have been successful at scouting out retail and drugstore clearance deals in the health and beauty aisles and pairing them with high-value manufactur-

ers' coupons. Many Web sites track the best deals on items, including my favorite, RefundCents.com (which also allows shoppers to chat about their deals and trade coupons). Just be sure you are buying things you will use, and don't hog items for the thrill of it. Overconsumption is *not* the goal.

4. Free after rebate

Some folks despise the effort involved with purchasing a product on the premise that it will be free after a mail-in rebate. Several online and retail outlets, however, make this an easy choice for shoppers. Many large chain drugstores feature three to six monthly brand-name items for nothing out of pocket (but tax) after rebate. Rebates are easy to obtain, thanks to their dependable tracking system and online submission forms (which sometimes won't require even the cost of a postage stamp). With unique incentives (like 10% bonuses for rebates that are placed on gift cards, for example), it's possible to buy your favorite items for completely free, including the price you paid in tax. If you are getting items that won't rot in the back of your closet, you can add $10–20 to your health and beauty budget. With items ranging from hair dye to cold medicine, I have found it to be an excellent deal.

....

5. Bulk-buy with a buddy

I'm no sucker for those giant bottles of mouthwash packaged together at the warehouse stores. They are a great deal if priced separately, but how long would it take me to use all of it? I've found the best way to save money at bulk co-op outlets and warehouse stores is to go halves with my mom. She buys pretty much the same stuff I do, and by splitting both the cost of the warehouse club fee and divvying up the goods, we make out like bandits on items that rarely go on sale or don't offer much in the way of manufacturers' coupons. (Carpooling also saves us gas money and makes for a fun afternoon!)

....

6. Dispense with care

Many of the products we use every day are packaged poorly. They are designed to allow a large amount of product to come out at a time, increasing your usage and forcing you to buy more often. If you only need a "dime-sized" helping of shampoo, why does a "half-dollar" come oozing out? One way to save money is by changing your usage habits. We do this at home in several ways. My favorite is to buy some inexpensive foaming hand pumps for products like face wash. A nifty toothpaste tube flattener helps us use every bit of paste, and keeps the kids from trashing the sink. Storing bottles upside down in the shower lets us get two or three more days from most items.

Saving money doesn't have to be a hardship. I've never been one to ask families to make their own beauty products for the sake of frugality (although it can be a fun hobby!). I also despise generic beauty products and don't believe in watering down the goods. It is possible to stick to your favorites and save at the same time! — **Linsey Knerl**

5 Cheap and Simple Sunburn Remedies that Really Work

Oops, I did it again. Thinking that just one unprotected hour in the sun would be all right, I fried my fair Danish skin. I really know better, but it can happen to the best of us. Sunburn isn't just a painful nuisance—it can wreak havoc on healthy skin and put you at risk for getting skin cancer later in life. (In fact, two or more severe sunburns before age 18 greatly increase the chances, as skin has a sort of a "memory" of burns and tans year after year.) While the best treatment is prevention with an effective sunblock, sunscreen, or a proper physical barrier from the sun, things can sometimes go wrong.

So what do you do when you return home from an outing and you resemble a well-done lobster bake? Try one of these time-tested home remedies, and give yourself a chance to heal.

. . . .

1. Vinegar
. . . .

Apply vinegar (or a half-water, half-vinegar solution) with a spray bottle or dab on with a towel. Then cover the area with a tea towel for overnight relief. While a bit stinky, it does wonders to "cool" down the burn.

. . . .

2. Aspirin
. . . .

Recommended for adult sunburn victims with a known tolerance to aspirin, this is the treatment I used most recently. Simply crush a couple of aspirin in a bowl or cup with the back of a spoon. By adding a small amount of water, you can create a paste which can be applied directly to the burn. (Be sure to crush the aspirin very well.)

A variation on this is to add it to Maalox (the tummy stuff) instead of water and brush it on with a basting brush or a cotton ball. Since aspirin alone can cause burns, be certain you don't have an intolerance to it being applied topically, and don't let it sit on your skin any longer than overnight.

If in doubt, simply take the aspirin orally as recommended. (Be aware of your tolerance to aspirin, first.)

. . . .

3. Tea
. . . .

Whip up a batch of tea (either from boiled tea bags or sun tea), and cool it in the fridge along with some ice. Spray directly on burned skin or dab with a soft rag. It instantly cools and relieves the burn, so keep applying for best results.

. . . .

4. Milk
. . . .

Apply gauze dipped in lukewarm milk to the burned area. Leave on for a minimum of 20 minutes, and rinse the area when it starts to get a bit funky-smelling (or no more than an hour or so later).

5. Aloe vera

Growing up, we always had an aloe plant in the home for minor burns and afflictions. Break off a piece of the plant and squeeze it so that some of the goo (gel) drips out the end. You can rub this directly into the sunburn for the same kind of soothing relief you can get from those "after-burn" gels and over-the-counter commercial products (only better). When the gel starts to dry, the area may become stiff, so keep applying or cleanse the area and apply some new gel.

Extreme Sunburns

I'm no doctor, but I'm also no stranger to sunburns. If prevention has failed, and you experience a nasty burn, stay home, stay hydrated, and stay rested. Using simple techniques to relieve pain and maintain the integrity of your skin, it is possible to get back to your daily routine the next day. If you experience any of the following symptoms, see a doctor for proper care:

Dizziness
Vomiting
Fever/chills
Intense fatigue

You will also want to be aware that some prescription medications increase your sensitivity to sunlight

and put you at added risk of getting burnt. These include certain:

diuretics
antibiotics
tranquilizers
birth control pills
diabetes medications

Medicated soaps, perfumes, and Retin-A can also make you susceptible to overexposure.

Take it easy year-round to prevent sunburns and other dangerous skin conditions. A regular visit to your dermatologist can keep skin concerns under control and decrease your chances of cancer-related illness or death. — **Linsey Knerl**

50 Ways to Get More from Your Health-Care Dollar

In *Stay Healthy, Live Longer, Spend Wisely: Making Intelligent Choices in America's Healthcare System*, Dr. Davis Liu describes how health insurance premiums grew 73% compared to wage increases of 15% from 2000 to 2005. Here are 50-plus ways to save money without compromising your well-being, drawn from Dr. Liu's book and my experience, research, and wisdom of the Wise Bread community.

1. Skip the annual physical but get specific screening tests recommended by the U.S. Preventive Services Task Force (USPSTF).
2. Save on prescription medications if you meet certain eligibility guidelines found at Together Rx Access (togetherrxaccess.com).
3. Review all medical bills and question anything that doesn't seem right, especially services that should be covered under your insurance plan; talk to your insurance agent, employee benefits counselor, and/or insurance company representative to make sure that covered items are paid correctly.
4. Call your physician's office to ask about a nonurgent problem (or to see if a symptom requires immediate treatment) rather than scheduling an appointment
5. Ask your pharmacist about medications including prescriptions, over-the-counter drugs, and behind-the-counter remedies; you'll get free, valuable advice from a health-care professional who has spent many years studying medicines.
6. Compare your physician's recommendations with clinical guidelines (e.g., pediatrics, obstetrics/gynecology, urology); ask about anything that you don't understand or seems to be unusual care.
7. Do self-exams.
8. Get high-deductible health-care insurance rather than forgoing insurance because the uninsured have higher death rates from chronic disease and accidents.
9. Carry continuous coverage so that exclusions for preexisting conditions will be limited according to

federal law associated with HIPAA (Health Insurance Portability and Accountability Act).

10. If you may lose your job or already have lost your job, compare the cost of COBRA coverage (extended to displaced employees but includes the employer's *and* employee's cost) to other options such as purchasing insurance on your own or getting coverage on a spouse's plan.

11. Open an HSA (Health Savings Account) linked to a high-deductible insurance plan and take a tax deduction for your contributions, subject to limitations as stated in the federal tax law.

12. If your insurance company does not cover USPSTF-recommended tests, question why it doesn't cover expenses proven to prevent disease and start a letter-writing campaign asking for coverage; write your insurance company and your state's insurance commissioner.

13. Take a tax deduction for medical expenses that exceed 7.5% of your adjusted gross income (AGI).

14. Go to a provider (physician, physician extender, or hospital) that is in your insurance company's network so that you can take advantage of discounted rates already negotiated by your insurance company.

15. If the provider that you prefer is not in your insurance company's network, ask the provider to join so that you can get discounted rates.

16. Choose a high-performing healthcare plan by checking out plan ratings by the National Commission on Quality Assurance (NCQA).

17. Select a physician who follows the standards of care according to evidence-based medicine; find those who meet the NCQA criteria in its searchable physician directory online (recognition.ncqa.org).

18. Get free blood pressure, blood sugar, and cholesterol checks at health fairs. Take the results to your physician for discussion and further testing if needed.

19. Wait at least 24 hours after the onset of a fever (with no other worrisome symptoms) before making a doctor's appointment.

20. Take free or nominal-fee health classes on topics such as childbirth preparation and diabetes prevention; beware that some of

these classes are sponsored by pharmaceutical companies.

21. Find free skin-cancer screenings but don't wait to find a free check if you think you may have a problem.

22. If there is a competitive market for health-care services (e.g., more than one maternity hospital in your town), negotiate prices, preferably before you receive services.

23. Check out the safety, effectiveness, and clinical soundness of home remedies, herbs, and supplements at PeoplesPharmacy.com and Consumer Reports-Health (consumerreports.org/health/natural-health.htm).

24. Evaluate hospitals using The Leapfrog Group's ratings (leapfroggroup.org).

25. Donate blood and receive free blood pressure, iron-level, and temperature checks.

26. Establish a relationship with a primary care physician through an "establish visit."

27. Get better, more informed, and quicker medical advice by preparing a written summary of your medical history (should include surgeries, medical conditions, medications, allergies, family history, and social history).

28. Communicate priorities during the initial part of the physician visit, rather than waiting until the very end of the visit to express your concerns about an important matter.

29. Help your physician arrive at a diagnosis with a minimum of tests by discussing your symptoms in terms of *when* you first noticed the problem and *when* it occurs; *what* it feels like (sharp or dull, constant or intermittent) and *what* seems to make the problem better or worse; *where* in the body it occurs; and *why* you are concerned.

30. Make sure you understand any diagnosis, additional testing requirements, treatment plan, and further assessments recommended by your physician before you leave the office.

31. Before allowing medical treatment (giving informed consent), determine the benefits, risks or complications, and alternatives to treatment plans.

32. Don't hesitate to get a second opinion not only on the diagnosis but also for the treatment plan if you feel uncomfortable with your physician's plan, and especially if you have a rare disease.

33. If you are waiting on test results, never accept the phrase, "We'll

only contact you if the results are bad." Ask for a callback or, preferably, written documentation of your test results.

34. Get immunizations to prevent certain diseases.

35. Ask your primary care physician what type of specialist treats the problems you are concerned about to avoid paying for a visit to the wrong type of specialist.

36. Make sure your physician is licensed by checking with state boards.

37. Don't be overly influenced by ads for prescription medicine: Ask about symptoms mentioned in commercials or ads rather than requesting specific medications; stick with your current regimen if it is working without complications. Heavily advertised medications are almost always more expensive than nonpromoted ones.

38. Consider generic drugs to replace name-brand drugs; for a list of generic drugs with their equivalents, check out the Electronic Orange Book (fda.gov/cder/ob/default.htm).

39. Compare drugs in the same class by price using Consumer Reports-Health Web site (consumerreports.org/health/natural-health.htm).

40. Cut costs on prescriptions through patient assistance programs; learn more at RxAssist.org or Partnership for Prescription Assistance (pparx.org).

41. Ask for free samples of medication from your physician.

42. Tell your physician about cost concerns and see if there is a less expensive but just as effective alternative treatment.

43. Read the labels and ingredient lists of over-the-counter medicines to make sure that you are not overdosing on certain active ingredients.

44. Say "no" to body scans that are more likely to lead to unnecessary testing and cause harm via radiation rather than detect deadly disease.

45. Take part in group visits with your physician or support groups for those with similar diseases.

46. Exercise, maintain a healthy weight, and don't smoke.

47. Research medical issues using reliable sources such as the MayoClinic.com.

48. Sign up for discount programs with non-insurance companies such as Merck's Prescription Discount Program (available to those who do not have prescription coverage) and Pfizer's program.

49. Visit a dental clinic associated with a dental or dental hygiene training program to save on fees.
50. Tap into hospital programs that offer aid for low-income, low-re-source patients.

This article is intended to provide readers with a general understanding of health-care issues rather than provide personalized medical, financial, or legal advice. Please consult your physician. — **Julie Rains**

6 Secrets for Nailing that Salon Mani-cure Look

A 10-finger discount? My painted nails redefine that term in a fashion that transcends all crimes. Without theft or fraud, I score big savings with my manicured hands.

Here's how: With art and artifice, my hands have a fraudulent appearance of expensive weekly spa dates. Through careful maintenance and do-it-yourself enamel, I have created a polished 10-finger discount.

CAREFUL MAINTENANCE

The first approach—careful mainte-nance—is valuable for extending the lifespan of salon or DIY nail color. With discipline and maintenance, I have stretched manicures for two to three weeks longer than the standard one week of brittle color. To do so, I follow these steps:

1. Let the paint dry

Meditate, breathe deeply, or count to 1,000. The goal: Keep your mind active and your hands still. This Zen approach to nail polish will preserve the finish of your painted nails. That's because nothing fades faster than smudged, nicked, or dented nails. So get your money's worth from a professional manicure by taking the time to let the paint completely dry.

2. Wear a top coat

A glaze of clear nail polish will serve as an invisible barrier between your manicure and the world. Coated by a clear top coat, your painted nails will remain bright and chip-free. Clear polish works like slipcovers on a sofa. It's all about preservation. Therefore, beginning 24 hours after a salon visit, I religiously apply clear polish every day. It's my buffer between the harsh world and my soft hands.

3. Clean with gloves

On the highway of life, our hands pay daily tolls. Washing dishes, gardening, and other daily activities can crack, scratch, and chip our hands. For protection, wear appropriate gloves—rubber, canvas, or cotton—while completing household chores.

DIY MANICURE

The second technique—a DIY manicure—is also a money saver. You can groom and polish your own hands for less than 50 cents a session, compared to salon visits that typically cost between $10 to $25 per visit, plus tax and tip. Here's how I give myself a manicure, including the trendy French manicure.

4. Pay attention

A careful study of salon operators will yield valuable insights. Professional manicurists have a variety of tricks for softening, filing, and painting nails. Watch and learn.

5. Buy the right tools

Invest in sturdy but easy-to-use manicure/pedicure tools. There are also great painting kits that make it easy to apply the two-color (nude base and white tip) French manicure. It's easier to create a salon finish if you have the right tools, including a nail clipper, a pumice stone, files, and enamel. Don't forget the cotton swabs and nail polish remover. Those tools make it easier to tidy up whenever you have painted outside the lines. That's what the pros do.

6. Be patient

Painting nails is like meditating. Focus, breathe, and concentrate on a small canvas of life. Don't be afraid of making mistakes; goofs can be removed or painted over. And finally, don't rush the process. Let the paint dry or else you'll ruin a perfect 10-finger discount. If you liked these handy tips, you can find more frugal beauty secrets in my new book, *The Frugal Duchess: How to Live Well and Save*, or by visiting www.frugalduchess.com.

—Sharon Harvey Rosenberg (The Frugal Duchess)

10 Frugal Ways to Care for Your Allergies

I've had allergies for as long as I can remember. I have spent more days sniffly, snorty, with a scratchy throat and sinuses that feel like they're about to explode than many entire families. I've ended up with more ear infections, sinus infections, and cases of bronchitis than I care to recount. In fact, I take so much decongestant that my husband decided that my mutant power is Producing Snot.

And I've tried everything, from standard medicine to acupuncture to herbal remedies to homeopathy to staying in the house and shutting all the windows. The following are some things that work for me and won't cost you an arm and a leg. In this, the beginning of allergy season (well, for most of you . . . here in SoCal it's more like "The Middle of the Allergy Season that Never Ends"), I offer these suggestions in hopes that they also work for you.

1. Alternate decongestants. Now that many companies are not selling deocongestant products containing pseudoephedrine due to the fact that it can be used to make meth, the new decongestant of choice is phenylephrine. The first works by actually thinning mucus while the second helps make nasal passages wider. Allergies can cause both symptoms, so your nose, throat, and sinuses will feel better if you treat them both. Since you aren't supposed to take them together, alternate dosages.

2. Cut 12-hour pills in half. Most pills containing pseudoephedrine are now the 12-hour kind. (Is it harder to make meth from these? I don't know.) Sometimes, they actually work for 12 hours. But if they don't for you (like they don't for me—they work for about 8 hours and then I'm miserable for 4 until I can take more meds again), cut them in half and take them at 6-hour intervals.

3. Buy decongestants at bulk stores. I don't notice a difference in quality, even when I buy the store brand, and I pay much less than I would at the grocery store, pharmacy, or even discount store. I can get both daytime and nighttime pills that will last me

between three and six months (depending on the season) for less than I would get 24 night-time pills at some stores.

4. Take lots of showers. I love a good, hot shower, and I've found that timing them well can mean not having to take deconges-tant. For instance, if I take a hot shower about an hour before bed, the steam loosens the crap in my sinuses and it has time to drain out before I go to bed. Then, I don't have to take the nighttime medicine, which can give me some of the . . . um . . . *strangest* dreams.

5. Drink mint tea. Apparently, this won't work if you have gastro espaphageal reflux disease (GERD). But if you don't, and you don't hate tea, this is a good way to open up your air passages. I will often drink it when I really need some more decongestant but can't take it because it hasn't been long enough since my last dose or I don't have any on me. It doesn't work for long, but it has gotten me through some hard times. Plus, it tastes good, gives me good breath, and is relaxing.

6. Use a saline nasal spray. My sinuses hurt the worst when they're dry. The saline helps keep them moist, which helps the mu-cus move through them faster. Once you have a sprayer, you can make your own spray. Otherwise, store brands are cheap and work.

7. Don't irrigate your sinuses. Sprays are fine, but shooting salted (or vinegared—yikes!) water through sore, dry sinuses just makes them more sore and more dry af-ter the water dries up. Not to mention, it hurts like the dickens when you do it! They get moist for a short time, but are more irritated in the end. And when they're full, the water doesn't loosen the mucus much, just makes it a little runnier and more likely to lodge in your ears. I don't know why, but it happens to me every time. I've had the same thing happen when I try to use the steroidal al-lergy nasal sprays, though.

8. Try homeopathic remedies. These are controversial and rightly so, as my experience is that many of them don't work. However, some of them do. And some of them work sometimes, with certain symptoms, and not others. These are usually a pill that dissolves under the tongue or a liquid that you dissolve in wa-ter. My recommendation is to go

with the pills, as they often taste *much* better than the liquid. You may have to try several brands to find one that works, but it's worth it if keeping chemicals out of your body is important to you. They're not as strong as traditional decongestants so they don't always work, but have saved my days more than once.

9. **Drink lots of water.** Sounds cheesy, but it's true. The more you drink, the looser your mucus will be as there's more water in your body for it to mix with. In addition, if you drink a lot of water, your sinuses will be more likely to be moist, which means they'll function better.

10. **Walk up stairs. Repeat.** There's something about the position your body is in when you're walking up stairs that is conducive to draining sinuses and nasal passages (body slightly tilted forward, head up). I'll do this in the middle of the night when I wake up because I can't breathe and it's too close to time to get up for me to take more medicine. It has never failed to drain my sinuses and help me get back to sleep. — **Sarah Winfrey**

7 Beauty Secrets that Cost Almost Nothing

Open the pages of almost any magazine, or turn on the TV, and you're bombarded with ads that claim (if indirectly) that their beauty products will make your life fuller, more rewarding, and all-around better. The message is pretty simple: Spend, and you'll look so much better.

There are, however, a few beauty methods that are nearly guaranteed to make you look and feel like a million bucks, and you don't have to smash your piggy bank to get them. It's tired to talk about how beauty comes from within, so rather than worrying about the purity of your soul, here are a few ways to bring out an inner glow that doesn't involve liposuction or deep contemplation.

1. Have safe sex

There's something about regular sex that makes people beautiful. I don't know if teenagers still talk about this stuff today, but back in my high school days, we believed that sex cleared up acne. Although there doesn't appear to be any direct correlation between sexual activity and zits, people who have regular, satisfying sex tend to have a glow about them.

Sex gets your blood flowing. Orgasms reduce stress and increase pain tolerance due to a natural boost in oxytocin and endorphin levels. Sexual satisfaction also helps you sleep better at night. In short, orgasms are good for your brain, and when your brain is happy, the rest of your body will respond in kind. Your mood, sense of self, and general well-being will be affected, and others will notice.

2. Exercise

This is another activity that gets your endorphins flowing. Something about that bordering-on-Zen feeling that follows a vigorous workout is really lovely. Sweating clears out your pores and helps to prevent acne. Even though I personally regard the gym as a chamber of torture, I find that I look like a million bucks about an hour after huffing and puffing through a weight routine, or 30 minutes of tripping over the elliptical machine.

But it's not like you have to push yourself to the limit to get benefits from exercise. A short routine of yoga will get your blood pumping, as will a long, meandering walk around a park or city street.

Our bodies are made to be active, and by doing so, we're sending the right signals to our muscles and cells to keep up the good work, and maintain health.

3. Laugh

You'd never know it from the popular media, but smiling is such a simple way to immediately look better. We spend so much of our days grimacing at the computer screen, or glowering at the line in the post office, that it can be tough to bring ourselves to smile in a genuine, open manner.

When was the last time you doubled over in laughter? Laughter, like orgasms and exercise, releases hormones that reduce stress and lower blood pressure. In fact, just anticipating a good laugh can help to reduce your overall stress levels.

Some people avoid smiling because they don't like their teeth, but even a genuine close-lipped smile on a normal face is more attractive than a blank stare or a glaring model with perfect features. Think about how wonderful a face that is shining with laughter looks. It doesn't matter if you laugh like a hyena or snort like a pig (like me), laughter enhances your beauty. Rent your favorite movies or watch comedy clips online. Hang out with your goofy friends. Stick duct tape on the bottom of your cat's paws and giggle at his antics. Whatever it takes. Laughter is infectious, and it is gorgeous.

4. Get some sun

No, I'm not talking about baking on the beach, because I'm an advocate of avoiding skin cancer whenever possible. Just 10–15 minutes in the sun every day can help your body produce more vitamin D than inhaling any amount of vitamin D supplements. Many people in the U.S. suffer from vitamin D deficiency, which causes bone loss, depression, and cancer. If you are worried about wrinkles and sun spots on your cheeks, put sunblock on your face and hands, but let the rest of your body soak up some nutritious sun.

5. Drink wine

Assuming you're not allergic to alcohol or prone to rosacea, having a glass of wine not only gives your cheeks a healthy glow, but can give you a good dose of resveratrol, a polyphenol with antioxidant properties. The alcohol is good for your heart, too (we're talking light to moderate drinking, of course). Sure, I might be looking for an excuse

to have a glass of champagne with lunch, but as long as I'm not driving around or performing open-heart surgery after a lunchtime aperitif, what's the harm?

6. Stay hydrated

I don't believe in drinking great quantities of water if you don't want to, and it's probably not necessary to take in the eight daily glasses that were randomly recommended to the general public for no reason. But drinking water helps keep your kidneys happy, your skin cleansed (again, the sweating helps here) and plumped, and the toxins flushed out of your system.

7. Go easy on the medication

It can be so easy these days to pop a pill for every little ache and pain, or to take meds when conditions start to trend in the wrong direction. Sometimes, though, doctors seem too busy to deal with the source of your problems and are more than happy to push a prescription across the counter at you. A couple of years ago, I counted the number of daily medications that I was taking, and they numbered eight, five of which were either unnecessary, redundant, or causing *more* problems that required other medications to combat. Overnight, I switched from a regimen of eight medications to three, and found myself feeling better, looking better, and experiencing none of the previous side effects that I had been plagued with.

Obviously, you should consult your doctor before changing your diet or medications, but don't be afraid to push your doctor to help you find ways around taking more medicine; on the flip side, be sure to listen to what your doctor tells you. If s/he tells you to lose weight or change your diet to avoid taking cholesterol medication, you had better take the advice seriously rather than simply continuing on as always.

So, you might be asking—I'll be better looking if I stop taking so much Ibuprofen, drink more water, and laugh uproariously while drinking champagne and having sex in the sunshine?

Well . . . yes. But don't quote me on the outdoor sex part.

— **Andrea Dickson**

4 Ways to Dress for Success and Still Spend Less

Ladies, are any of you out there like me? I hate buying clothes for work because I know that work is the only place I'll wear them. They aren't particularly comfortable, and they certainly aren't my style outside of the office. On top of that, work clothes tend to cost more than any other clothes I buy. In fact, sometimes I feel like I should get an extra stipend just because I have to buy an entirely separate wardrobe full of clothes I would never otherwise choose to wear so that I can be presentable at the office.

Over the years, I've learned how to stretch my money when it comes to buying work clothes, so I can spend more of it on things I really want. Here are some of my ideas.

1. One jacket, several outfits

Instead of buying a jacket for every suit or a blazer for every outfit, make the jacket itself your centerpiece. Then, you can find a jacket you love and create several work outfits around it. You'd be surprised at how many skirts and pants you can find that will go well with whatever jacket you choose, and no one will ever know that they weren't made to go together. And, if the outfits are different enough, people won't even notice that you wore the same jacket three times last week!

This is great in more ways than one:

- It saves you money, because you're not buying as many jackets *and* you're not buying overpriced suit combos.
- You get to choose your style, because you choose the jacket that's your centerpiece.
- You're more comfortable, because the jacket is so often the most uncomfortable part of an outfit.
- If there's a downside to this, I haven't found it yet.

2. Better yet, wear a button-down shirt as a jacket

Yeah, it sounds a little crazy, and it doesn't work with every button-down shirt in your closet, but you would be surprised at how often this does work (and I love it because of how it messes with people's heads).

Here's the plan: wear a tee or a tank with a dressy neckline, and pull on a matching button-down. Keep the buttons unbuttoned and wear your shirt like a jacket. No one will really think it's a jacket, but it will have the same effect in people's heads.

If you're game to try this, look for button-down shirts that are dark-colored or that have vertical stripes in neutral colors. Make sure the button-down you buy isn't too long or too short—it should fall to the place where you like your jackets to fall. Try it on with a tank or a shirt like the ones you'll most likely wear with it, just to check the effect.

3. Layers, layers, and more layers

Layering several different items, as long as it's done tastefully, can make some items of clothing that alone are too informal to wear to the office into something that's totally office-appropriate. Try a couple of T-shirts of different lengths under another with simple gathering or ruching. Or, wear a couple of different-colored tanks under a white button-down shirt. Those are just a couple of ideas. Seriously, the possibilities are endless.

On top of being less expensive (tanks and tees costing less than most work shirts), you'll be more comfortable this way. And when you're more comfortable, you'll feel more like yourself, and it'll be easier to be at work all day.

4. Sometimes, you can get away with a T-shirt

No one will ever tell you this, but when you're wearing a jacket, particularly when you're going to keep it buttoned, most people won't focus on you long enough to tell if you're wearing a T-shirt or something fancier. It's the same when you're layering a shirt under a button-down or a sweater. There's no need to spend as much on that under-layer as you do on what goes over it!

If you're worried, choose soft T-shirts made with thick material with decorations at the neckline. Just make sure it's something you'd be comfortable wearing outside of work, too, because that's how you'll save the most. — **Sarah Winfrey**

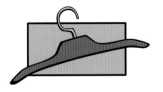

6 Cheaper Ways to Have Fabulous Hair

In high school, I watched a friend drop over $100 on a trip to her favorite salon. I'd always known that her hair looked better than mine, but I couldn't believe that it was simply a matter of money. I didn't want it to be, either. Even in high school, I had other financial priorities. There are frugal options for taking care of your locks, though. It's taken me a while to find them, but I use these tricks regularly.

1. Skip the repeat

"Lather. Rinse. Repeat." It's one of the greatest marketing phrases of the 20th century, but it's misleading. To get your hair clean, one lather-and-rinse cycle is plenty.

2. Eat a healthy diet

You can eat your way to better hair. If you eat a balanced diet—plenty of fruits and vegetables, as well as protein—your body will have the nutrients necessary to grow healthy hair. A balanced diet won't solve every hair problem, but it can head quite a few off at the pass. For instance, if you have an iron deficiency, your hair can thin out.

3. Go natural

Hair dye is expensive, and it can make keeping your hair healthy much harder. Consider going back to your natural hair color for a while and save some serious dough. The same goes for perms. I've also been known to dye my hair myself. It isn't hard, but I recommend having a second pair of hands around.

4. Shop around for products

The same tips for shopping frugally for groceries work on hair-care products. I buy on sale, clip coupons, and pick up bulk bottles. I do have a preferred brand that I tend to stock up on, but it's not the most expensive brand on the shelf. According to a few hair-

styling friends, the *expensive hair products aren't really any better* than cheaper options. Wholesale distributors will also often provide great deals, as do online vendors.

5. Barter

If you really do prefer the job a professional will do on your hair, you don't have to give up those regular visits. But it's worth finding a stylist willing to accept a payment other than cash. During high school, I traded babysitting for haircuts on a regular basis. I didn't have to pay for a haircut and I could generally do my homework at the same time.

6. Go organic

Sure, organic brands can be more expensive than their chemically enhanced counterparts, but many organic shampoos and conditioners do not contain sulfates. While sulfates do remove oil and other junk from your hair, they also strip it and create frizz and other problems. If you can switch to sulfate-free products, you can stop using other products—like anti-frizz mousse. There's a period of adjustment and your hair might be slightly oily in comparison, but after a few weeks, your hair should be healthier. — **Thursday Bram**

10 Killer Ways to Feel Like a Million Bucks

There are plenty of studies tying health to wealth (and vice versa), on a national and a personal level. Here are some tried-and-true suggestions for feeling better.

1. Stretch and strengthen your hamstrings

In a society where many of us sit for hours at a time, the hamstrings don't get either the exercise or the stretching that they need to hold it all together. Do you suffer from lower back pain? Mid-to upper back pain? Knee problems? Hip aches? Ankle soreness? All of these can be tied to weak and/or tight hamstrings. You can find some ideas for strengthening your hamstrings at home from About.com (physicaltherapy.about.com). You should feel both the stretching and the strengthening immediately in your lower back, though it may take two to three weeks to see results other places.

2. Drink water

I know you've heard this a million times. I've heard it a million times. But it's true. We all know that drinking water helps flush toxins from the body and keeps the kidneys healthy, but did you know that staying hydrated will help eyes stay moist, sinuses drain, stomachs digest better, skin stay soft, nails and hair grow healthily, brain synapses connect better, and blood cells fight off infection?

3. Spend some time every day in silence

Some people like to meditate, but some continue with their daily tasks, just without the noise. Most of us are so accustomed to the sounds around us—the air-conditioning, the typing of the employees around us, people talking in meetings—that we don't realize how tired it makes us. Noise can make it harder to breathe and harder for the heart to beat. Noise can make it hard for us to sleep. It can even make us more aggressive. But a few minutes a day of silence helps our brain to relax and find equilibrium again.

4. Make yourself comfortable

For me, this one is a little more intuitive than some of the others. Not only will we avoid repetitive stress injuries if we take the time to make our workstations ergonomically correct, but we will also be happier if we are wearing clothes and shoes that are comfortable. And, happiness correlates positively with health. It could also help you lose weight!

5. Tell yourself to be healthy

Have you ever had an experience like this? You have a big project due on Wednesday. Many people around you are sick, but you tell yourself over and over that you can't get sick until after the project. You stay healthy, turn the project in, and wake up sick on Thursday morning. I know it's happened to me. So, apparently, what we tell ourselves really matters. On a larger scale, positive self-talk leads to reduced stress, which leads to better health.

6. Take a walk

Human beings weren't made to sit for long periods of time. In fact, sitting for long periods of time (at work, on a plane, in a car, etc.) can cause all sorts of injuries, from the obvious back pain to the less obvious blood circulation and reduced heart and lung efficiency. Scary!

There are several series of slightly goofy-looking exercises you can do when you're in a situation where you have to sit for a long time, or you can just get up and walk. Walk around your cube, around the office, to the bathroom on the other side of the building. Just take the pressure off your spine and move around! In addition, walking is as effective (or more!) than running for physical fitness.

7. Relax your muscles the natural way

Sure, muscle relaxants are good when you're in severe pain, but who wants to walk around like a zombie all the time? (Don't answer that!) But there is a natural way to gently relax muscles. Quinine, generally given to combat malaria, also relaxes muscles. And the best part? It's available in tonic water (regular and diet) and bitter lemon, both of which you might have left over as mixers from your last party. A glass of tonic water before bed can help you relax into your sleep.

. . . .

8. Cultivate happiness

Whatever makes you happy, do it (unless grisly murders make you grin—then consider your unhappiness a sacrifice for society's sake). Why? Because happiness has a strong correlation to health. No one seems to know quite why this is so, but studies show over and over that it is.

. . . .

9. Relax your jaw

Sort of like your hamstrings, your jaw is connected to lots of other parts of your body, though it particularly influences the muscles in your neck and shoulders. Relax the jaw and the tongue (make sure it's lying on the bottom of your mouth and not pressed up against the top), and feel the muscles in your neck and shoulders let down. Apparently it's so effective, they're encouraging pregnant women to do it while in labor!

. . . .

10. Avoid pollution as much as possible

Most pollution is toxic. It's made up of things that are bad for your body. Even if it doesn't cause cancer or something else life-threatening, a cough, a sneeze, or a runny nose all get in your way. It's true that you often don't know when you're around a pollutant if it's not bothering you, but avoiding the ones you do know about is a great place to start. Look for improved respiration, circulation, and happier eyes and nasal passages.

As they say in Ireland, "May you live a long life, full of gladness and health, with a pocket full of gold as the least of your wealth."

— Sarah Winfrey

5 Tips on Toilet Paper Usage

Is there a strategy for using toilet paper? Is it worth our time? When I spend money to literally flush the product down the drain, I often wonder . . . how much should I be flushing? Am I wasting money?

As an adult, I had never given it much thought until a comedian I was listening to pointed out that even hard-nosed conservationists seem to forget their scruples in the stall. Why use a few sheets when a massive wad of paper will do the job just as well?

My mother worked out, pretty quickly, that regardless of how good the toilet paper was that she bought, we'd use the same amount: way too much. So instead of buying the luxurious double rolls with extra absorbency, she'd get standard rolls. And as kids, we never really noticed the difference, and would still pull armfuls of paper from the roll, leaving the cardboard tube spinning on the holder for a good 10 seconds.

So, what to do? Pardon the pun, but even to a frugal guy like me it seems a little anal to have a toilet paper strategy. I mean, I don't have much of a life but I'm not at the point where I'm counting TP sheets . . . at least, not yet. But there are a few things I can suggest, especially with kids around.

1. Skip the luxury

Think twice about getting those expensive, luxurious rolls of paper for the kids' bathroom. Regular paper works just as well, and kids will use either one with zeal.

2. Try baby wipes

Consider having a box of baby wipes in the bathroom. For those times when things get a little messy (stomach flu, anyone?), a baby wipe or two will do the work of handfuls of toilet paper. They're designed to handle much bigger messes than regular TP. Of course, buy *flushable* wipes if you're flushing them along with the regular TP.

3. Buy standard-sized rolls

Double rolls actually run down quicker than two standard rolls. The reason being, we see more of the roll and subconsciously use more because there's plenty. It's the reason you keep seeing manufacturers up the size of the roll, so that now we need extra equipment to fit these jumbo-sized rolls onto the holder.

4. Go with store brand

There is very little difference, if any, between name-brand and store brand; especially in this instance when it all ends up being flushed down the drain anyway.

5. Practice restraint

There's no reason to attack the roll and pull masses of paper away with the force of Rambo starting a speedboat. Grab what you need and nothing more.

These few simple tips will save you money on a product every single one of us uses on a daily basis. Let's save a few trees and a few bucks at the same time. — **Paul Michael**

5 Ways to Trim Haircut Costs for Kids

Let me preface this advice by saying that I'm not above cutting my own kids' hair. We often cut their hair (especially the boys'), and in the summer, we prefer to shave it down for coolness and to avoid tick dangers. I have found great results with a mid-range Wahl hair-cutting kit, complete with all the bells and whistles. There are times, however, when it is not appropriate for me to cut their hair: My daughter is entering tweendom and needs something more stylish, or my youngest needed his first "real" cut and had more cow-

licks than I could handle, etc. How do you manage to keep up the coif and keep it under budget? Start with these simple tips.

. . . .

1. Use a coupon

. . . .

This should be a no-brainer, but I'm amazed at how often I forget. Many of the larger chains offer incredible savings on cuts via clippable coupons in your local paper inserts. Great Clips, for instance, drops the cost of their kid's cut from $11 to $6 at several times during the year (right before school, for example). You must have the coupon, however, to get the savings.

. . . .

2. Get a group rate

. . . .

Planning on bringing in all four kids and the hubby for a trim? Schedule a time in advance on a day when they don't do much business. Ask if they can give you 20% off for having all the cuts done on the same day. (Don't forget to tip.)

. . . .

3. Use a barber

. . . .

Salons aren't the only ones equipped to handle cleanup. Our local barber has been doing boys' and men's cuts for decades, and he still charges rates from the 1970s. You'd be surprised at how all that experience can translate into a gift for keeping the little ones still. (And they get to sit in that "Big Boy" pedestal chair!)

4. Hit the beauty schools

You may not trust a beautician-in-training with your hair (although I've gotten nothing but fantastic results), but that doesn't mean your toddler can't take the risk. With prices at 25–50% off retail, you can get all the kids' hair done for the price of one salon cut! (And if there happens to be a "mishap," you can blame it on your child's imaginary friend.)

5. Cruise the retirement circuit

Someone's grandma used to be a hairdresser. The key is finding her. (Ask around.) Since zoning ordinances may prevent private individuals from conducting hair business from their home, it may not become a regular thing. For an emergency trim or for in-between cuts, that "has-been" stylist could really come in handy! Sometimes they will forgo payment entirely in lieu of a nice trade (the same goes for any private stylist—not just those who are retired).

Stay creative and remember that you only have a few short years where the kids won't care how their hair looks, and that means a smaller hair-care budget! — **Linsey Knerl**

FUN & ENTERTAINMENT

$

What's life without the thrill? While not absolutely necessary for survival, a good time now and again can keep you hoping and dreaming (and make the mundane tasks of balancing the checkbook and monitoring credit card balances a bit more tolerable). Do the most memorable of moments have to cost an extraordinary amount of money? We don't think so. In fact, we have made it our mission to experience the best the world has to offer on a less-than-modest income. This chapter is sure to open your eyes to just how compatible fun and frugality can be.

12 Fabulous Frugal Party Ideas

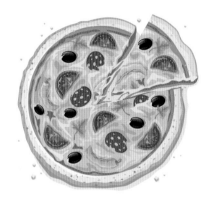

Need ideas for having a fabulous party with minimal money, time, and catering abilities? If you've got gracious friends, just a bit of cash, and time to clean your home, you'll likely enjoy these 12 ideas for having a party to remember.

....

1. Topping-optional party

....

One of my all-time favorite parties was a nacho party. Guests enjoyed trying nachos topped with various types of cheese, beans, and veggies. You can do this with pizza and baked potato,

too. Anything that can use a wide variety of toppings will work.

....

2. Soup and sandwich party

....

This is perfect for cold days and nights. Make simple but classic sandwiches like grilled cheese and PB&J. They can even be made to order, cutting down on your party prepping work. Chicken and noodle soup is usually a crowd-pleaser. For a more grown-up event, whip up this onion soup recipe (you'll need 4 medium onions, chopped, canola oil, 2 cans beef consommé, toast cut into 1–2-inch pieces, and mozzarella cheese; sauté onions until soft, mix onions with consommé and 2 cans of water, and simmer for an hour or so; serve topped with toast and cheese).

....

3. Lasagna and spaghetti pie can serve many

....

If you're not in the mood for cooking, try one of your grocer's frozen lasagnas or go low-key with frozen raviolis. If you want to save money, bake a spaghetti pie (you'll need 8 oz. spaghetti, 16 oz. spaghetti sauce, 6 oz. of mozzarella cheese and cheddar cheese, and parmesan cheese; layer half of the sauce, uncooked noodles, and cheeses two times; bake covered at 350° for an hour; then uncover and bake for 15 minutes). Serve with bread and salad.

4. Breakfast or brunch

Breakfast/brunch servings can be smaller and lighter. Serve bagels or egg and sausage casserole with orange juice and coffee.

5. Afternoon tea

You may need to spring for a teakettle or you can use the microwave to boil water (beverage setting). Select specialty tea at your favorite grocer. Have sweetener (honey or sugar), milk, and lemon on hand. Serve with a few treats such as your favorite jam and slightly softened cream cheese with specialty crackers or goodies from your favorite bakery.

6. Dessert party

Bake your favorite desserts, which usually can be made days to weeks (if you freeze desserts) ahead of time so that getting ready for the party is a snap. If it's warm outside, you can serve ice cream with a variety of toppings in the backyard or on the front porch. Bonus: You won't have to clean up much inside.

7. Limit liquids

A chef friend has taught me to limit choices and I think this concept is applicable to food *and* beverages. Buying every combination of soft drinks (regular, sugar-free/caffeine-free, caffeine-free-only, etc.) can put a huge dent in your budget, so you may opt to serve lemonade or hot Russian tea, depending on the season. Add a pitcher of water and you'll easily accommodate many guests' beverage of preference.

8. Time limit

Parties don't have to last hours. You can schedule a quickie before or after a big event, such as dessert after a holiday show or hot chocolate after an evening of sledding or Christmas caroling. People won't arrive expecting a large food spread.

9. Require RSVPs

One of the biggest expenses associated with a party is the extra food and drink for the guests *who might show up*. Knowing how many people will be attending (and not having to guess at many more showing up the day of the event, or calling at the last minute) helps you to buy and prepare the right amounts.

10. Accept help

Some of your guests may have a special dessert or outstanding appetizer they would love to show off. You don't have to require a dish to attend, but if guests offer help and ideas, don't be shy about accepting. A few extra dishes that guests are happy to provide would help you a lot.

11. Allocate accordingly

Set a festive table and make sure you have plenty to offer guests, but you don't have to place everything you have on the table from the start. It's best for guests to take small portions and keep returning for more, rather than tempting them into grabbing more than they can finish.

12. Local access

If your home cannot accommodate the number of guests you'd like to have, consider facilities at a city park (some have indoor space for rent with great views and often include tables, chairs, and other equipment), community center, YMCA, or place of worship (generally available for free or discounted rates for members). Prices are *usually* much less expensive than meeting room space at a hotel, restaurant, or convention center.

— **Julie Rains**

8 Affordable Romantic Dates

Has budget dating become a real drag? Looking for ways to be really romantic while you're really broke? It's a challenge for married and unmarried couples alike. Here are eight easy ways to light a stylish spark without driving your budget into the ditch.

1. A matinee and happy hour

This is basically dinner and a movie in reverse. By simply switching the order and time of day you do this, your cash outlay reduces dramatically. Depending on what time in the afternoon you go, you might even have time for a double feature. Then check out your local eateries and see what happy hour deals your favorite places offer. With both entertainment and food at such a discount, you're able to keep the date under budget even if you want to indulge a little more.

2. Share a foot-long

Some popular sandwich chains offer 12-inch subs for five dollars. Get the meal deal, go easy on the ice in the drink, and take it to a scenic spot for a more modern version of the scene from *Lady and the Tramp*. Sharing an entree in general is a great way to be able to eat out affordably.

3. Open mic night

This is basically a no-brainer. Most of these I've been to are either at a hall where you pay a minimum donation, or a club or coffeehouse where you can go for drinks-only. Hey, it's cheaper than a hundred-dollar dinner out, right? Order a pitcher of draft and share it with another couple on a double date.

4. Stroll and snack

This one can be successfully modified for a variety of situations. Beach walk and an ice cream, cruising the piazza while sharing a portable panini, or sharing a hot giant pretzel while walking the street performers' circuit are just a few ideas.

5. Picnic in the park

Before you assume this can only be humdrum, here are a few ideas. First, pair the picnic with some form of free entertainment such as Shakespeare under the stars, a free concert, public dance performance, children's theater presentation, etc. Next, put some effort into planning the picnic menu so it will feel like more of a date. Wine, cheese, and bread with sliced fruit; biscotti and iced coffee with pressed sandwiches . . . you get the idea. A plateau overlooking Petra in Jordan and the piazza in Pisa, Italy, are a couple of memorable picnics for our family.

6. Camping

Since you are doing this as a date, get a great campground in a fun location with a decent number of included amenities. KOA Campgrounds (koa.com) are a good example. They have tree-canopied campsites with electricity and water, fire pits and picnic tables, swimming pools, clean showers with changing areas, laundry, high-speed wireless service, and more. You'll be able to get away to a simplified environment without having to "rough it" to the extreme. Bonus? It's an excellent litmus test for how you'll problem-solve as a couple.

....

7. Couples massage, DIY style

....

We actually own a professional massage table. As necessities go, this would not be at the top of many couples' lists. But it's one of my favorite indulgences, and with the treatments I like to get, the massage table paid for itself within three uses. While it's not my husband's favorite vacation activity, he does occasionally indulge for relaxation. What we found, though, was that once we bought the table and the spa cost of a massage was no longer an issue, we enjoyed them more and indulged more often. It's a great at-home date that's way more of an intimacy builder than movie night.

In terms of cost, the table is really the largest expense of a home massage

setup. If you decide to incorporate this as a regular part of your dating routine, upgrades such as hot stones, face-rest pillow covers, and essential oils for homemade massage products are all easily incorporated into your budget. It also provides an overall gift theme for things you can pick up for each other affordably, such as soothing background music, massage instructional videos for special techniques, etc. Toss in a few affordable bathroom upgrades, and you'll have an at-home spa in no time.

....

8. Photo shoot

....

If you each have a digital camera, fantastic. If not, it's an excellent opportunity to promote greater intimacy through sharing. Pick a place that's ripe with photo opportunities and take playful shots of each other and the area in general. Remote waterfall, picturesque piazza, hip downtown historic district . . . you get the idea. Incorporate lunch or a brown-bag picnic. Review your photos together at the end of the day and pick your favorites to play in a digital frame. Or have a little extra creative fun by editing a travel-style photo essay together. — **Myscha Theriault**

8 Tips for Getting the Most from All-You-Can-Eat Buffets

Food can serve many purposes. For some it is merely for nourishment. For others it is a form of art or a means of entertainment. For still others, it fills an emotional need and could even be considered an addiction or vice. For the purpose of this article, I'd like to point out that my advice is for the most basic of needs: good nutrition, a bit of indulgence, and a chance to fellowship with your family or friends with no dishes to clean up! Here are the eight ways we make our dining dollars a great investment.

. . . .

1. Kids eat free (or almost free)

. . . .

Yep, with four of them, it's important that we at least get a generous discount, if not a total write-off on the little darlings. In my area, Tuesday is usually the "Kids Eat Free Day" and requires that at least one adult purchase is made for every one (or even two) free kids' meals. Be sure that if you are dining at a chain restaurant, you call ahead to see if they honor national promotions.

. . . .

2. Lunch is served
. . . .

If at all possible, eat the lunch buffet. There is usually at least a $2–$3 difference in the pricing of lunch and dinner, and usually the offerings are similar. In rare instances, an evening buffet may offer something special, like nicer steak, crab legs, or a themed dinner. Weigh your options to decide if this is worth it. I won't justify the extra for a cheap steak, but a couple of jumbo crab legs might seal the deal.

. . . .

3. Skip the beverage (or plan accordingly)
. . . .

Drinks can make an otherwise affordable buffet downright expensive. If drinks are included in the meal price, go for it. If not, you may want to stick to water with lemon, or decide on only one drink. (Some places will let you get a soft drink with your meal and a coffee afterward, but may charge you for two drinks.)

. . . .

4. Fill up on fresh
. . . .

I know that those hot wings are tasty, and I'm also digging the homemade mac and cheese, but the best way to get your money's worth at a buffet is to eat as fresh as possible. Melons, berries, broccoli, and avocados are yummy ways to eat healthy and increase the value of your buffet. Encourage kids to eat one full plate of fresh stuff before they even head toward the french fries and fried shrimp. They will get loads of nutrients, and you can feel good knowing the extra cost gave them more than any fast-food kid's meal could really provide.

5. Take your time

Buffets are not a dine-and-dash type of atmosphere. If you are squeezing in your meal between two other pressing matters, pick another day to buffet. We like to take a weekday with nothing else to do, go early, and stay late. We snack, talk, and enjoy each other's company while sampling all kinds of new foods. If we do it right, we can have a lunch/dinner combo that knocks out two meals in one. We try to leaving by 4:30, so as not to get charged for dinner, too! We think of it as the same concept as a brunch, but with the two later meals combined. And if kids get hungry at home later, we snack on yogurt and granola, or another kind of light breakfast food before retiring for the evening.

6. Know what's safe

Even the most talked-about buffets can be a health risk. Be aware of your surroundings, and watch for common food-safety issues that may make you sick later. Aim for foods that are fairly popular, get switched out often, and appear fresh. If anything doesn't look right, please don't eat it! And let a manager know of your findings. Raw fishes should be approached with caution, and any salad made with mayonnaise should be eyed carefully. (It's a bad idea to go for that tuna salad with the orangish-looking crust on top.)

7. Explore your options

There are many types of buffets that appeal to our family. We like Chinese, American, and Italian the best. In areas that offer more diverse options, I'm sure there are many more kinds to choose from. Encourage your family to try new things while at the buffet. After all, if they don't like their first choice, they can just try another dish—and you won't be out any more money.

8. Be courteous

While buffets are great for saving money, they also seem to attract dining dunces that have little to no common sense or courtesy. While most all of you will know these, I feel they are at least worth saying:

Just because it is a buffet, doesn't mean you don't have to tip. Even if they only pick up your plates, your servers deserve the minimum for your region.

Don't take more than you can eat at one time. Wasting food is a no-no, no matter where you are.

Don't let little kids get their own food. Most places have a 10-years-or-older policy for the buffet line.

Clean up after yourself. It's a restaurant, not an abandoned lot. Pick your trash up off the floor, and try to make the server's job at least tolerable. They work hard, too.

We look forward to our monthly outings at a buffet-style restaurant. When a family of six can eat well for under $20—that's a great deal! And with a wide variety of dining options, buffets can fit any style or budget.

— **Linsey Knerl**

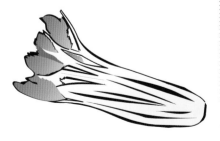

55 Ways I Saved Time and Money Planning My Wedding

One gorgeous wedding, one "flashed by so fast I can barely remember it" reception, and one glorious, relaxing honeymoon later, I'm back. It was fabulous. Truly fabulous. Sure, it had its glitches and panicked moments, but the memories I have in my mind are of being surrounded by people I love on one of the most important days of my life, and those I'll cherish forever.

On a more practical note, I started totaling the receipts from the whole affair yesterday, and was pleasantly surprised by what the numbers are saying. We did pretty well. How? Keep reading. Where we used a strategy, I tried to note it. Others were suggestions we pursued, and that would have saved us money, but that we rejected for one reason or another.

BEFORE YOU PLAN

1. Decide between time and money (wedding planner vs. doing it yourself)

Honestly, that's the decision you face. You can save your time and hire someone to do most of the legwork for you, or you can do it yourself and avoid paying a planner's fees. Your time, your money, your choice. I did it myself, and wouldn't have it any other way. Then again, I also like to be in control. Go figure.

2. Decide what's important

Where do you want to spend your money? On what? What have you dreamed about having in your wedding for so long that to forgo it would make the very event something other than a wedding? For me, these were my dress, my pictures, and my flowers.

3. Decide what's not important

There's a lot of hype surrounding weddings. One trip to a wedding convention, or even a perusal through a wedding magazine will give you multiple introductions to the wedding industry, also known as "those people who try to make you want stuff for your wedding so bad you'll pay outrageous prices for it." Beat them at their game by deciding what you won't spend money on. Mine? Cake, church decorations, and the reception.

4. Prioritize what's important

Even among the important things (or if everything's important), impose some sort of hierarchy. What is necessary? What would be wonderful but isn't necessary? What can go, if push comes to shove? My list: dress, pictures, flowers, cake, reception, church decorations.

5. Purchase a "bargain" book (but only one)

These really are helpful, particularly if you shop wisely and select one that has good information for your area and on the topics that are most important to you. I lost my planning book somewhere in the process (after its main period of usefulness and before I moved), so I can't tell you what it was. Do only buy one, though; they tend to be repetitive, and could create a substantial hole in your budget. Better yet, borrow one from a friend (or get her to give it to you—like she needs it anymore).

6. Find a planner that will work for you

Depending on what you chose in #1, this either means a person or a book. Either way, choose someone/something you can work with, and whose interpersonal skills/interface works for you. I ended up making my own, out of a three-inch notebook and some plastic dividers, because I couldn't find one that didn't a) stress me out entirely; b) confuse the crap out of me; or c) make me want to puke with the number of pastel flowers on its cover. Sure, it's an initial expense, but most of them let you see how much you're spending in different areas and allow you to budget easier.

7. Decide on the "look" and "feel" of your wedding

This keeps you from buying things that later don't fit with what you want. Do you want something casual or formal? Classic or trendy? Carefree or chic? Mine was casual, laid-back, and carefree, while still being simple and elegant.

8. Determine how much you can spend

This can be a little awkward and unwieldy, what with your money, your fiancé's money, any money from parents or other relatives who want to contribute, and any investments you might be including, but it's worthwhile to do, early on, so you don't get your heart set on something you just can't afford, or find that you can't have *any* flowers because you already chose such an elaborate cake.

9. Make a budget, but make your own budget

Many bridal services will tell you that you should spend a certain percentage of your available wedding funds on X, another percentage on Y, and yet another on Z. I tried this, but it didn't work. I spent *way* more on my dress than I should have, given my budget, but *way* less than they recommended for my reception. But I spent based on my priorities, and I was happy with the results.

10. Find people to whom you can delegate

If you find them at the beginning, you won't have to find them at the end. And they're essential. Give them a little something special for helping out.

11. Laugh a little

Seriously, relax. I realized part of the way through my planning process that

a) I was going to have a wedding and b) I was just going to have a wedding. It wasn't going to be the social event of the year, but it didn't have to be. Consequently, I laughed a lot more and did things the way I wanted them done, not the way I hoped others would like. My way was cheaper and more relaxed.

CLOTHES

12. Research, research, research!

I got my dress for several hundred dollars less than retail because I spent several hours (spread out) researching it and the places I could buy it. It was perfect, and I didn't have to spend a fortune.

13. Rent them

Look on the web for sites that rent children's formal and dress clothing at a reasonable price and for a reasonable amount of time. There's not much of a point in spending $80 on a child's tux you can keep for three days, when you can spend $20 or $30 and have it for three weeks.

14. Make your own

If you are a seamstress, or know someone who is, make your own clothes, particularly for the flower girls. There are a million cheap and easy patterns out there, and cute material goes on sale quite often. My mom made my flower girl dresses, and they were darling.

15. Shop fabric and craft store sales

At the end of a season, these stores sell all the fabric that's obviously from the previous season at truly amazing prices. My flower girl dresses are a linen-look fabric from this summer that I purchased at half-price in September. Because I live in LA, it was still appropriate for the wedding.

16. Houseofbrides.com

I purchased my wedding dress from them and I couldn't rave more about the service they offer. It's a "no frills" sort of thing, and you have to give them enough time and trust that it will come. If they carry your dress and you're ordering far enough in advance, they can save you a bundle.

17. Don't buy boutique, but do try it on there

Boutique markups are ridiculous (or funny, if you're me and you already know you can find it cheaper somewhere else), and honestly, they have to be for the places to make a profit. It's good business. It's also good business for you to find one that carries your dress, try it on there, and get the size and any other information. It was a relief for me to know that the dress would fit when it came.

....

18. Look into dresses made out of different materials

....

Heavy satin is the most popular and, therefore, one of the most expensive materials right now. I ended up with a dress made out of taffeta, which was lighter (perfect for my more casual wedding) and cheaper, and made me feel like I belonged in a ballroom.

....

19. Find a seamstress who sews as a home-based business

....

People who do this are often cheaper, and can work around any scheduling difficulties you may have. I asked for recommendations at work, and found a woman who did all my alterations for $100! (That's unheard of, in the wedding world).

....

20. Avoid bridal chain stores

....

Seriously, it's tempting, but you can resist. Really. I have faith in you.

And you can most likely find what you're looking for somewhere else. If you truly can't, buy your dress there, but watch out for any other "special pricing" they may offer you on other items. The fact that your bridesmaids get 10% off their dresses because you bought yours there sounds good, but they'll still most likely be paying too much for their dresses. And alterations? Don't even get me started!

....

21. Make your own veil

....

It's easy. I promise. If you're worried, find a friend who can sew and get her to help. But really? It's cake. My best friend and I even did some hand-beading on mine, and that was easy, too.

....

22. Rent tuxes as a group— you'll get one free.

....

If you don't, go to another tux shop. Men's Wearhouse is, by the way, a great, easy place to rent quality tuxes.

CAKE

....

23. Club stores

....

Club stores will do decorating for you, and their cake doesn't taste bad (that, from the girl who doesn't like cake). They won't stack or do anything fancy, but what with the current penchant for individual cakes on individual stands, their 10-inch rounds are perfect. I had three (with a dessert table . . . see below) and they were great.

24. Decorate the cake with flowers

Why pay extra cash for frosting flowers on the cake when you could have real ones, often at a fraction of the price? If your florist wants to charge an arm and a leg for cake flowers, get them to drop off some extra petals and have an artistic friend arrange these on the cake. It's classy and tasteful, and your guests won't have to deal with mouthfuls of that awful frosting (unless, of course, you like frosting . . .).

25. Have a dessert table vs. cake alone

Originally, I wanted brownies alone. I ended up with brownies, mints, and cake, and it was perfect. And cheaper, because we bought the brownie mix and my mom made them. It wasn't too much work for her, and the overall effect at the wedding was more fun than that of cake alone.

26. Make your own cake stand

I used two hurricanes (of different sizes) and a small candle holder (upside

down). Classy, cheap, and fun. Just like me.

27. Make all your cakes the same flavor

The more cake flavors you have, the more you'll pay. Instead, pick your favorite and serve that. Bonus? No siblings arguing over who gets the chocolate!

28. Pass on the fondant

It's expensive *and* it tastes nasty. It looks nice, but not as nice as you would expect it to, for the cost. Other frostings look almost as nice, taste hundreds of times better, and cost much, much less.

29. Cut the round cake, but serve the sheet cake

We didn't do this, because of the brownies, but it's a tried-and-true way to save money. Put a smallish, decorated, round cake on the stand to cut. After you smear each other with frosting, have someone disappear with the cake, to "cut" it. A few minutes later, have them reappear with pieces of cake, and no one will ever know you swapped it out. Seriously.

DECORATIONS

....

30. Accessorize your flowers with bouquets from a club or warehouse store

....

These stores sell bouquets with great colors, year-round. Purchasing flowers here for pew decorations, centerpieces, and buffet tables can save you a bundle.

....

31. See if your church or reception hall has decorations you can use

....

Often, people leave their decorations behind and a church or hall will save them. You may not love them (ask me about the hideous lace bows—I dare you), but they just might do, either if you get in a pinch, you just don't care anymore, or you don't want to spend anything else.

....

32. Ask your friends (tulle, anyone?)

....

As my friends have gotten married, they've passed around these two plastic garbage bags of tulle. We've all used it at our weddings, and it still looks great. By the way, wrinkles easily steam out of tulle.

....

33. Shop creatively

....

I "designed" my centerpieces in a discount craft store. Twenty each of table mirrors, hurricanes, blue glass pebbles, white candles, and 5 lbs. of dried lavender, all for less than one fully-designed piece. You just can't beat that.

....

34. Buy in bulk

....

Often, if you buy at least some minimum number, you get a discount. Hence, the above savings.

....

35. Give your centerpieces away

....

An easy way to save on prizes for reception games or gifts for your volunteers. Now, I wish I'd thought of it before the wedding.

....

36. Find out if your church or reception hall has a relationship with a local florist

....

Often, players in the wedding industry hook up to create package deals, or one will give you a discount if they know you're using the other. It didn't work out for me, but it's worth the time it takes to ask the question.

....

37. Be willing to substitute expensive flowers for cheaper ones with the same look

....

My wedding was in California, within a week of the Rose Parade. Many of the flowers I'd planned on having were sold out, because someone used them in a float. I was a little nervous about letting my florist make substitutions, but she did really well and the overall effect was still what I wanted. Also, it ended up being cheaper because she used some more obscure blooms.

....

38. Let your florist make the decisions

....

She is the professional, after all. I told my florist the overall look I wanted, my colors, and the fact that I was trying to save money, and then I let her make the decisions. The flowers couldn't have been better if they'd been all exotic blooms!

....

39. Simple elegance beats (and is less expensive than) lots of frills

....

Enter Sarah's Soapbox: Some florists want to add frills (extra bows, pearls, pieces of lace) at a substantial extra cost. Don't let them. Flowers should look like flowers, not frosted replicas of themselves. Besides, flowers are cheaper than bows, pearls, and lace.

....

40. Dried flowers are perfect!

....

My favorite scent is lavender, so I used dried lavender as one of the unifying themes of the wedding. The flower girls threw it, the church and hall were decorated with it, and the guests threw it at us as we left. It was cheaper than using real flowers in all of those areas, and united the different parts of our wedding festivities in a way I wouldn't have thought possible.

....

41. Find people who grow the flowers you want in their yards

....

Ask several of them if you can cut a few. True story: My friend got married in Seattle, where purple hydrangeas grow well. Her florist wanted to charge a ton for them, so she and her sister went door to door where they saw them growing, asking if they could come back and cut two or three blossoms the day before the wedding. So many people agreed to it that she had more flowers than she needed, all for the expense of a little legwork!

42. Go for a "different" look (don't use roses)

Because roses are commonly associated with weddings, they tend to run much more expensive than anything else (that's not exotic or imported). For my boutonnieres, I used baby gerbera daisies, because I like them. What I didn't know when I chose them was that they're also dirt cheap.

INVITATIONS

43. Club store paper center

Dave and I more than paid for our entire year's worth of membership in the deal we got on our invitations. And we got it all, down to the envelope liners and the little pieces of tissue paper between the invitation and all of the goodies that come with it. I got so many compliments on them, and people were shocked to find out I'd purchased them at a club store!

44. Skip the engraving

Unless your wedding is as formal as it possibly can be, engraving is an expense you can spare. There are several other (cheaper) kinds of lettering that look and feel like engraving, and create just as exquisite an effect.

45. Print reception cards yourself

Because they involve another whole folded piece of paper, reception cards often add a lot to the price of the invitation. I printed ours on vellum I purchased at a local paper store, and they fit right in with the rest of the invitation without pushing the cost up too much.

HONEYMOON

46. Ask your friends and their friends

Dave and I went to Sayulita, Mexico, which is a small town about 30 miles north of Puerto Vallarta. We stayed in a small condo with a full kitchen. We never would have heard about the place if it weren't for a friend of my mom's, who vacationed there last year. She knew that the condos were nice, but cheap, and where to get the best food for the least dinero. So ask around. What you really want just might be available.

47. Decide what kind of honeymoon you want

Dave and I knew we wanted something where we could choose to be alone or among people, and where activities were available but not necessary. We almost spent a bunch of money on a package deal, until we realized that the small-town atmosphere Sayulita offered was more "us." No matter what you want, you'll be able to find the best deals if you know what you're looking for.

48. Look into all-inclusive packages, especially in the off-season

This is what we almost did, and we almost got a killer deal and a five-night stay on the Mayan Riviera.

49. Look for privately owned condo-style housing

Often, you can rent condos by the day or by the week, with the week's price being cheaper than seven days would be. Way to save yourself some serious money!

50. Plan the honeymoon way ahead

Like with any travel, good deals are often available ahead of time. If you find one you like, snatch it up before it runs and gets away. We didn't have this option, as we were engaged for less than six months.

51. Plan the honeymoon last-minute

A little contrary to the above, but also true. When things don't sell, they tend to go on sale. If you're adventurous and not picky about where you go or what you get, you very well might stumble upon something fabulous!

52. Find a place where you can cook your own meals

Food is expensive. In some areas of the world, it's less so, but it still costs money. If you can cook for yourselves (and don't mind doing it), you may pay a little extra for the kitchen, but you'll save overall. We did this, and found that it came in very handy when I had food poisoning too badly to eat anything even vaguely Mexican.

53. Get off the beaten track

Why? Because you get to see more local color. And? It's cheaper. At Sayulita, we got all the beach, water sports, and surfer vibe we could handle, without Puerto Vallarta's prices. Yahoo!

54. Kayak.com

If you haven't used Kayak, you should. For any plane tickets. I did some site comparisons when we were purchasing our tickets, and found that they matched or beat any deal I found anywhere else, including with the airline itself. Puerto Vallarta, anyone?

. . . .

55. Bookit.com

. . . .

If we had purchased the fabulous "honeymoon in a package," we would have purchased it here. Again, I did the price comparisons, and they're the best. And no, I don't have any idea why they aren't more popular.

— Sarah Winfrey

How to Throw a Fun, Inexpensive Kid's Birthday Party

The most fun, memorable and inexpensive birthday party for your child may be, figuratively and literally, right in your own backyard. I've attended and hosted fabulous but simple parties with cake, ice cream, and a few balloons, and participated in much bigger backyard extravaganzas. But, just because a party is at home doesn't mean that it will be cheap and easy to orchestrate. I'll share a few tips for throwing a happy event that's light on cash outlay and effort.

Be aware of but not intimidated by the fervor around children's birthday parties. A few days ago, I picked up a parenting magazine for families in my area. In this 46-page publication, there are 15 ads from birthday party purveyors, ranging from magicians to nearly complete packages at a butterfly farm, party palace, and an art studio. Prices start at about $300 for eight children.

My kids have attended parties that involved:

- Dinner at a nice restaurant
- Mad Science presentation
- Backyard carnival with cotton candy fishing booth, and more
- Backyard petting zoo and pony rides
- Activities led by Taekwondo instructors at a martial arts studio

- Bear component selection and assembly at a Build-A-Bear Workshop
- Gaming at GameFrog
- Going to a movie and then hanging out with friends at a sleepover
- Bowling at the bowling lanes
- Baseball and cookout

There are loads of choices, or rather, there are lots of businesses who are ready to take your birthday money; even my local "Y" is offering parties now that "will guarantee a perfect day for your child's birthday."

It is the charm of the hosts and pleasantness of the guests that matter. One of the nicest parties my kids and I have ever attended was held in the apartment complex where the family of the honoree (five-year-old girl named Samantha) lived. Ten or so kids and many of their parents gathered in the family's living room, played (or supervised play) inside, walked together to the on-site playground, trekked back to the apartment, enjoyed cake and ice cream, and talked.

The parents were kind enough to allow me to bring my younger child in addition to my older son (the invited guest); in fact, they welcomed everyone and remarked that my then-two-year-old, who enjoyed building

and taking things apart and pushing buttons (which some people find annoying), would likely become an inventor and live off royalties, just like Samantha's uncle. What made the party great: party hosts who seemed to truly enjoy their guests' company, unstructured play, and the chance for parents to mingle.

But backyard events are not always so simple. A few years ago, I planned what I thought was going to be a frugal, fun party: a few guests; cake and ice cream; and some cool games. I bought Harry Potter paper goods, decorations, and party favors from a birthday celebration catalog. I figured since I was holding the party at home at no cost, I could afford a themed event at a cost of about $100.

Researching, evaluating, and organizing a series of activities took awhile. Supplies for the games added some to my expenses. A game that I thought would occupy the kids for a half-hour lasted about five minutes; another game that I was sure would be a huge hit (sticker tag) was rejected by one child, shortening its life at the party.

Since then, I've opted for single activity-based parties: a basketball party for a handful of kids held on our driveway; a baseball party for a slew of classmates held at a public park (rental fee of $10); and a sleepover with enough children to entertain themselves without causing property damage or personal injury. What I like most about these types of parties is that the kids are occupied but still have plenty of chances to socialize.

Consider all the costs (money and time). I have finally realized that there are many components to party planning and each has a dimension of time and cost to consider:

- Venue
- Activities
- Food
- Decorations
- Treat bags

Having a party at home can be the most frugal option or can cost you plenty, depending on your choice of activity or entertainment, extravagance or absence of decorations, food, and treat bags or party favors. For me, getting my house and yard in shape for guests is often a time-consuming challenge, though others may have spotless, ready-to-have-a-party homes. Decorations for a themed party can be pricey, so learn from my mistake, and make sure that the money you save on having a party at home isn't diverted to paper goods, Mylar balloons, and trinkets with images of fictional characters.

Other free or very inexpensive options include reserving space at a local park, the clubhouse in your neighborhood, or even your place of worship. Check rental fees and reservation requirements well ahead of the big day: The baseball field at a nearby park cost just $10 but it could only be reserved a few days in advance (also, don't assume that public spaces are cheap: some sites can run $100 or more).

It's obvious that if you hold a party on a baseball field, then you'll play baseball or perhaps softball or kickball; skate at the skating rink; bowl at the bowling lanes; swim at the swimming pool. But you might rent space at a public facility and arrange for entertainment and activities, in which case your time and cash expenditures increase.

Evaluate the package deal. You might decide to pay a fee (or a series of fees) for a party package or menu of services. Most price lists are very specific about what is provided. Still, a busy parent might not notice that the goody bags provided by the bowling lanes are empty or that party guests will most likely share space with shoppers at the Build-A-Bear Workshop.

Here are questions to help you evaluate the deal (relevant whether you are planning a party for a 5-year-old or an 80-year-old):

What is the price and time limit for the room or facility rental?

Can I bring as many guests as I'd like or is there a maximum number?

Will I have space dedicated to my party or will I share the space?

Is there a minimum number of guests (that I need to pay for whether they come to the party or not)?

Are decorations included?

Is food included?

Are treat or goody bags included and, if so, are they filled or empty?

Do you need to bring a birthday cake or is one provided?

Treat bags are optional. You don't have to give treat bags filled with very small, probably useless toys (which I am sure I did at least once). Here are some alternatives:

- A book (give everyone the same title)
- Pencils and candy (parents will like one; kids, the other)
- Deck of cards or other inexpensive but nice-to-have item
- Crayons or markers purchased at back-to-school sales with a coloring book from the dollar store
- Random items given as prizes throughout the party

What I've learned:

1. More kids usually means more fun.

2. Younger children (three to four and younger) may enjoy a very small party that is more of a play-date with cake rather than a big birthday party.

3. Certain activities can be overdone (for example, one of my child's guests attended two bowling parties in one day).

4. If you have to choose, spend money for a cool activity or a place for kids to have plenty of space, rather then decorations.

5. Kids who are usually ravenous don't eat much at parties (I still make sure we have plenty but typically have leftovers).

6. There are a surprising number of children who do not eat cake *and* ice cream.

7. Take pictures to make the day memorable. — **Julie Rains**

13 Free Ways to Wrap Your Gifts with Style

Beautiful gift wrapping doesn't have to cost a fortune. You can easily find ways to wrap gifts with everyday items around the house. Not only will you save money, but people will also appreciate your thoughtfulness and creativity.

1. Use the Sunday comics section. Extra points for having a *Calvin and Hobbes* strip prominently displayed.

2. Leftover wallpaper or fabric from your home improvement projects can add a touch of class to any gift.

3. Hat and shoe boxes for sentimental gifts, especially mementos or keepsakes.

4. Spray-paint boxes with bright holiday colors. This works great for large gifts that already come in their own boxes.

5. For the rustic look, use craft or construction paper and dress up the package with twine, strings, sprigs of greenery, or pinecones.

6. Dress up any plain wrapping with stickers, stencils, and stamps.

Use things related to the gift

7. Use pages from magazines related to your gift. For example, *Vogue* for clothing, *Rolling Stones* for CDs, *National Geographic* for business travelers' gifts, *Wired* for gadgets, etc.

8. If you wrap anything with the *Onion*, the wrapping becomes a gift in itself.

9. Use old school dot-matrix printing paper for computer products.

10. Use maps for gifts related to traveling.

Use child labor

11. Children's drawings are great for gifts to relatives. Hey, it's about time your kids earn their keep.

12. Put children's handprints on white construction paper. Acrylic paint is usually the best choice for these projects. If you have a baby, little footprints would also work (Warning: this might be nauseatingly cute, and messy).

13. Have extra pictures of your kids lying around? Fold them in half and use them as gift or greeting cards. — **Will Chen**

4 Tips for Cutting Out Cable TV Without Missing Your Favorite Shows

Think your cable bill isn't that big a deal? Think of it this way: "It's like buying a new 50" TV each year and tossing it in the dumpster," asserts CancelCable.com.

Fortunately, it's now easier than ever to enjoy a good picture and a wide range of programming without paying the cable company. Here are the changes and services that are allowing more and more people to cut the cable.

. . . .

1. The digital TV transition: clearer picture, more programming

. . . .

You can send away for coupons at DTV2009.gov to get those digital TV converter boxes for pretty cheap. I've been putting off buying mine (in fact, I let the coupons expire—doh!) and grumbling about the inconvenience of it all—until recently. That's when I heard that once we hooked up this box, we would receive the kind of clear picture that cable subscribers receive—on many more channels.

In fact, when I checked a helpful site called AntennaWeb.org, I found that my zip code should receive *tons* of stations, including five different versions of PBS. One reason some folks pay for cable is to get quality programming for the kids. With five versions of PBS, I feel pretty confident I could find something they want to watch at about any time of the day.

. . . .

2. Free programming

. . . .

Hulu.com and network TV Web sites like CBS.com, NBC.com, and ABC.com. And don't make me remind you about the library, people!

The one thing we miss most by not having cable at our house? *The Daily Show*, of course. So lately we've made it a little night-night routine to watch *The Daily Show* on my laptop via Hulu.com in bed. Yeah, it's yesterday's episode, but is getting the same episode 24 hours earlier worth $60 a month? Not to me.

And since I'm busy tomorrow night during the season premiere of *Grey's Anatomy*, I'll be watching it Friday—on ABC.com.

3. Low-cost programming

Netflix is the one thing that makes me wonder why *anyone* has cable. Then I remember all those poor football fans being held hostage by the Cable-Athletical Complex.

But back to me: With Netflix, anytime we feel like vegging out in front of the tube, we usually have something we're interested in sitting here to watch. And if we're between movie deliveries, there's also Netflix's streaming service. Or, you know, Blockbuster.com, Redbox, whatever floats your boat. Whichever you choose, you're looking at a monthly cost from $0 (if you use Redbox coupon codes) to $4.99 (Netflix's cheapest tier) to $19.99 for Blockbuster's top plan. Beats the pants off cable.

Need more instant gratification? You can also buy TV episodes one-by-one from iTunes.com for $1.99–$2.99 a pop.

4. Find alternatives to cable for your favorite shows

Now you have the tools you need to figure out if canceling cable would save you money: Write down what shows you watch. Use the Show-finder gadget on CancelCable.com (cancelcable.com/db/showfinder.php) to figure out where you can get those shows besides on cable TV. Take the cost per episode on Netflix, iTunes, or whatnot, and multiply it by the number of episodes you watch per month. Is the product less than the cost of your current cable package?

For example, if you pay for cable in order to get HBO shows, you'd have to download 31 "premium" episodes a month to run up a bill that matches the $93.99 that Comcast charges for a digital package with HBO.

I'm guessing that almost everyone will feel that cutting cable would save them money, even if they watch a lot. Then it's just a matter of the reception quality. If you don't have one of those digital converters, I urge you to stop by the home of a friend who does and take a look at their picture. If you like what you see, there's your answer. I know what mine is. — **Carrie Kirby**

Frugality Makes the Heart Grow Fonder: 5 Ways to Spend Less and Love More

Hot dates are often stereotyped as being expensive. Fine wines, fancy dinners, high-priced hotels, and posh resorts top the list of ways to reconnect with our significant other. Even though frugality isn't generally considered sexy, it can bring about intimacy in unexpected ways.

1. Share a ride

I know a young married couple who work in the same building and share the same work schedule with each other. They also commute 45 miles everyday separately! The fact that they don't carpool blows my mind. When asked why they wouldn't share a ride to save on gas and car expenses, the answer is simply, "We don't like spending that much time together." It's surprising they're married at all!

Carpooling can be a great opportunity to discuss the day's events, catch up on an audiobook together, or just sit in silence and enjoy the scenery. Done daily, it can bring a couple closer without really trying.

2. Split a plate

Saving money while eating out can be difficult. It is so tempting to order two oversized meals that you will never finish. Try sharing a plate. You can even use the same fork and feed each other. (Just get a table near the back where it isn't as obvious, please.) If you encounter uppity restaurant policies that prohibit plate-splitting, have one person order a side salad as their main course, and split that, too.

Sharing gives you the chance to experience the same foods from a different perspective.

....

3. Divide the work
....

Sure, I could sit inside doing my housework while hubby is in the yard doing his, but why? I know that I could help him somehow (stacking firewood, raking leaves, etc.), and he enjoys my company. By doing our own yard work, and not hiring out, we save big money, and working up a sweat is great for your love life! (We also get to wear adorable matching leather work gloves.)

....

4. Create a spark
....

When the weather gets chilly, avoid the temptation to turn up the thermostat. Grab a blanket and cuddle for optimal warmth. During the evenings you can keep your house 10 degrees cooler and still remain comfortable with proper layering and some snuggling!

....

5. Conserve water
....

Cut your number of showers and baths down by half, to save big money on water and electricity or gas. Since most people's showers last as long as there is hot water to run, make it a date and give your hot water heater a break on that second run!

There are so many ways that sharing resources can connect two people. Keeping this in perspective when cutting back will make it feel like an experience worth remembering, and not any real sacrifice, at all! — **Linsey Knerl**

SHOPPING & BARGAIN HUNTING

Who doesn't love a good deal? With so many ways to shop, it's no wonder many people find it hard to resist. What if you could learn the best ways to shop, without spending more than you needed, and only on those things that would truly be a good investment? This next chapter lays out all of the ins and outs of bargain hunting, bartering, and (sometimes) even walking away from that fabulous deal.

Bulk Buying 101

Most of us have known for some time that purchasing in bulk provides decent financial returns. The problem? Bulk buying sounds way simpler than it actually is. Where do you store it? When does it make sense to buy in bulk versus small quantities?

It's enough to make your eyes cross and your brain start to feel pickled, particularly if you've never shopped this way before. What's more, it's far from the sexiest financial subject matter out there, which can make it very difficult to analyze and apply to your personal situation. Here's a nuts-and-bolts article covering what I see as the five major areas of consideration.

....

1. Storage
....

What to store it in?

Some items actually come in packaging that makes them easily stored as is. For those that don't, the first order of business is making sure the container is as airtight as possible. From there, the next level is bulk storage versus daily usage containers. For the larger amounts of things, I like the 5-and 25-gallon white plastic buckets with the matching snap-on lids.

While the larger buckets are great for safe long-term storage of large-quantity dry goods, they can be a bit cumbersome for daily use. For easy grab-and-use access in the kitchen, I love clear containers. These can take a variety of forms depending on your personal taste and budget. What's important is that you have manageable access to things you need on a regular basis, such as sugar, tea, spices, flour, beans, coffee, etc.

Freezer issues are a bit different, but the overall concepts still apply. Some things can get tossed in as is, using only the packaging they were purchased with. Others might require freezer storage bags.

Where to store it?

Where to store it requires flexibility and ingenuity, particularly since everyone's situation is different. Here are three ideas I think everyone can use to some extent:

Sleep on it. Literally.

Pick up a set of bed risers and create a pantry from the unused real estate under your bed. If you really want to get fancy, you can invest in some wheeled under-the-bed storage containers, or make your own out of mismatched dresser drawers and castor wheels. If not, just go with the raising-up-on-risers trick and go nuts with bulk toilet paper, cases of vegetables, and tomato products.

Hang it off the door.

There are all kinds of products out there at various department stores that hook over the tops of doors, keeping even the pickiest rental landlord happy. Some of them have fabric pockets. Some have the sturdy wire shelving for canned goods. Either way, it's typically unused real estate when it comes to storing extra goods. This may not work for the more formal home decorators out there. But those of you renting may find it valuable for reaching larger financial goals sooner.

Shove it in a corner pantry.

I've drooled over the one my friend has in her kitchen for years. The major benefit of these things is that an unbelievable amount of stuff can be stored in a convenient location where the square footage is usually ignored. Include a canned goods rotator, and you're really in business. Renters can make one of these on the cheap by using a rod or tension cable across the corner and hanging a long curtain in a fabric that makes sense for them. Using a folding screen room divider would also be another way to go.

2. What to buy?

While individual items will undoubtedly vary from household to household, I've come up with three flexible categories that I believe everyone can relate to: non-food consumables, family favorites, and something I call "consumable infrastructure."

Non-food consumables

This is different for every family, but can include things like batteries, cotton balls and swabs, shampoo, deodorant, feminine products, laundry soap, toothpaste, and the like. Basically, this category includes any non-edible items you have to replace on a regular basis.

Family favorites

These include any items your family goes through on a regular basis that are unique to your home. For us, canned tomato products are high on the list, as are frozen 1-pound bullets of turkey sausage, 10-pound bags of chicken legs, bar items, bulk canned clams, and pasta. Again, this list will differ from family to family. Honor your own style.

Consumable infrastructure

What goes into this category also fluctuates from family to family. There are some fairly predictable subcategories, however, such as oils, sweeteners, vinegars, seasonings, flours, grains, and other base ingredients. In short, these are items you use to put other things together, such as marinades, baked goods, dry mixes, casseroles, homemade salad dressings, dips, sauces, and other menu items. Obviously, some homes will stock up on such things as tofu, coconut milk, and curry powder, while others might concentrate more on frijoles and cornmeal, or perhaps cardamom and eggplant. This system works regardless of your preferred cooking style.

3. Why buy in bulk?

Emergency savings extension

Food storage and pantry stocking is a powerful part of your three- to six-month emergency savings plan that in my opinion should not be ignored. Bulk buying, if done diligently, can be markedly less expensive and also go a great distance toward supplementing that emergency savings fund in times of need. No need to take valuable time away from job hunting or caring for an ill loved one to shop for sales (or shop at all). You'll be ready to rock and roll if you are stocked up for any occasion. Unexpected crisis situations really increase your personal vulnerability level, which for me is when I'm more likely to overspend due to lack of time and energy to spend on such things as budget grocery shopping. Being stocked up protects me from this.

Household harmony

In a nutshell, if you have the cash in your budget already, why go through the hassle of commuting, shopping, and waiting in line multiple times a month or week when you can skip the aggravation and deal with it once every couple of weeks or less? The peace of mind and ability to roll with the punches that comes with being well stocked is one of the greatest perks to stocking up. Youngest child forgot to tell you about tomorrow's bake sale? No problem. Your spouse has an unexpected case of the sniffles? Got it covered. Everything's on hand for those emergency batches of cookies and chicken soup.

Extra liquid cash

Eventually, the savings of bulk buying will carve out enough cash to really matter. You'll have enough to take advantage of larger up-front savings, invest more, or have a little more mad money. It's up to you what you do with it, but having more available liquid cash is always a good thing in my book.

4. How much to buy?

This sounds like a simple question until you start factoring in all the variables for you and your various family members. The three main factors I like to consider when making these decisions are:

1. Consumption rate. Usage patterns will vary per person and item.
2. Available storage space.
3. Your specific situation (financial goals, available cash, other monetary priorities).

While you'll need to work out the actual amounts for yourself, considering the above factors that are unique to your home should help guide you.

5. Challenges and strategies

Carving out the up-front cash

If you're having trouble finding the extra two dollars for bus fare, setting aside funds for bulk shopping can be pretty daunting.

It's okay to start small. Bulk toiletries such as large-quantity bottles of shampoo provide an excellent value for your start-up dollar, as do beans and rice. To get the biggest bang for your bulk-buying buck, however, my money's on yeast and spices. Use the extra funds saved from those purchases to make a few more precision purchases with each new shopping trip. While you won't be super-stocked overnight, it will add up overtime, and you will eventually be in the driver's seat.

Staying focused and making It a priority

Some folks have a hard time avoiding feelings of discouragement and deprivation. How do you set yourself up for success? One strategy is to choose start-up bulk items with a high personal "wow factor" or a huge initial savings return. Then, combine this strategy with short-term financial goals you can easily accomplish with the savings you achieve. Being able to get excited about the initial returns will go a long way toward staying committed for the long haul.

Getting (and staying) organized

This is a challenge shared by nearly everyone, regardless of the amount of space, storage infrastructure, and start-up cash available. Start small and pace yourself. You want to be able to get a handle on the situation, as well as stay on top of the new system. Bulk buying is one of those concepts that sounds simple until you start trying to implement it across the board, and realize all of the "sub-issues" that come along with it, not the least of which is figuring out where to put everything you just brought home.

Also, not having a system that is user-friendly can sabotage the best-laid plans of any beginning bulk buyer. Sticking that case of creamed corn in the back of the closet might seem like a good idea at first, but if you can't get to it when you need it (or forget it's there altogether), it does you absolutely no good to have it on hand. Further, don't forget to honor who you are and how you live your life. Choose an organizational and implementation system that flows with your particular home and lifestyle.

Analyzing the deals

Not every bulk-purchasing opportunity is a smart buy. A strong working knowledge of the per unit costs on items you regularly buy is extremely helpful. One item that can assist you with this is a price book.

Keeping it sexy

Basically, how do you remain excited enough about bulk buying and pantry stocking to stick with it and not get bored? The consumable infrastructure category really comes into play here. When you have the base ingredients to make most things, it's easier to get excited about strolling for the perfect avocado or planning a romantic dinner. I know I have more fun under those conditions popping into the grocery store for a few things if we want to have a "date night" quality dinner, than if I am trying to do that

along with stocking up for the month or quarter on certain items. Having the freedom and flexibility to try a few new things keeps us focused.

That's bulk buying 101 in as much of a nutshell as I can put it. If you've been holding off on this powerful money-saving strategy, this article should hopefully give you an affordable jumping-off point.
— **Myscha Theriault**

11 Strategies to Shop Your Way to Financial In-dependence

Love to shop? Just can't stop? A slight shift in your paradigm and perspective could lead you out of debt . . . and straight to the bank.

Shopping is something we all need to do. There's no way around it. We shop for food, clothing, vehicles, home repair supplies, gas, credit card rates, long-distance plans, school supplies, and more. How can this be turned from financial drain to financial gain?

The key lies in changing shopping from a hobby into a job. This is critically important, so let me rephrase and repeat. Shopping, from a financial independence standpoint, is not a hobby. It is a job. A responsibility to be taken seriously. Following are some power-shopping strategies to put you in the driver's seat.

1. Shop your service plans and other accounts

Service plans, account packages, and card rates change all the time. Companies are rarely, if ever, going to track you down and let you know that they have a better plan or package for you. Calling a card company to negotiate a lower interest rate (if you carry a balance), asking what new plans are out there to save you money, or evaluating your changing usage of a particular plan to select a new one (cell phones are a good example of when this is necessary) are all ways to carve out extra cash. If you spend an afternoon evaluating and researching new account options, including those you may no longer even need, and find an extra 50 bucks a month, you are actually finding an extra $600 annually.

2. Maintain lists for home information management

What items do the kids need for school? What grocery items (including semiannual bulk purchases) are you running low on or out of? What are the sizes and measurements of each family member? What types of lightbulbs, air filters, etc., do your home systems and vehicles take? This is all critical information to have if you want to shop sales effectively.

3. Know the sale trends

Certain things traditionally go on sale at particular times of the year, such as August for camping equipment and athletic shoes, July for picnic condiments, and January for gift wraps and holiday items. If you know of something you want, can be disciplined enough to save ahead, and are able to wait for the sales, you can save major money.

4. Celebrate clearance sales

No, this does not mean you get to max out your credit card every time there's a seasonal shoe sale. It does mean that there are big savings to be had, particularly on classic items of good quality. This is an excellent strategy to partner up with the second suggestion on the list. Having your home and family needs lists current enables you to pick up those items inexpensively if you run into a slamming sale on the fly.

5. Treat it like the job it is

Once you've established the mind-set that shopping is a responsibility and a job, start considering what someone who has this type of job would need to do to pull it off successfully. Establishment of line items, awareness of whether your budget has been over or under for a particular line item each month, workable filing system for bills . . . these are all areas you need to be aware of and have the tools to implement properly.

6. Develop a knowledge of liquidation value

This strategy can be applied to educational materials, literature, vehicle purchases, and other critical items in your life. One area where it might not occur to everyone is with antique shopping. I'm not talking about the ultra-high-end antiques necessarily, although this applies to them too. I have repeatedly seen antique bureaus, tables, and chairs for the same price (and in some cases, less than) as some of the newer furniture items in popular stores and galleries. Some items are even equivalent in

price to lower-end assemble-yourself particleboard items from department stores.

Why is this important? Antiques hold their value, and in many cases increase in value. If you are going to spend 180 bucks on a lower-quality particleboard bookcase or kitchen table anyway, consider hitting a roadside antiques shop. You'll at least be able to get your money out of it later if necessary, and you know it has a better likelihood of standing the test of time.

7. Be aware of regular and exceptional market prices

You may be able to keep the prices on items you regularly purchase in your head. For others, you may want to implement a price book. The point is, if you are informed, you never have to pay full market value again. Ever. No more getting sucked into a bogus buy-one-get-one free special at the grocery store that has actually increased your per pound rate by 70 cents. No more inflated so-called "discounts." You will know an excellent deal when you see one.

8. Develop a regular shopping circuit

By this, I mean those favorite few stores that are on your regular path for errand running, as well as the occasional stop at a mega-savings store that is worth your while to hit once every four to six weeks. It's a good idea if your shopping circuit includes a few thrift and secondhand stores, as well as discount retailers and grocery warehouses.

If you have a few extra minutes anyway, stopping by a place that's on your way to check out a seasonal pocketbook or blazer doesn't cost you a ton of extra gas or time. It doesn't mean you should stop in and shop just for the sake of shopping. But if you know you'll have a need for a particular item in the next few months, it pays to start casually shopping in advance for a great price. This will also give you a sense of what the regular prices are, how often a particular hard-to-find item becomes available, and when you've found a deal you are not likely to see again.

9. Calculate your ROI

Your ROI is your return on investment. This can apply to larger retirement investments as well as money-saving items you are considering as purchases. For example, if you think a food processor is going to save you money, figure out how much money you can easily save each month through its use and divide that into the full price of the item. After that return is reached, you are looking at pure extra cash on a regular basis. This extra cash can be used for fun, travel, savings, investing, or anything else you feel fits into your "living large" goals.

10. Get excited about percentage rate savings

When I see someone who regularly turns their nose up at 10% savings opportunities, I am seeing someone who could probably retire much earlier than they actually will. They are avoiding a savings percentage rate they would most likely be thrilled to receive on a liquid savings account or CD. When you decide you need a brand name of a particular item like a baking spice, and it costs $1.20 versus $1.00 for the store-brand equivalent, you are choosing a fairly large percentage difference.

These smaller types of decisions add up, especially on items we buy regularly. The example I used is a small one. Let's go a bit higher and apply it to something like new blinds for the house. If you could pay $1,000 versus $1,200 for a new set of window coverings, which would you choose? What is your cutoff amount for a savings to be worth your while? For me, anything I would be thrilled to receive as a percentage rate on a savings or investment account has my full attention.

11. Accept the power of secondhand shopping

If you can incorporate secondhand purchases into your lifestyle even minimally, it will make an enormous difference to your overall financial picture. I've previously gone for more than five years without paying over $10 for any single outfit. Many cost far less than that. It isn't necessarily fun, easy, or even something most people would feel comfortable with. It was something extreme that I felt was worth it for early retirement. If secondhand clothing is not something you are willing to explore, consider other secondhand items that are in your comfort zone: power tools, automobiles, non-upholstered furniture, a home, appliances, etc. Get the picture? Larger-ticket items can make a huge difference when purchased secondhand. The savings can add up to a staggering amount in a hurry.

The bottom line is that by treating shopping as a job and responsibility instead of a recreational activity, we all have the power to take more control over our financial futures.

— **Myscha Theriault**

5 Marketing Ploys Grocery Stores Use to Steal Your Money

The cost of food isn't going down, and for some, it is making the task of feeding a family more painful than ever. It doesn't help that ad agencies and PR companies are getting better at creating snazzy gimmicks to get you to buy. Instead of providing you with better food at larger quantities, some of them are selling slicker packaging and empty promises. Here's a look at some of the biggest marketing trends designed to keep you spending.

1. Preportioned food

I'll admit that it is very tempting to snag one of those 100-calorie snack packs that go on sale frequently at my grocer. Individually wrapped portions keep us in line by making sure we don't overindulge in cookies, crackers, or chips. Seriously, folks, who are we kidding? If you look at how much they are charging per portion, it is insanely overpriced. I could easily dole out 13 crackers at an equal 100 calories on my own and toss them in a reusable plastic baggie, thus saving money and the damage to the environment. *What about the health benefits of watching your portions?* If your penchant to overeat is so easily restrained by the workings of a flimsy cellophane bag marked "100 calories," then you are a better person than I am.

. . . .

2. Soup causes
. . . .

Any company that works alongside an honorable charity has my full support. However, I would like to clarify that I have been disappointed in the recent rash of breast cancer promotions by my favorite brands. Pink soup cans, pink appliances, and pink candies have me a little overwhelmed and confused. Are we expected to pay more for these premium brands simply because of a promise that a tiny percentage of the purchase price will go to breast cancer research? Personally, I would rather use a coupon or buy the store-brand mushroom soup, and write out a nice

$15 check to the charity of my choice. I get more groceries for my money, and it's tax deductible. By exploiting a "relationship" with the Susan G. Komen fund, many companies have managed to sell plenty of stale merchandise at quite a premium. For more information on how companies are profiting from these campaigns, visit ThinkBeforeYouPink.org.

. . . .

3. It's "healthy"
. . . .

Remember when yogurt was just yogurt? Now you have yogurt "for digestive health" and yogurt for "immune defense." There is a growing debate over how much influence these new products will have over your health, and the definitive verdict is that you will only experience benefits if you continue to use them. With a cost of two to three times more than their "regular" counterparts, many people can't make that kind of commitment. Several recent lawsuits have many experts reminding consumers that yogurt alone isn't the cure for all digestive ailments. While they won't be discouraging yogurt use entirely, it is important to remember that there is no miracle cure for your health.

Additional healthy food trends that will become popular this year include the inclusion of DHA omega-3 into baby food, pomegranate and blueberries into juice, and calcium into hot cocoa. Many of these foods can be viewed as "new and improved." Others are just exploiting the same benefits they (and other brands) have always offered.

4. Animals are friends

As consumers demand to know exactly where their food is coming from, meats, eggs, and dairy will hold a new spotlight. Foods from "humane" sources are in high demand, and with that comes a higher price. Consumers need to have an understanding of how standards are applied, however, before they can assume that pricier foods will meet their ethical standards. Eggs, for example, can carry the label "cage-free," "free-range," or "certified organic" and still not be "certified humane." For details on what each label means, the Humane Society of the United States (www.HSUS.org). If you're going to be paying three times more for that egg, it's good to know if it will actually meet your standards.

5. It's all included

New breakfast kits, lunch kits, and snack packs are hitting store shelves every week. Some of them include everything you need for a healthy meal (or so it seems). In addition to

being calorie-rich and preservative-laden, many of them are also missing some key components. Several complete cereal packages are an attempt to give kids a healthy start to their day. While a great idea in theory, it seems disappointing that parents can't even get it together enough to pour a bowl of cold cereal and throw down a glass of juice for Junior. And did anyone else notice that these "complete breakfasts" are missing the milk? (I won't even address the horrendous amount of packaging this product comes in.)

As marketing companies struggle to come up with new ways to sell you the same food, be aware of trends that become widespread over several brands. With markups at over 200% of the cheapest brands, it may be wise to do a little additional research before succumbing to the temptation to buy. Generally speaking, the more advertising money a company has thrown at a new product, the more they are going to charge—and consequently, the more they *need* you to buy it to keep them well within their profit zones. — **Linsey Knerl**

6 Ways to Avoid Tricky Traps at the Supermarket

Going to the supermarket and sticking to a list is an exercise in discipline and requires fortitude and resilience of epic proportions. Employing tips like "don't shop when you're hungry," "look for the no-name brand," and "avoid the checkout counter displays" are simply damage control for an experience that categorically breaks the budget.

But most of us still need to shop, and supermarkets often offer the best prices and selection. In some cases, the supermarket is all we have. Here are six tips on how to get in and get out without going over your budget:

1. Put blinders on

Staple foods (like eggs and milk) are often located at the back of the store. And for good reason: The only way

to get there is to walk through aisles upon aisles of temptation. If all you need is a quart of milk, then do not allow yourself to get sidetracked by an "amazing deal" on something you don't really need.

2. Be wary of amazing deals

Many people (myself included) look for sales, and will often formulate the week's menu accordingly. However, the supermarket marketing gurus are on to us. When your eyes scan the shelves looking for the sale stickers, take a peek at the original price before you decide that it's a steal; you may find that the amazing deal is a discount of a whole whopping 8 cents. Now I'm all for a deal, but 8 cents is not enough incentive to buy that can of corn for a dish I may not have otherwise used the corn for.

3. That special display is just for show

The gondolas (displays at the end of each aisle, and racks of product hung where shelves join) and other special displays—be they seasonal promotions or just a mountain of cases of pop in the middle of the floor—are also tricky traps. You may automatically assume that they are featuring sale items, since they are prominently displayed and have a neon sign highlighting the price. Again, buyer beware: Check the original price and compare it to other similar products. Often the items displayed on gondolas are actually more expensive, be they on sale or not. Only after some due diligence should you decide if that pretty pyramid of product is really meant to compliment your shopping cart.

4. "Complementation"—the ultimate distraction

Coffee or tea is on your list. And before you know it, a package of yummy-looking biscuits that are temptingly displayed next to the coffee and tea is also in your cart. Then you head for the pasta aisle, and walk out with an overpriced pesto sauce that simply looked too good to resist. Be wary of items which complement each other that are positioned near one another in the supermarket. If you aren't the sort to rigidly stick to a list, complementary items will jump off the shelves and into your cart before you know what happened.

5. Watch the checkout like a hawk

You may not remember the exact prices for everything that is in your cart, but you likely have a good idea of what you will be charged, especially if you picked up a few sale items and are proud of it. But upon reaching the checkout, you could well discover that those items you thought were on sale are not scanning through as such—either because the actual sale item was next to or below the one you picked up (a very sly maneuver on the part of grocery stores), or because the scanner codes were "accidentally" never adjusted.

If there is a huge line behind you and you don't want to cause a stir with the checkout clerk (who will likely have to call for assistance and stare belligerently at you while you both wait for somebody to run around the store doing price checks), then simply march your items and receipt up to customer service and politely point out the discrepancy.

6. Try a cupboard special

After reading this, are you angry at supermarkets for their little ploys and marketing decoys? Great! Skip your next scheduled trip to the supermarket! See what you can scrounge up from the dark corners of your cupboards or frost-bitten freezer, and get creative. Some of my best meals have been dubbed "cupboard specials," making use of what I have on hand when supplies start to dwindle. — **Nora Dunn**

10 Things I've Learned by Grocery-Shopping on a Budget

I used to consider myself a frugal shopper, without following the cardinal rule of setting and sticking to a grocery budget. Inspired by Wise Bread and other Web sites, a few months ago I finally took the plunge and set an $80 a week budget. I know that some people manage to spend as little as half that to feed a family of four (the two kids are little enough that they don't eat much), but for us $80 has been a challenge.

Despite the challenges, I was pleased to find that the budget goal (some weeks it's been merely a goal) has taught me a few things about shopping and about myself:

1. Coupons really do make a difference

I used to think that coupons would only tempt you into buying more expensive name-brand items, but lately I've learned to do some online research, check my grocery flyers, and match up those coupons with items that are already discounted. I was delighted to learn that most stores will accept coupons even if the items are on clearance. The result is that almost every shopping trip, I get a couple things completely free.

2. While most cheap food is unhealthy, a lot of healthy food is cheap

When you're using coupons, you'll notice that some of those freebies are for food that a health-oriented person would not touch. Then there's the

fact that the meat that gets marked down to less than $1 a pound is often fattier and almost never hormone- or antibiotic-free, grass-fed, or anything at all healthy.

But the flip side of this sad story is that some of the healthiest food is also some of the cheapest. I load up on in-season fruit and dried beans, and try to save a little room in the budget for some wild-caught salmon or some grass-fed ground beef. If I can't spend $6 to $8 for a pound of the good stuff, I'd rather eat something else, at least when it comes to beef (that's a side effect of just having finished *The Omnivore's Dilemma*).

3. When you buy less, less goes to waste

Seems obvious, no? But I used to feel that I should grab as much as I had time to buy at the grocery store. After all, getting to the store, waiting in line, etc. is time-consuming, and I wanted to make as few trips as possible.

What I didn't account for is that when you buy more than you can eat fresh in a week, you have to take time to prepare it for the freezer, or you'll be spending time dumping it into the trash. Cleaning out the fridge is work, too—and if you are regularly dumping leftovers, you are wasting money. Sometimes I open a friend's fridge and I can't see the back or the walls because there is so much food stuffed in there. They don't even know what they have—so of course a lot of it is going to end up in the garbage.

4. A budget gets you excited about freebies again

Relive your college days! Remember when all a college group had to do to ensure turnout at a meeting was to post a flyer offering free pizza? When I was a broke college student, nothing (well, almost nothing) made me smile more than a free meal.

This weekend, my in-laws visited, and, while I was away for the day, they all shopped and cooked barbecue at my house. I came home to a fridge *full* of leftovers, and I was just tickled pink that I don't have to shop for a couple days. Because that means I'll either be able to go under budget, or I'll be able to spend a few bucks on an indulgence. Which brings me to . . .

5. Booze is expensive

Time and again, I find that the weeks we go over budget are the ones when we picked up some wine and beer. The hubs and I both enjoy a drink after the kids go to bed, and it's not an indulgence we're interested in sacrificing. I know that beer is cheaper than wine, but I've often wondered how a cocktail (we use store-brand seltzer water with a little liquor) compares to a glass of wine. Inevitably all my research notes get mixed up or spilled on and I've not been able to come up with a good economic model on this point.

Solutions? So far the only ones we have are: get a case of inexpensive wine when you come upon a sale and get boxed wine. And, be really nice to people who tend to bring a bottle when they come over.

....

6. Shopping frugally can lead to cultural adventures

I used to live in China, and oh did we eat cheap over there. Now, I can't figure out how to make biweekly shopping flights to Beijing work out economically, but I have found that exploring neighborhoods dominated by immigrants can be both money-saving and fun.

The budget has pushed me to walk a little farther out of my neighborhood and check out the grocery store closer to a Hispanic community, where there is always fresh chorizo and menudo on display. I love this store! One of the things I love is that instead of putting soon-to-expire foods in the dumpster for the freegans, Fair Share Foods just puts them on a fire sale. My kids love individual containers of yogurt, and I can usually get them at this store, with a coupon, for 25 cents or less. They'll expire in a couple of days, but they'll be gone by then, and anyway, yogurt lasts awhile past the date.

The only thing I don't like about this store is that the shopping carts don't have seat belts, so I usually go with the stroller. But despite the fact that most of the other shoppers do not look or sound like me, I always feel comfortable and welcome there. So explore a little and, who knows, you might get to try some fun new foods too. In our old city, we also used to hit such a grocery store and our daughter would have a good time riding the 25-cent merry-go-round with little Spanish-speaking friends. In toddlerese, it's all the same language, right?

Similarly, if you live in a city with a Chinatown, you will find produce markets with better prices and fresher goods than the supermarket.

....

7. Yes, we will eat all that cereal
....

When I stocked up on a dozen boxes or more of on-sale cereal, friends always laugh and ask how on earth we will eat it all. C'mon! Cereal lasts forever, has a million uses (especially in a house with little kids), and is normally kind of expensive. Every once in awhile, a store will have a great sale event where it goes for around $1 a box. When that happens, I'm yelling, "Buy, buy, buy!" I will go in with all the coupons I've been hoarding for weeks and I have never bought too much. After all, you can always donate any excess to the local food bank.

8. A price book would be great, especially for staples

All the smart frugal shoppers keep price books, where they note down the best price they can get for any given item. That's been on my to-do list for, oh, half my life. But since I started shopping on the budget, at least I've been looking over my receipts at the end of the week and getting a good idea for my target prices for the things I buy the most: cereal, milk, cage-free eggs, chicken, and of course, produce.

This is actually a big change for me, because in my old, "shop as frugally as possible" mode, I just compared prices *in that store* and *on that day.* That is, I figured I needed at least three pounds of meat for the week, so I would buy the three cheapest meats available. Now that I'm aware that I can pay $1 a pound or less for conventional meat and poultry, if there is nothing under $2 in the store, I just don't buy meat that day. This may seem like a waste of time, since I'll have to hit a different store if we want any meat. But on the other hand, I spend a lot *less* time comparing "price per ounce" to find the absolute best value in the cooler.

9. Just because the caviar's half-price doesn't mean it's affordable

I used to bring all kinds of goodies back from club store runs—ready-to-heat organic mushroom ravioli, for instance. I figured since I knew it was a good deal, I barely had to glance at the price. But that doesn't work with a limited amount to spend each week, and this has been one of the key reasons the budget helps me spend less. Instead of worrying about getting the best possible deal for a given item, I think more about how to get a week's worth of nutritious and filling meals for my budget.

That means some delicacies are never going to come home with me, unless it's New Year's Eve or it's practically free after a coupon. It also means that I buy a lot more chicken than beef, and that I almost never buy juice or soda.

10. Shopping frugally is worth the time

A lot of my friends tell me they don't have time to be frugal. Actually, a friend who is unemployed and has no kids recently told me that, which kind of blew my mind. Personally, I sometimes worry that I'm spending too much time pinching pennies when I could be taking on more work from home and coming out ahead.

However, as a stay-at-home mom of two kids below school age, one thing is certain: I can't make any more money than I already do without spending money on a babysitter. Clipping coupons, making extra grocery trips (on foot with the stroller) to buy loss leaders, reading the sales flyers—these are all things I can manage with the children with me. At first flipping through a coupon file while controlling the kids in the store was difficult, but now I have the hang of it and it's working out. Actually, my four-year-old has kind of gotten into helping me, and this is how she now asks for something:

"Mommy, if such-and-such is on sale, and you have a coupon, can we get it?"

That's my girl. — **Carrie Kirby**

8 Tips for the High-End Cheapskate

Here at Wise Bread, we're not just about saving money and reducing budgets. We're also about provid-ing ways to live a more luxurious lifestyle within a reduced set of financial parameters. In other words, we show you how to be a high-end cheapskate. Here are eight tips to do just that.

1. Decanters

Don't feel like justifying your brand choices to new acquaintances? Prefer the look of fine crystal or cut glass to bottle labels? Decanters are a great way to add class to your bar or entertaining area and make sure the brands of spirits you choose are nobody's business but yours.

2. Heirloom and estate jewelry

Whether it's handed down, purchased at auction, or picked up at pawn shops, previously owned jewelry is a great way to establish a nice collection for a significantly reduced price. Think pearls and studs for women, pocket watches and tie clips for men.

3. Maximize gourmet purchases

There are two ways to get the biggest bang for your gourmet buck. First, stretch fancy items as far as possible as an accent ingredient. This can be done with truffles, shaved specialty cheeses for pasta dinners, sliced steak salad to serve four people on one piece of meat, etc. The second way is to combine one or two high-end items as featured meal elements or make a high-end side or appetizer. For example, one pound of shrimp can make a decadent dinner for two, or shrimp cocktail for several.

4. DIY

Using or getting your own skills can hide any-sized budget from others. Take some classes in photography, sewing, flower arranging, etc., and you'll find that having a personal area of expertise can really bump up your lifestyle a few notches.

5. Bartering

This is related to the previous tip, but rather than using your skills for yourself, you can offer your skill to others, for the same price of their skills. This doesn't just apply to swapping casseroles for homemade jellies. Consider stretching your parameters a bit. How about a custom interior paint job in exchange for a bathroom remodel minus the cost of supplies on each? A few quarts of gourmet hummus swapped for an hour of professional massage therapy? Refurnished serving buffet for a professionally painted family portrait? Using those DIY

skills as a form of currency can help you get what you want without laying out cash.

6. Budget ingredients with high-end style

Frozen spinach for a Mediterranean cheese log, boxed wine for marinades and mulling, basic dry goods for biscotti on the cheap, repurposing and refinishing thrift furniture, salvage and hardware materials for custom storage and DIY pot racks . . . lots of options are out there to implement the unexpected for a high-end result.

7. The classics

Whether you pay closer to full price and own fewer clothing items or hunt for classic wardrobe items online and at thrift stores, the styles will be stable and the quality above par. Having fewer items to take care of that will stand the test of time is the way to go. You can also apply this strategy when power-shopping for vehicles. Certain classic models (even used) hold their value better than others. Volvo is a good example.

8. Explore

Be open-minded about every penny-pinching method available, particularly when they are methods that won't necessarily show, like perfume or brand changes on basic items. Buying in bulk, whether generally for the freezer, or with an assembly-cooking strategy in mind, can be a great way to carve out extra cash as well.

These tips only scratch the surface. Frugal discipline does not have to mean deprivation. It is possible to have a life of abundance without spending more money than you'd care to. — **Myscha Theriault**

A Sneaky Way to Win eBay Auctions and Save a Fortune

Many people find that eBay.com is a fabulous resource. Not only can you find almost anything, but you can usually get it a whole lot cheaper. Usually.

There are, of course, many ways for the savvy shopper to turn that "usually" into an "always", and in the case of eBay, it's sniping an auction.

So, what is sniping? Well, it's a nasty word, but the explanation is simple. In a regular eBay auction you place a bid (up to your max) on an item you want. If other parties are interested in that item, you may get into something called a bidding war. And for the frugal shopper, that's your basic nightmare. The price rockets, and before you know it, you're almost paying the cost of retail. Ouch.

With sniping, you place a bid at the very last second, to avoid the bidding war altogether. If the other party doesn't know you're planning on bidding, he/she may be less inclined to place a high bid. Slip in your bid at the last possible second and no one else has the time to decide to outbid you.

This is also effective in managing your ceiling price (you won't fall into the temptation to bid just a little bit more than you planned on, because you've been outbid by a few bucks). If your final offer is still under the highest bidder, you can let the item go without any regrets.

There are two ways you can snipe on eBay. You can do this manually, which means constantly refreshing your browser and then timing your submission just right (remember you have to give the system time to process your bid). It's a little more stressful, and can take some practice, but it's free.

The other way is to use a sniping service. There are a variety of sniping services available. The one I use is Bidnip.com. You state the maximum amount you want to pay and the time you'd like the bid to be placed. I usually choose three seconds before the close of the auction. Then, you sit back and relax. As far as eBay is concerned, you haven't yet placed a bid. Your bid doesn't appear in the system. Thus, no bidding war. And three seconds before the close of the auction, your bid sneaks in at the last second. The opposing bidder has no time to place a new bid on the item and bingo, it's all yours.

Sneaky? Well, yes. But this technology is out there for everyone, so I'm certainly not the only one using it. I recently won an auction for 99 cents, on an item that usually goes for $20–$25. How much does it cost to snipe an auction? Just 25 cents per snipe, and *only* if you win the auction. If you lose (and it can happen, but it's very rare), then you don't use a snipe credit. And on average, you'll save around 25–35% on every auction.

Bidnip.com gives everyone five free snipes when they open an account, and it's free to sign up and use. No credit card details, none of that hassle at the start. Once you're happy with the service, you just buy extra snipes and add them to your account. Easy.

Do yourself a big favor and learn the art of sniping. It'll save you a ton of money, and you can avoid the bidding wars forever. Happy sniping.

— **Paul Michael**

Miss the Big Sale? Claim Your Savings Anyway

The sudden aggravation of my son's allergies became the last straw for this frugal family. While we had suffered through a summer or two in our old farm home with little to no air-conditioning in most rooms, this year was going to be different. Credit card in hand (we enjoy collecting on those rewards points), my husband headed to our local retail store for the 12,000 BTU beauty.

Soon after he arrived, he called me from his cell phone—a bit more than aggravated. "Linsey, it's showing $50 more than what you said it was going to cost." I reached for my sale ad and realized that the great price on the very last one in stock had ended —yesterday.

"Tell them you want it anyway." I figured it couldn't hurt, right? After all, I had been reading so much on haggling lately (but never really tried it). How hard could it be?

The happy ending to my story is that I got my A/C for yesterday's sale price. We slept in two hours of dehumified and cooled air last night (I set it on a very conservative cycle to save energy). My son woke up without his little pink eyes today (he had white ones, instead). We are very happy.

We also learned a bit about real-world haggling techniques.

1. Know "the" price

This is different from "Know *your* price." Your price (what you're willing to pay) may be higher than what you can actually get it for. Or it may simply be way too cheap for the store to make any money on it. A better way to approach this is to know the bottom-line price the store is willing to let the merchandise go for. Sale ads are great resources for this. If you know that a chair went on sale for $99 last month, then you know that this is a price they are probably comfortable selling it for.

2. Bring evidence

In addition to competitors' ads for the same week (which many stores honor without haggling), keep a record of sale ads for that same store for the past six months or so. If you see an appliance on sale in March, but don't have the money, save the sale ad until you do. Bring that same ad with you when you're ready to make your purchase, and you have just proven that you know your stuff. Most stores won't deny you their own best prices—especially if it moves merchandise.

3. Start high

While many upscale stores may have trained their entry-level sales associates on how to give discounts, don't assume that it will be easy. If you can locate a manager right away, don't be afraid to approach them directly with your offer. It will take much less time, and by doing so, you will build a relationship with that manager (which will come in handy when you ask for another discount at a later date).

4. Leave the door open

After you have made your sale purchase, clarify the store's (or manager's) policy on similar transactions for future items. Would they be willing to discount another large purchase in a week or so? What kind of items do they see going on sale next month? Did you thank them kindly for their discount? By building a relationship with your favorite stores, you are doing more than haggling. You are networking a future of savings opportunities.

Once you make your first successful "off-sale" purchase, you will become confident in your abilities. Why shop the old way ever again?

— **Linsey Knerl**

25 Great Gifts for $5 or Less

Having struggled with gift-list limiting (I have 1 husband, 2 children, 2 parents, 9 nieces and nephews, and 12 in-laws) and being hopeless at crafts, I have opted for creative gift buying with some occasional holiday baking. Here are 25 non-crafty gift ideas, all for less than $5, and suitable for nearly everyone on your list.

1. Fruit basket

These are pricey if you order them fully prepared and decorated from a gift basket company, but it's easy to make your own. You'll need a source of good-quality (preferably in-season) fruits for a good price—$3–$4 should get you a nice offering. Put them in a dollar-store basket and you've got a fruit-basket gift for just under $5.

2. Flashlight

Everyone can use a flashlight, right? This gift will be especially useful for the outdoorsy type, but is great for anyone who needs to see outside at night or who happens to find him/ herself off the grid or without power. Find one at your favorite hardware store or look for bargains online at Amazon.com or Buy.com.

3. Classic books

Dover Thrift Editions have been one of my holiday traditions for nieces and nephews. Titles include *A Christmas Carol* available through Amazon.com and *Anna Karenina*, which you can find at the Dover online store.

4. Children's books

You'll also find great buys on classic children's books at Dover. Check out the Dover Evergreen Classics, where you can find *The Fables of Aesop,* or Children's Thrift Classics to buy *The Adventures of Old Mr. Toad.*

5. Oven mitt

Ever notice at potluck dinners how oven mitts are nearly always stained and ragged (even those owned by the most persnickety perfectionists)? A green oven mitt (or red or other suitably festive color) can be paired with red and green Hershey kisses for a holiday-ready and most useful gift.

6. Kitchen towels

If you like the kitchen linen idea but want something more elegant, consider buying a set of kitchen towels (or cloth napkins); tie with a nice ribbon.

7. Bowls

You can also buy a set of bowls and give them individually; add a decorative touch of ribbon or home-cooked treat.

8. Measuring cup

For a super-practical and nearly everlasting gift (perhaps for newlyweds who forgot to put a measuring cup on their registry), get a Pyrex glass measuring cup. I use mine for measuring *and* boiling water in the microwave.

9. Coffee mug

Someone starting out is most likely to enjoy a sturdy coffee mug. Most clearance shelves will have a variety of fun and quirky cups. Classic white goes with nearly any china pattern so even more established recipients can use it.

10. Handmade recycled drinking glass

Jahanara Cottage Industries is an artisan group in rural Bangladesh supplied through Ten Thousand Villages (tenthousandvillages.com). Ten Thousand Villages works with artisans in developing countries and impoverished areas worldwide. Artisans are paid a fair wage (that is enough to support their families and educate their children; hence, the term "fair trade") in an arrangement that gives artisans merchandising direction, provides supplies and payment advances, and guarantees payment of completed work. There are shops throughout the United States and Canada, an online store, and partner stores (where some, but not all, merchandise is supplied by Ten Thousand Villages). You can find a variety of beautiful pieces, including a drinking glass that is made with recycled glass, for $5 or less.

....

11. Conversation piece (bird whistle)

....

While you're visiting Ten Thousand Villages, you can check out their terra-cotta whistle that imitates a bird's song or peruse the clearance section to find handcrafted bargains.

....

12. Ornaments

....

I participated in a Christmas ornament exchange with a childhood friend for many years. This very informal arrangement allowed us to select a suitable, affordable gift; when I am decorating my tree, I get to remember the ornaments she bought or made for me. You'll find ornaments anywhere, but I like shopping at family-owned gift shops for memorable, one-of-a-kind ones.

....

13. Chocolate chess pie

....

This gift involves cooking but is simple, absolutely delicious, and freezes exceptionally well. I've been buying them at my church bazaar for a few years and finally snagged the recipe,

which makes two pies for a cost per pie of about $4.

Here's the recipe:

Ingredients: 4 squares unsweetened baking chocolate; 2 sticks butter; 4 eggs, lightly beaten; 2½ cups sugar; ½ cup warm milk; 1 teaspoon vanilla; 2 x 9-inch pie crusts.

Instructions: Melt chocolate and butter over low heat. Temper the eggs with the chocolate and add to chocolate/butter mixture (add a small amount of chocolate to the eggs). Add sugar, milk, and vanilla. Mix well. Bake at 300° for 40 minutes; turn oven off and leave pies in for 5 more minutes. Remove to racks to cool.

....

14. Potato soup jar

....

This potato soup is a dried version that lets the recipient create a homemade lunch at a moment's notice by adding boiling water.

Mix all the ingredients (1¾ cups instant mashed potatoes, 1½ cups dry milk, 2 tablespoons instant chicken bouillon, 2 teaspoons dried minced onion, and 1½ teaspoons of Italian seasoning), place in a quart jar (you can buy a canning jar or plastic quart container, or clean out a spaghetti sauce jar); add a bow on the top and a tag that gives instructions: "Bonewarming Potato Soup: Place ½ cup mix in soup bowl and add 1 cup boiling water. Stir until smooth."

You can make this soup for approximately $3.50 per gift.

15. Movie-night basket

Assemble a movie-night basket (or gift bag) with DVDs found in the bargain bin at any entertainment store; add a few packs of microwave popcorn and your favorite drink mix.

16. Jump rope

If your gift recipient wants some intense exercise, a jump rope is an excellent choice.

17. Deck of cards

Who couldn't use a deck of cards for some non-wired fun? Even if you have a deck at home, carrying these on trips can help pass the time during your travels or give you a game to play when you reach your destination. You can pick these up at the drugstore, the dollar store, your favorite mass merchant, or order online. You can even play solitaire with them.

18. Puzzles

Puzzles are appropriate for all ages. My cousins used to always have a large puzzle set up on a card table in their den for leisurely puzzle-solving mixed with conversation. Prices can vary on these, but you can usually snag inexpensive ones at the dollar store or your favorite mass merchant.

19. Sudoku

Sudoku books are equally appropriate for all ages. You can pick these up at the bookstore, grocery store, or find one at Amazon.com.

20. Coloring book with crayons

Here's more fun but this time for kids only. If you stocked up on crayons during the back-to-school sales, you're nearly ready for this gift; if not, I recommend buying a sturdy brand of crayons (I like Crayola, as other brands I've tried tend to break easily) and pairing it with an inexpensive coloring book, often found at the dollar store.

21. Die-cast toy cars

Die-cast cars are great for busy hands. Even little ones appreciate the sturdiness of these types of cars, which tend to race faster than the cheaper variety. A well-selected edition should create some excitement.

22. *Star Wars* (LEGO) key chains

For the *Star Wars* fan on your list, you can buy Princess Leia keychains from LEGO Shop (shop.lego.com) along with many other characters, such as Anakin, Chewbacca, and Darth Vader.

23. T-shirts

If you're lucky enough to have a warehouse or discount store nearby, check out its selection of T-shirts and sweatshirts, often seconds but usually with name-brand labels. I've also noticed that craft stores carry inexpensive T-shirts in a variety of colors.

24. Photo albums

Find inexpensive ones at craft stores or drugstores, decorate and fill with photos. It's a personal and lasting gift.

25. Picture frames

I like getting picture frames and I like getting photos of family members, but I love getting family photos in a frame. I can keep the set as-is or place the photo in an album and re-use the picture frame. — **Julie Rains**

Get Huge Cell-Phone Discounts with Your Work or School E-mail

You might be able to get a discount on your personal cell-phone bill simply by using your school or work e-mail address. Nearly all cellular providers have deals with businesses and schools that extend discounts to their employees and their families, according to Jonathan from MyMoneyBlog.com.

Here's how it works. You (or your spouse or kid) work for XYZ Inc. XYZ has a business account with Verizon.

Your family has a shared cellular plan. Verizon and XYZ might have a deal that extends discounts to employees' families. You punch in your (or your spouse's or your kid's) work-issued e-mail address to see if you qualify. You'll get a response detailing the discounts for which you are qualified. You can get as much as 25% off under certain agreements.

Just to clear up any confusion, we're talking about *your personal cellular account!* Yes, your personal account that you signed up for outside of your company. That's the beauty of the discount. These discounts have always been available, but not a lot of people know about them. Bad marketing on their part means when you tell your friends this trick, you can feel all smart and savvy.

Check for your discounts now by visiting the Web sites listed below. It just takes a few seconds, and with a potential 25% off discount, there's no reason not to go do it now!

AT&T / Cingular:
www.wireless.att.com/business/authenticate

Verizon:
tinyurl.com/verizon-discounts

T-Mobile:
tinyurl.com/tmobile-discounts

Sprint / Nextel:
www.evpdiscount.com — **Greg Go**

10 Things I Never Buy New

I don't like buying new. It's not that I consider myself to be some kind of Scrooge. I just have a hard time paying more for something than I need to, and often we take that extra hit when we pay for a brand-new item. So, I buy secondhand things a lot of the time. Here's my guide to the main items you should always consider buying used.

DVDs/CDs

Why bother paying $21.99 for a new DVD or $14.99 for a new CD, when you can pick up a barely used copy of the same title for at least half the price? The improvements in modern DVD and CD players also mean that scratches and smudges don't really matter—the technology can deal with them. It's the best way to get your home entertainment. Even places like Amazon.com offer avenues to get the titles used. No more excuses; stop buying new DVDs and CDs.

Video games

This is just like DVDs and CDs, only the deals often come quicker and with greater discounts. I recently picked up a used copy of an Xbox game for $1.99 that was still selling for $19.99 in the store. It played perfectly, it still had the manual, and for an extra $1, I got insurance so if the disc did malfunction I could get a replacement or refund.

Cars

Car experts and sites like Edmunds.com and KBB.com will tell you that brand-new cars lose around 12%–15% of their value the second you drive them off the lot. That's thousands of dollars up in smoke for your average midsize sedan. Why should you take that financial loss? Instead, buy a car that's a year or two old. It will usually have low mileage, a good chunk of the factory warranty left on it, and the depreciation isn't anywhere near as bad for you. That's smart spending.

Yard toys

I encourage my kids to play in the garden, and there are toys and games for them out there. But why buy new when they'll get scuffed up and worn out in days? Once again, places like Craigslist.org and Freecycle.org are good places to find some excellent yard toys for the kids. The slide in our backyard was free and has so far lasted three years. It still looks as good as the day we got it (very good in fact), from someone who had previously had it for five years. They're built tough to withstand all weather and all kids.

Workout/exercise equipment

This is an area where you can monopolize on impulse buying and laziness. People will buy a big treadmill, a health rider, an exercise bike, or a weight bench in hopes of getting super-fit and ultra-trim. The problem is, it takes hard work and dedication. And most of the time, it's easier to let the new purchase rot in the basement or garage after a few weeks of use. That's when the garage sale comes around, and you can pick up an almost-brand-new piece of equipment at a fraction of the price for a brand-new one. Many people offer them free if you'll just haul it away and stop them from feeling guilty about their overoptimistic purchase.

Most furniture

Have you ever seen *Antiques Roadshow*? Desks, chairs, shelves, bed frames, sofas, and tables last a long time. Well,

they do if they're built well anyway. I scour Craigslist.org when I'm looking for furniture. You can often find a solid oak desk with great craftsmanship for a lot cheaper than you can get one of those nasty MDF things that you put together yourself. Sure, you'll need a way to get it home. If you don't have a big truck, just rent one from UHaul for a few hours for $20. You'll end up with a great piece of furniture you can hand down to your grandchildren, rather than something that ends up in the garbage after two years.

Sports gear

Footballs, tennis rackets, bicycles, soccer balls, badminton nets—you name it, you can find it all used.

They're usually in excellent shape and a whole lot cheaper than store prices.

Houses

There's a huge caveat on this one: Make sure it's been checked out by an inspector and has the green light. You don't want to take on major plumbing problems, damp basements, or termites. But, if the house is sound, the current economy makes a used home very, very desirable. Sometimes it's just a few years old; there are homes in my area that have decreased in value by $70K in just a few years. Ouch. But not for you. Of course, the used-home sales market is also affecting new home sales. If you insist on buying new, make sure you battle hard with the realtor and look for inventory houses. They just want them sold, so you can often negotiate serious discounts and tons of free upgrades.

Plants

I do not have green fingers. No one in my family does. So, I like to let someone else do the hard work of establishing a plant and giving it healthy roots. Then I'll pick one up cheap at a garage sale or off Craigslist.org.

Artwork/ornaments/mirrors

Stores like Goodwill are perfect hiding places for gems like these. There was a story recently about a woman who found an old painting at Gooodwill, got it valued, and it was worth over $1 million. That's not the point though. Most of the time you can pick up beautiful framed works of art, often original, and much cheaper than in department stores. The same goes for figurines, mirrors, and other home embellishments. Buy them used; no one will even know. — **Paul Michael**

Easiest Way to Save 3 Months' Salary

Want an easy way to save three months' salary? Don't buy a diamond engagement ring. If your fiancée, friends, and family scream hellfire, calmly explain:

It's just marketing. The whole "A Diamond is Forever" and the idea of a diamond engagement ring is not an ancient tradition to be revered and followed. It is Sprite's "Obey Your Thirst." It is Nike's "Just Do It." It is Gary Dahl's "Pet Rock." Not only did the diamond importers understand it had to control supply (buying up and closing down any diamond mine discovered); also they had to control demand. They had to make it sentimental. And Americans were the perfect suckers. They targeted the U.S. specifically for our marketability. This campaign is less than 70 years old yet has become so ingrained in our culture that the diamond engagement ring has become the ultimate symbol of *how much* the relationship, the girl, and love itself is worth.

Diamonds aren't rare. Fine, using marketing tactics can't be blamed since that's part of the game of capitalism. But another part of the game is competition. It's all well and good if marketers can convince consumers to buy them instead of the competition based on a nice slogan, but the competition should be there to protect the consumer. All gems are valued based on their rarity (as are most things in life). But diamonds are abundant. One company has a huge vault where they keep most of the world's supply of diamonds. If it ever got released into the market, diamonds would be worth nothing. It's literally a pretty rock.

Diamonds have no resale value. The reason a "diamond is forever" is because you're basically stuck with it. You'll never be able to resell it except to a pawn shop. Even a jeweler (the few who would be willing to buy it) would offer a fraction of what you paid.

Synthetic diamonds will flood the market. Synthetic or "cultured" diamonds are already being made and within the next few years, will be efficiently made for the mass market. These are real diamonds. They are made in a machine that replicates the environmental forces that make diamonds. The only difference is that they're better. They have less flaws. And they cost a fraction of the going rate. Want a 2-carat pink diamond? That'll be a few thousand dollars.

Moissanite looks just like a diamond. Jewelers had to upgrade their equipment to detect Moissanite from diamonds when it came into the market. It's undetectable with the naked eye. And it's actually more brilliant. A 1-carat ring is under $1,000.

Who is the ring for, anyway? Seriously. It's fun to show off for about 30 seconds. After that there is little to show for the debt incurred for the shiny piece of rock. That money could have gone into furniture, an amazing trip (or many nice ones), or your future kids' college funds!

What are conflict/blood diamonds? Conflict/blood diamonds are used by rebel groups to fuel conflict and civil wars, and by terrorist groups to finance their activities.

The Kimberley Process is just PR. The Kimberley Process is an agreement that is supposed to prevent conflict diamonds from getting into the market but ended up being more of a PR stunt since it's based on a system of self-policing. The UN reported in October 2006 that due to poor enforcement of the Kimberley Process, $23 million of conflict diamonds from Côte d'Ivoire alone entered the legitimate market.

Jennifer Connelly says in the movie *Blood Diamond*, "People back home would not buy a diamond if they knew it cost someone their hand." Now you know. — **Lynn Truong**

How to Complain and Get a Good Result

As a professional advertising copywriter I've learned a thing or two over the years about persuasive writing. I've used that knowledge in my personal life on many occasions, but the place where it's really paid off is in letters and e-mails to customer service departments. I've put together a little guide for writing a letter of complaint that will hopefully get you further along than a typical rant and rave.

I should point out that this is advice only for those involved in the most minor of problems. If you get rear-ended by a bus and get hospitalized, you'll need much more than a letter of complaint. But, if you get a bad attitude from a store clerk, this may help you get something other than a snotty reply, or in most cases no reply at all, from the customer service rep.

First up, do you have a genuine complaint?

Silly question, right? But I've talked to many customer service reps in my time, and some of the things they get screamed at for are ridiculous. It's not the company's fault that you ordered a car with cruise control and expected it to be autopilot (that's a real one by the way . . . the mind boggles). Are you ticked off for a genuine reason, or do you just want to lash out because you made a bad purchase? If you feel

you have a genuine, realistic gripe, it's time to take action.

What do you want out of the complaint?

Be reasonable. A bad attitude from a grocery clerk is not going to get you a year of free groceries. A stale bag of chips will not get you a lifetime supply of your favorite snack. Ask for something equal to your disappointment. A bad experience in a restaurant equates to a free meal next time, so try for that. A poor product deserves a refund or replacement. I recently had very, very poor service at a gas station. I wrote and explained what happened, politely, and asked what the company would be willing to do to help restore my faith in their company. I received two gas certificates in the mail a few days later, and I'm happy to go back and try them again.

You catch more flies with sugar than vinegar

Not that I'm calling CSRs flies; that's just an old saying that illustrates a point. If you start spitting venom in your complaint letter, all you're doing is letting that company know that you're irate and probably a lost cause. It's far better to be a loyal, disappointed customer who really wants their faith restored in a company so they won't take their business elsewhere. Also remember that these people have to sit and read complaints day in, day out. Another average "I'm pissed off—what are you gonna do about it" letter is hardly going to cut through the clutter.

You must get across that you are a customer who still wants to come back and use that company's products or services, but need a show of good faith in order to do so. Act a little wounded if you must. The outcome will favor you much more.

Threats and rants will get you nowhere

I've worked closely with CSRs over my many years in advertising, and they've all had threats of varying proportions. From legal action to verbal abuse and violence, it's all been done many times. And those reactions fall on deaf ears. You may get lucky and get a result, but usually you'll get an apology letter, if anything at all. More often than not, threats go nowhere because people know you write them in a state of anger and frustration, and 99% of people will never see the threats through. They just want to vent. So, calm down before you write your letter, take a few deep breaths, and put everything in perspective. You'll get much further

from that starting point than with steam shooting out of your ears.

Handy phrases to use in your letters

Try a few of these next time; they're worth their weight in gold. And use this tone of disappointment, not anger, throughout your letter.

- Since I can remember, I've been a loyal customer of . . .
- I have always enjoyed your products/services but was really disappointed when . . .
- I was shocked to see such bad service from a company I've grown to trust . . .
- I feel let down by this incident. It's so unlike your company . . .
- Can you restore my faith in . . .

You get the idea. Let them know they are a good friend who has let you down. Someone you care about, and want to trust again. That's a good story to tell, and a good way to get someone to listen. It's far easier for a company to save an existing customer than spend more marketing dollars acquiring a new one. As long as you indicate that you want to be saved, that is.

Letter checklist

- Include your contact details. They need to know who to reply to.

- Have respect for the person you're talking to.
- Don't make idle threats or wild claims.
- Be brief. No one wants to read *War and Peace*. Get to the point in one page or less.
- If you need to provide proof, keep copies or better yet, send copies.
- Keep a copy of your letter. You may need to reference it later.
- Avoid generalizations. Be specific about the one incident.
- Be honest. Really, only complain if you have a real complaint.

Nice feedback is also appreciated

As I said earlier, the customer service folks are on the receiving end of some pretty nasty calls and letters for most of their working day. So imagine their reaction when they get a letter or call that is simply a note of thanks for a great product or service. Not only does it make them feel good about their company, it also has more chance of making it higher up the corporate ladder. Who knows, it may even get to the CEO, and you may find yourself getting something in return for your kind words. It's not uncommon for nice feedback to result in a T-shirt, gift voucher, pen, or free product that you like so much. So, next time you eat a really tasty meal or are knocked out by the quality of service somewhere, think about letting that company know. It's a win-win situation for everyone.

— **Paul Michael**

$ GREEN LIVING

If spending money wisely is a representation of how you care for your resources, then expanding that concern for the world around us should seem natural. Everyone says they are "going green," but how can that apply to you and your finances? Since many of the "greenest" tips also help you save cash, it's easier than ever to feel motivated about making positive changes for the future.

10 Ways to Go Green and Save Money at the Same Time

Want to help the environment, but not too keen on all of the expensive suggestions floating around out there? Here are 10 frugal ways to incorporate green living into your life without throwing your well-laid budget plans to the wind.

1. Safety razors

Giving up disposable razors for the old-fashioned safety razor is a great way to save money and the environment. The multipacks of flat razor blades are not only inexpensive, but they come without all of the extra plastic housing that ultimately ends up in landfills. We've been doing this in our house for a few years now, and have noticed a tremendous savings. An added bonus? We don't have to carve out extra storage in the cabinets when we stock up. Flat packs of blades store very efficiently in a minimal amount of space.

2. Mineral salt deodorant sticks

You can find these at nearly any health food or natural living store. They last an incredibly long time, don't contain any harmful ingredients, and as with the safety razor idea listed above, don't come with a ton of obnoxious plastic packaging to toss in the landfill. My husband and I used this product on a recent six-month trip around the world. It lasted the duration of the trip and is still going strong. It also takes up minimal room in the backpack.

3. Reusable coffee filters

Just imagine never having to buy or run out of these babies again!

4. Give up paper towels

Okay, I'll be honest. This is not easy in the beginning. The trick is developing a simple, workable system for having clean rags on hand. To store clean rags, I'm using several of those fabric sleeves with elastic on both ends. You know, the kind most people use to store empty plastic grocery bags for quick access? I hung one in each place we routinely used paper towels. Then, I raided the pile of old T-shirts we had set aside to go to Goodwill and cut up a bunch of cleaning rags. These were what I used to fill up each of the disposal "sleeves." When we need to reach for something to wipe up a spill or do a quick cleanup of a particular space, we can now reach for a washable cleaning rag instead of a paper towel.

5. Recycle old athletic socks

Not possible you say? I beg to differ. Cut each old sock off just slightly above the ankle, and below the ribbed leg section. The leftover foot portion is what I use instead of those expensive disposable dusting mittens. These things are great for getting around stair banister railings, and gripping table and chair legs to dust. You won't go back, I promise you! The other ribbed section, particularly if it is ribbed the entire length of the piece, is great to slice up one side and use for a great moisture-holding dishrag. The ridges give you extra scrubbing power too.

6. Shopping for secondhand goods

Anything you are comfortable buying secondhand keeps that same item from ending up in a garbage dump. This applies to furniture, clothing, toys, kitchenware, and to a certain extent, automobiles. This personal finance procedure goes a long way toward helping out the planet and your pocketbook at the same time.

7. Think before you print

Save money on ink and paper by checking to see if you really need a paper copy of a particular document before hitting the print button. Still think you really need it? Check out the economy mode for printing which will at least use less ink and save you money in the long run on those refilled cartridges.

8. Celebrate the power of tie-dye

This is a great affordable way to give lightly stained, lighter-colored linens and clothing items a second shelf life. Some ideas? Old sheets, curtains, pillowcases, socks, and T-shirts, to name a few.

9. Find a second use for those plastic grocery bags

These things really can help out a time or two more after making it home from the grocery store. Use them to line small trash cans (one less item to buy), pick up after your dog in the park, or provide extra cushioning in those holiday postal packages.

. . . .

10. Consider a personal filter for your kitchen faucet

This will enable you to skip the extra packaging that comes with large cases of bottled water, and carve some extra cash out of your personal budget at the same time. We've been using one for at least five or six years now and really like not having to find extra room for those bottles. **— Myscha Theriault**

7 Secrets to Gas-Efficient Driving

Your gas mileage depends more on the way you drive than on what car you are driving (of course, smaller is still better). Do you ever wonder why you don't seem to get the gas mileage that is advertised as the EPA rating for your car? Those tests are conducted under ideal conditions (weather, traffic, car condition) driven by an ideal driver. Most of us don't realize how much our driving

habits affect our mileage, and what little effort it takes to improve it significantly. Here are just a few tips to get better gas mileage, saving you money and helping our environment at the same time.

. . . .

1. Inflate your tires

Fueleconomy.gov states that keeping tires inflated to the recommended pressure can improve fuel economy by up to 5%.

. . . .

2. Stop aggressive driving

Speeding, cutting in and out of lanes, tailgating, and other smart-ass maneuvers save you very little time and end up costing you at the gas station. Don't floor your gas pedal when you start moving and slam on the brakes right in front of a red light. By anticipating stops and accelerating moderately, Edmunds.com found that you can get up to 37% in gas savings. This not only saves you gas, but also keeps your brake pads working longer and helps you avoid speeding tickets and accidents—not to mention it's better for your blood pressure!

. . . .

3. Lower your highway speed

The biggest factor influencing fuel economy at high speeds is wind resistance, and going above 60 mph significantly decreases your fuel efficiency. According to fueleconomy. gov, each 5 mph you drive over 60 mph reduces your fuel economy by 10%.

4. Windows vs. air-conditioning

The debate over using the A/C versus having the windows down has to do with how large the effect of drag on a particular car is. Air-conditioning places a 5–10% extra load on the engine. The drag caused by having windows down on a sedan can go up to 20% , while SUVs are only affected by about 7% (this is due to the poor aerodynamics of SUVs to begin with). It's generally accepted that when driving at low speeds (under 40 mph), it's better to have the windows down, while efficiency favors the A/C at higher speeds. But when you're driving an SUV, it may not make much of a difference no matter what the speed.

5. Stop idling

You use up gas when your car is on idle (going zero miles will drop your average mpg). This doesn't mean turning off your car in the middle of the road when you're in traffic or at a red light, but keep in mind it's better to turn off your car and restart than

to leave it on idle for more than 30 seconds. So if there's a long line at the drive-through, consider parking and walking in.

6. Keep it warm

First, there's no need to warm up the engine before driving. Cars today warm up faster and more efficiently by just driving rather than idling (which wastes gas as mentioned above). Second, plan your errands and drive to the farthest destination first, so your engine can completely warm up. It hurts your engine to make frequent stops (making your engine cool and have to warm up again), especially in cold weather. If you allow your engine time to warm up completely before stopping, there will be less loss of heat and it'll take less time to warm it back up when you go to your next stop.

7. Lose weight

If you're carrying excess pounds in your trunk (no pun intended), get rid of it. Weight contributes to your gas mileage too, so remove any unnecessary load.

Driving efficiently so you can save money at the gas station is great incentive to be more mindful when you drive. But more important, it's a very easy and cheap way to contribute to saving our environment. Not to mention it'll make the roads a little safer and a happier place to be.

If you want more tips to help raise your fuel economy, get our FREE e-book, Wise Bread's Wise Driving Guide: 108 Tips to Raise Your Fuel Economy, at www.wisebread.com/108-best-fuel-economy-tips. — **Lynn Truong**

10 Ways to Hold Off on Heating

Heating costs hit us every winter, but in my household we've implemented 10 strategies for keeping warm just a wee bit longer, sans heating unit.

1. Open the shades

Let the sun warm the house by opening the shades during the 10:00 AM–5:00 PM hours. Free heat feels so good.

2. Put an end to line drying

We enjoy hanging our clothes out on the line when it is warm. When the frost has fallen, we reverse our think-

ing to utilize the heat our dryer produces. Since our dryer wasn't vented outside our home, we use a lint receptacle to "catch" the lint. These kits are under $15 at a hardware store, and in addition to the benefit of having the dryer heat in our home, the added moisture is nice during the winter months. (Be sure to keep this system in check with weekly cleanings and adequate water to the trap. Families with allergies will need to be especially diligent.)

3. Dress in layers

I still see kids walking to school in shorts, despite the 35-degree mornings. This is ridiculous to me, as clothing is the cheapest way to stay warm in this season of transition. Once the first frost appears, I rid my

kids' drawers of shorts and sleeveless tops, packing them up into plastic tubs for winter storage. They are free to choose from any of their winter clothing, and I encourage them to dress in a T-shirt under their warmer clothes for added warmth. They don't complain about the cold when they are properly dressed (including socks and indoor shoes).

4. Make your bed

We also switch our sheets to flannel for the winter. We supplement each bed with a wool blanket and an extra quilt or two. In the upstairs room (where it is coldest), the adults have an electric blanket set on low or a heated mattress pad for the really cold nights. It's amazing how peacefully you can sleep with a chill to the air and your body comfortably warm.

5. Top it off

My ultra-sexy nightwear consists of sweats or long underwear with wool socks. I also wear a stocking cap on the colder nights. It keeps me feeling snug, and I have less bed head in the morning. (Plus, my husband thinks it's cute!)

6. Spice things up

Cold sandwiches take a sabbatical for the winter at my house. We bust out the chili recipes, Crock-Pot fare, and make all of our evening meals a bit zestier than normal. Most of it is purely psychological, but it does help keep a warmth about the dinner table. (Another perk is the economics of spicy meals. Many of them are dirt cheap.)

7. Keep hydrated

Our hot cocoa bill is higher than normal during the winter. We replace our chocolate milk with hot chocolate. (Ovaltine works well for a vitamin-packed alternative.) I enjoy herbal teas and decaf coffees in the evenings. Hot apple cider kept simmering on the stove not only tastes delicious, but it also keeps your home smelling yummy. Replacing your cold drinks with hot ones can keep you toasty any time of day.

8. Snuggle

I'll admit to letting my kids jump in bed with us a bit more in the winter time. The toddlers are like radiant heaters that require no electricity. Just toss a three-year-old in the mix for an instant 10-degree warm-up. (Cuddles are the cheapest form of heat I know.)

9. Use a space heater (wisely)

I'm not a huge fan of the small electric heaters. They are good for some things, but quite dangerous in other situations. Use your head on this one, and under no circumstances should you leave one running overnight, in a child's room unattended, or when you are not in the home. If nothing else, I like one running in the bathroom first thing in the morning. (It takes the edge off that cold seat, if you know what I mean.)

10. Go to Grandma's

I'm not saying that my house is too cold. Many wouldn't be comfortable in anything as chilly as 55 in October. But on days when I'm not particularly enthusiastic about watching TV in a cooler-than-average home (or once a week), I'll head next door to my mother's house. She's glad to see us, and she has cable. (It's also 10 degrees warmer by default. If she's already paying for gas, why not?)

Call me cheap or stingy, but I don't see any reason to crank up the heat until I really have to. With 35-degree nights turning into almost 70-degree days, starting up my woodstove would leave us baked by midafternoon. These tips help us in the month or two between seasons, keep our annual heating bill low, and help us to appreciate that roaring fire when it finally gets burning each year.

— **Linsey Knerl**

7 Ways to Lower Water Heater Costs

According to fypower.org, your water heater can account for 13% of home energy costs. The good news is that there are small, easy tweaks you can make to lower those costs and conserve energy at the same time.

1. Reduce your use

It is usually the shower that keeps most people raising the dial on their water heaters. Use low-flow showerheads, take quicker showers, turn off the water when you are soaping up, and stick with mild, lukewarm water. You'll realize you need a lot less hot water than you think.

Also consider using cold water to wash your clothes. About 90% of the energy used in a clothes washer goes to water heating. Cold-water washing also helps clothes last longer!

2. Turn it down

Your water heater maintains its temperature 24 hours a day, 7 days a week. That takes a lot of energy. According to the U.S. Department of Energy (apps1.eere.energy.gov), for every 10°F you turn down on your water heater, you save 3%–5% in energy costs. Turning it down to 120°F could cut your costs by 6%–10%. As long as you are reducing your use with the tips above, you won't even notice. Make sure to consult your manual for proper instructions on adjusting the thermostat. For example, the electricity should be turned off before adjusting electric water heaters.

3. Turn it off

If you're going off on vacation, turn the temperature way down, or completely off. When you get home, you'll just need to wait about an hour to reheat before the hot water gets back in service. If you have a gas heater, make sure you know how to relight the pilot light before turning it off (or just turn it down without completely turning it off).

4. Insulate

Adding insulation is inexpensive and can reduce standby heat losses by 25%–45%, saving you 4%–9% in water heating costs. Check to see if your heater has an R-value of at least 24 (if your water heater is less than 10 years old, it's likely it's already optimally insulated). You can also do a touch test—if it's warm to the touch, it needs additional insulation. Make sure to check your manual for insulation instructions.

5. Set a timer

Again, a lot of energy is used to keep the water hot 24 hours a day. And really, you only need it a few times a day. If you have an electric water heater, a timer can be installed to turn it off during off-peak hours (at night after you go to bed). This can save 5%–12% of energy. For gas heaters, you can keep it turned down most of the time, and then manually turn it up about a half-hour before you need it. Timers cost about $60 and should pay for themselves in about a year.

6. Reuse

Hot water that goes down the drain carries away energy with it. That can be 80%–90% of the energy used to heat water in a home. Drain-water (or graywater) heat recovery systems capture this energy to preheat cold water entering the water heater or going to other water fixtures. Heat can be recovered from hot water used in showers, sinks, dishwashers, and clothes washers. Prices for drain-water heat-recovery systems range from $300 to $500 (and you'll need a qualified plumbing and heating contractor to install the system). It can take 2.5 to 7 years to recover that cost in savings, depending on how often the system is used.

7. Buy a more efficient one

If your water heater is old, it might be good to look into getting a new one. New water heaters today are considerably more energy-efficient than those of 20 years ago. In addition, Energy Star models can be 15% more efficient than standard models. Look for one with heat traps, which prevents convective heat losses through the inlet and outlet pipes. Find the best type of water heater for your home and look for rebates and incentives at fypower. org for energy-efficient appliances and equipment. — **Lynn Truong**

6 Clever Green Gifting Strategies

Need to find a gift that's affordable, desirable, and green? Here are six of them.

1. Activities

This gift idea has the added benefit of including things the recipient might not be able to carve out cash for currently, but would love to be able to do. When we are really pinching pennies, fun is one of the first things to be cut from the budget. Get your friend national or state park passes to go hiking or take the kids and dogs on a picnic, season theater tickets, restaurant certificates, massage appointments—get the idea?

2. Seeds

This was what we gave out as wedding favors. Rather than going with the little plastic trinkets that do nothing but get pitched in the trash, we went with seed packets printed with a wedding wish and decorated tastefully on the front. They were for a perennial flower, so people could take them home and plant them, knowing they would come up every year.

3. Handmade

I'm not just talking tea cozies here. This could be anything from a set of designer-style drapes, to a custom paint job in your living room, to a hand-done mural. Are you great at Web design, or data management? If you have a skill that people would routinely pay for, then chances are somebody would appreciate receiving a gift that benefited from them.

4. Engraved, refillable pens

Use for graduations, new jobs, anniversaries, etc. These are really classy and special gifts that people will use. Think of all the cheap plastic pen casings that won't be out there in the landfills!

5. Green consumable products

Think fair trade coffee, soy-based candles, or eco-friendly bath products. This goes back a bit to the first item. When people are on a budget, they don't necessarily feel comfortable indulging in treats. They're affordable, and support the environment and small vendors.

6. Repurpose family heritage

Look through your attic and find things connected to your family history. Repurpose them. Turn an item of clothing from a grandparent into several smaller treasures for younger family members. Digitally archiving old family photos so everyone can enjoy them is another cool strategy that blends family history with newer technology, like digital photo frames.

— **Myscha Theriault**

A Simple How-To Guide to Regifting

We've all been there. You open a present with giddy anticipation, rip-ping the gift wrap away like a 10-year-old on a sugar high. And then, as you open the box and peek inside, your brain searches for a way to act really happy . . . because the gift you have received is just, well, awful. And when the dust settles and the event is over, it's time to start thinking about regifting. But be careful; there are rules to follow.

Some people see a big stigma attached to regifting. Personally, I think it's fine if you follow a few simple guidelines. You don't want to hurt the feelings of the person who gave you the gift, or the person who gets the regifted item. But look at the alternatives: You can just let the offending item rot in your basement or garage; you can give it to charity; or you can put it out with the trash. So if you know someone who would really like the gift that just didn't do it for you, where's the harm?

I've combined my own rules with some research I did online and at my local library (yes, there are books and news stories on this—I kid you not). Generally, there seem to be some major guidelines that regifters follow to ensure everyone is happy. Here's what I have uncovered.

1. Don't let anyone know this is a regift.

It's amazing how often people have made it quite clear that I was receiving a gift that was from their reject pile. Sure, they dressed it up nice enough, with language like "I just would never have used this cool gadget but I know how much you need one." It still makes you feel like you're getting crappy old hand-me-downs. Of course, if someone's giving me a brand-new, state-of-the-art laptop or cool pair of sunglasses, my hurt feelings fly out the window. But if it's a nasty crystal picture frame or a hideous painting, I'd rather not know you hated it as well. Ignorance is bliss.

2. If you get an unwanted gift that is meant for display, do the right thing first.

As much as you don't want to put that chintzy glass clown or fiber-optic lamp on display in your lovely abode, you may have to bite the bullet for a few weeks. The person who gave it to you will like to see it on display the next time they come over; otherwise they'll instantly know that you were lying when you said "It was just fabulous." So put it out on a hutch, coffee table, or kitchen counter for a while. But keep the box, if it has one, and all the accompanying packaging and tags. Once your gift-giver has seen the item on display, they feel appreciated. Then when it disappears from view, you can make up an appropriate excuse (a little white lie) like "Oh, the kids kept messing with it so it's up in my bedroom."

....

3. Beware of the previously regifted gift.

....

Sometimes you'll receive a gift that doesn't quite feel right. Your Spidey Sense will tingle and you'll realize, perhaps after some investigation, that this gift has already been through the regifting process. Now you've got problems. The last thing you want is for the gift to end up back in the hands of the person who originally gave it; not only will you look embarrassed, but so will the person who gave it to you. And we don't want friendships strained. My best advice: If in doubt, regifting is out.

....

4. Keep tabs on the gifts and the people who gave them.

....

When you receive a gift that is destined to be a gift once again, label it as soon as you can with the name of the person who gave it to you, and when they gave it to you. This is a simple habit to get into, but an essential one for regifting. Post-it notes are okay; although if they fall off you're relying on your memory. I would suggest something a little stronger, maybe a

Post-it in combination with an elastic band. Don't use strong tape on something that will rip or tear the gift or packaging. If you want, you could use a small notebook instead. Log items in the same way you would to write thank-you cards for wedding presents and baby shower gifts.

....

5. Keep everything in the original packaging.

....

Keep all the original packaging, including instructions, twisty-ties and anything else that accompanied the gift to keep it in that *new* condition. Even if you've never used it, a coffee machine or spanky-new DVD player is less impressive when the instructions are missing and it's rattling around inside the box. You can get away with packaging loss on some items, such as ornaments, photo frames, and so forth. But generally, if the packaging has gone bye-bye, so has your chance of regifting the item.

....

6. Some items are bad regifting choices.

....

Some people say candles fall into this category, but I'd have to disagree. For a start, they can make up part of a larger gift, especially a gift basket. And some people genuinely like candles; if you know one of those people, find a nice gift bag for the waxy present and pass it forward. However, you'll need to be creative, very creative, with any of the following, so beware: books that have no tie to the person you're giving them to; CDs or DVDs that are equally random, obscure or awful; clothing without the tags; shoes, or sneakers (unless they're spot-on for both size *and* style); useless appliances (come on, who really wants a Clapper?). If you feel a little uncomfortable or guilty about regifting any item, it's probably best not to do it. Of course, if you really don't like the person you're giving it to, but have to give a gift (like those Secret Santa deals), I'll look the other way as you pass on a crappy DVD with a random autobiography taped to it.

7. If it's used, it usually doesn't count as a regift.

Sorry, but a sweater you've only worn a few times is not a regifter, even if you do have all the tags and the original gift box. Same goes for all other clothing, most appliances, anything, in fact, that you can get actual "mileage" out of. Gift cards are also included here. It doesn't matter if you only used $5 of a $30 card—that's just tacky. However, I say "usually" because there are some exceptions to this rule. If it's meant purely for display, like a photo frame,

candlestick, painting, or something in that same vein, you can "usually" get away with it. Make sure you give it a quick dusting first, though, as that's a dead giveaway. Of course, if that person saw the item on display in your home, you're in a whole heap of awkwardness.

8. Don't wait too long to regift.

Time may be a great healer, but it doesn't really do the regifter any favors. The older the brand-new item becomes, the more obvious it becomes that this is a regift. If you can no longer find the product in the stores, if the packaging has been updated, or if the company that made it went out of business ages ago, you're stuck with that item. By all means, try to sell it or give it to charity, but as a regift it stinks of "Here's an old thing I found in my basement, but hey, it's never been used!"

9. If you can't regift, there's always craigslist.org or eBay.com.

The Web has opened up a world of choices to regifters. Now, if an item does go beyond its "regift date" or has been gently used, there's the option of the free classified ads on Craigslist.org, or the wider reach of eBay.com.

In some instances the item you have for sale could now be a collector's item and you could get back more money for it than it was originally worth. This is also a great way to attack the idea of regifting if you're just against it in principle. Simply sell an unwanted gift to raise money for a brand-new gift for that special someone in your life. You're happy, they're happy, and the person who originally gave you that gift . . . well, what they don't know won't hurt them, right?

10. Replace old, ripped or scuffed gift wrap.

This is obvious. Don't try to regift with the same wrapping paper, even if you were careful with opening it in the first place. And if there's a gift card with your name on it, well, do I need to say more?

To sum up, regifting is a great way to pass on a gift if you're watching your budget or want to see an unwanted gift go to someone who could genuinely use it. And as my mum and dad always told me, it's the thought that counts anyway. As long as it's done with someone else in mind, I don't see the harm. Better to do that than throw it away or mindlessly chuck it in the spring-cleaning bag for Goodwill. — **Paul Michael**

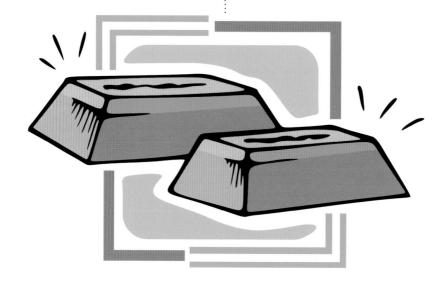

EDUCATION & SELF IMPROVEMENT

$

Referring to education as a financial "burden" may be an understatement. Many professionals today are unable to pay off their school loans even though they are earning decent incomes. We would all love to cut education costs, but how do you go about it? Whether you're struggling to pay for homeschooling materials or are filling out that college financial aid application, we've got the inside scoop on how to cut costs today!

How to Use Your Experience to Save Time and Tuition

Are you experienced, workshop-educated, community-involved, and/or moderately traveled and still working toward your bachelor's degree? Write it down! You may be able to trade a nominal portfolio assessment fee for credit hours worth thousands at your college or university. I've helped many people who have saved time (by completing degree requirements through credit for prior learning rather than taking semester-long classes) and tuition expenses in exchange for documentation of their past experiences.

To get started, find out if your school has a credit for prior learning (CPL) program and more specifically, a portfolio assessment process. Next, get a copy of the guidelines. Then, prepare your portfolio. If you get stuck, look for available school resources like counselors or other faculty members to provide guidance.

Guidelines vary, but work, volunteer, and travel experiences, professional and technical training, and even hobbies may qualify as educational. The portfolio program tends to favor older adults with years of varied experience, but even a year or two of working between high school and college, or time off for traveling can qualify as prior learning.

Identify and document your experiential learning.
....

Work experience
....

Describe the company and your position(s), duties, and accomplishments.

Include quantifiable information. For example, list the sales for the company, business unit, territory, or assigned accounts, operating and capital budgets, and/or number of customers, manufacturing facilities, vendors, and distribution sites.

Present your accomplishments. What goals did you meet or exceed and under what challenging circumstances? What new programs did you design or introduce? What have you improved in your department, business unit, or company?

Explain what you learned. It could be as simple as "I learned how to increase sales by better assessing customer needs" or "I learned how to resolve conflict between coworkers."

....

Training

List every non-college course you have ever taken including professional development (leadership training) and technical training (CPR, Photoshop, Bloodborne Pathogens); these may include one-day seminars, series of courses leading to professional certification, and self-paced computer-based or independent study.

Explain what you learned and, if possible, how you have applied this knowledge to your career and personal life.

....

Volunteer activities

List all extracurricular activities including company task forces and committees (if not mentioned under work experience), trade associations, civic groups, and interest groups.

Describe what you did (planned social events, arranged guest speakers) and what you learned (how to get multiple bids for catering, types of speakers who appeal to certain audiences).

....

Travel

List all travel experiences that are relevant: locally, nationally, and globally.

Describe your travel experiences (e.g., went camping in the mountains, took a mission trip to Guatemala) and what you learned (e.g., how to cook a meal over an open fire, improved your language skills).

If you need to develop a theme to which all of your experience relates, consider the common elements of your experiences (which may be easier upon reflection rather than before you start the process). A theme may be that you've enjoyed learning about the historical situation of a problem before proposing a solution, or you've used visual tools to communicate with people. This is where counselors or faculty members could be very helpful.

You may need to prove that your learning corresponds directly to a specific course offered by the college or university; or, you demonstrate only that you have learned something of value and/or relevant to your academic goals.

Warnings:

You will most likely need to pay an up-front portfolio assessment fee, which may be nominal or it may equal tuition expenses associated with the credit hours (in which case you will have saved time but not money).

Credit is not guaranteed.

Credits earned through CPL may not be eligible for transfer to other institutions. — **Julie Rains**

6 Ways to Pay Less Money for a College Degree

A four-year college degree can be one of the most expensive purchases in a person's lifetime. In fact, many hard-working professionals continue to pay for their college education long after graduation. Here are six ways you can expect to pay less money for a traditional four-year college degree.

1. Start early

Some colleges allow high school students to begin taking college courses while attending high school. Home-schooled students and those attending a participating high school can take up to 12 semester hours before graduation. By paying for and completing these classes early, it can help to offset costs later on.

2. Attend a community college

With costs at half of their pricier private and state counterparts, community colleges are a great buy. If getting a degree there doesn't interest you, consider their generous transfer programs. They allow a student to initially obtain a large number of credit hours at the cheaper college cost. You would still be considered a graduate of the state or private college.

3. Do it in three years

Several colleges offer summer class options to their students. By combining the summer semester with two 20-hour regular semesters, it is possible to graduate well ahead of schedule. Even with the summer semester costs, it is far cheaper than going the full four or five years.

4. Challenge the requirements

Many colleges allow students to "test out" of required classes. To do so, a student must prove that they already know the course material, and therefore, they do not need to take the class. Providing documented life experience or taking a competence exam will often be enough to skip a course entirely.

5. Let your boss pay for it

An increasing number of workplaces offer tuition reimbursement programs and will pick up the tab for up to 30 credit hours a year. Some employer plans require that you maintain a satisfactory grade level (C average or higher) and that you work a minimum number of hours. In addition, you may have to pay up-front costs, which will then be reimbursed by your place of employment.

6. Go in the off-season

It may be possible to get a 50% discount on your college courses if you're willing to attend during unpopular class times. Early morning, late evening, and holiday class offerings are often more difficult to fill. Some colleges will reduce the price for these classes to ensure adequate enrollment.

In addition to the traditional methods of scholarships, grants, loan forgiveness, and work-study, there are less traditional methods of saving college money. Tailor a unique schedule or program at your school, and it is possible to pay far less. By being as flexible as possible, you just might avoid the highest price tag on today's college education. — **Linsey Knerl**

7 Great Jobs that Offer College Loan Forgiveness

Paying for a college education can last up to 20 years post-graduation. While the cost is usually justified through higher earnings, it can still be burdensome. These seven careers are not only growing in opportunity, but they can sometimes offer partial to complete loan forgiveness!

1. Teaching

There are many arguments as to whether teachers get paid enough these days. If you could add in up to $17,500 in student loan forgiveness, however, it can make this high-demand career more appealing. Teachers that work in designated "low income" school districts for a minimum of five years can see some of that college debt wiped away. More debt forgiveness is offered to those teachers with an emphasis in math, science, and special education. (Visit www. studentaid.ed.gov for full details of current programs.)

2. Social work

Social workers who dedicate their time to agencies servicing families in low-income or high-risk geographical areas may see total forgiveness of their Perkins Loan. An increasing amount of debt will be forgiven for each of five

years served in these areas. Licensed clinical social workers will see the most money forgiven through government programs. (Visit Socialworkers. org for more information.)

3. Volunteering

Popular programs such as the Peace Corps, AmeriCorps, and Volunteers in Service to America (VISTA— which is now part of AmeriCorps) all offer deferment or partial payment toward loan debt. Each program differs in its formula for awarding payments. Participants may see up to 70% of select government loans

forgiven. (While not technically considered a paying "job," a stipend is usually offered in the compensation package for these programs.)

4. Military

The Montgomery G.I. Bill, offered through the U.S. Armed Forces Recruiting program, may pay up to 60% of college tuition costs. Those active in the Army National Guard may be eligible for a payment of up to $10,000 toward loan debt. Additionally, many veterans and private military associations offer funding through scholarships and grants.

5. Child care

Many child-care providers are eligible for up to 100% of outstanding loan debt. To qualify, they must have received an associate's or bachelor's degree in early childhood education. Their services must be used by a community of low-income families for two consecutive years. The program is open to new borrowers of federal education funds. (Note: This program has recently stopped taking applications for new participants. If you have received benefits in the past, however, you may still be eligible. See the program details at www.studentaid.ed.gov.)

6. Medical professionals

Doctors, nurses, and physical therapists can take advantage of several programs offering loan forgiveness in select geographic areas. By providing services to depressed regions, up to 100% of their loans may be deferred. Additional areas of need include clinical research and dental care. (A great list of resources can be found at nhsc.bhpr.hrsa.gov.)

7. Law

Law students and newly graduated lawyers who offer their services at free and reduced cost can take advantage of partial loan forgiveness. By working for agencies that provide public-interest or nonprofit services, graduates can make a difference in the lives of those who can't afford legal representation. Equal Justice Works (EqualJusticeWorks.org) has more information on these programs.

As the need grows for more professionals to serve our communities, there will be an increasing reward for those who answer the call. Loan forgiveness can be a big motivator toward commitment in these fields. Participation in forgiveness programs can add value to your degree and will make college affordable for thousands more each year. — **Linsey Knerl**

How to Sound More Confident in One Simple Step

I recently took a class on public speaking. It's not something that I thought I needed, but it turns out that I'm a terrible public speaker. Most people are, but I always thought of myself as relatively eloquent. Turns out, it's not so much what you say, but how you say it.

The woman who was teaching our class is a voice artist with over 50 years of experience. The first thing that she taught us actually took pretty much the entire class to learn, and will probably take even longer to master. But it's so simple and important, I felt it needed to be shared.

Own your name

Our teacher told us that when she is in charge of hiring other voice artists based on video résumés, she only has to hear the first line of their introduction to know whether or not she can work with them. This might seem harsh, but it's her methodology, so I'm not going to argue with its validity.

She asked us all to introduce ourselves and tell the rest of the class what we did for a living.

"Hi," I said. "I'm Andrea Dickson, and I'm a writer—"

"Stop right there," intoned our instructor. "Why are you asking a question?"

"Huh?"

"When you told us your name. You said, 'My name is Andrea Dickson? and I'm a writer . . .'"

"That's just basic inflection. People talk that way when we have more to say."

Think about it. When you're telling a story, your voice will tilt upward at the end of a phrase, indicating that the story is continuing.

This is fine for much of our normal conversation. But as our instructor pointed out, we use upward inflection only when talking about things that aren't as important as the climax of the story. When I introduce myself as "Andrea Dickson?" I am putting less emphasis on my name than I should.

When you are introducing yourself to another person, one on one, you will say your name with downward inflection, like a statement. "I'm Andrea. Good to meet you." But when you introduce yourself in front of an audience, you start with your name and move on to something else.

In those contexts, it's important to make sure that you introduce yourself as though your name is a statement. Your first name should inflect upward, and your last name should inflect downward. So it should sound more like "My name is Andrea? Dickson." Follow with a slight pause, then continue with the rest of your introduction. Actually, don't use my name, unless you want to be mobbed by thousands of screaming fans.

Try it by yourself a few dozen times, and then try it out next time you have to give a talk or introduce yourself to a group. You'll be pleasantly surprised at what a difference it makes in the overall tone of your introduction. — **Andrea Dickson**

13 Ways to Be Nice that Will Cost You Nothing

It's not expensive to be nice—in fact, it often costs nothing. Here are 13 easy ways to be nice that will cost you nothing.

1. Say "take your time" and mean it.

Truly, I am not one of those people who wait until the cashier finishes ringing up all purchases before *starting* to look for a form of payment; my card-sliding, coin-counting (pre-sorted), and button-pressing prowess has not stopped the next in line from pressing forward, snooping over my shoulder as I finish my transactions, clearly violating my space, and acting as if the millisecond of waiting for my receipt shows that I am hopelessly slow and not worthy of occupying a square inch of shopping-floor space. Though I am not patient naturally, my disdain for the hurry-uppers has calmed me and seems to be contagious. However, don't take kindness and patience as license to be oblivious to the needs of others.

2. Ask your friends if they want to borrow your stuff, not randomly, but upon detection of a need.

For example, I offered my pet carrier to neighbors who needed something to transport a newly adopted dog. My sister-in-law bought the carrier for our family so it seemed natural to share this gift. And, when my son's friend

went on his first-ever ski trip, it made sense to offer an extra pair of long underwear; they're expensive to buy and easily outgrown by a teenager. I've also been the beneficiary of an offer when a friend let my family borrow his tent for our first Scout camping trip; we've since bought our own but it was nice to test drive one (and let our son decide if he wanted to stick with Scouts).

3. Invite someone to join your group.

It can be one that meets regularly, such as your book club or mom's group, or an impromptu gathering for a bike ride or potluck dinner. You might be turned down, but you also might be surprised, as I have been, at the impact of a quick phone call. I invited someone to my women's group at church several months ago and was surprised that 1) she had really wanted someone like me to issue an invitation in order to feel welcome, and 2) she had been one of the charter members, but had gotten busy over the years with work and single parenthood.

4. Use your turn signal.

Judging from my experience on the road, the turn signal is an underused but highly valuable device. Whether it is a hand movement on a bicycle or a flashing light on a motorized vehicle, the signal tells the world what you intend to do, enabling other drivers to avoid accidents *and* more easily accommodate your desires.

5. Wave.

A friendly wave accomplishes two things: 1) says hello, and 2) shows that you acknowledge another person's presence. A cycling buddy waves at cars with drivers who pass carefully and patiently wait at intersections. I have adopted his habit and feel that I have joined a cadre of cycling ambassadors.

6. Tell someone what others think of them.

Make sure it's pleasant and accurate. A kind word can change someone's perspective and help forge or reinforce friendships.

7. Wait up.

Having been waited on and having waited for others, I can say that a slower pace can mean more meaningful conversations. There are times, though, that I have asked others to go ahead and wait for me at the finish line.

8. Return things you've borrowed.

Just because the lender hasn't asked for it back doesn't mean it wouldn't be appreciated to have it back.

9. Respond promptly to invitations.

It's okay to say "no" but please do it as quickly as possible.

10. Say "please" and "thank you."

Another thing that is underused but highly valuable.

11. Be sensitive.

Just because you have parents to watch your kids while you go to dinner or spend a weekend away; plenty of money for vacations each year; family members with no medical issues; a great career in a profession widely respected—doesn't mean everyone else does.

12. Call or e-mail the parents of your teenagers' friends if you have something important to say.

Even the best-raised kids and most well-intentioned parents aren't perfect and don't know everything: you may need to alert them to a major school project, a class registration or scholarship application deadline, unsecured guns in a neighbor's house, or drug possession.

. . . .

13. Bring extra to share or just share whether you have extra or not.

. . . .

You might bring extra water, Clif bars, or salty nuts on a hiking trip, or a spare tube and CO_2 pump on a bike ride. Being prepared is great; being prepared *and* understanding is even better. (This one may cost you more than nothing, but not by much.)

— Julie Rains

10 Tips for Winning College Scholarships

Winning a scholarship takes effort, even to snag an award that is relatively small ($500–$1,000) compared to the cost of attendance at a state university (more than $16,000 per year). But if you can acquire multiple awards (which is easier once you land the first scholarship), you can rack up big savings. Sorting through the volume of information on scholarships can be overwhelming, though. Here are a few tips from professionals.

I spoke with Kimberly Stezala, author of *Scholarships 101: The Real-World Guide to Getting Cash for College*, and Betty Wagner, director of admissions at Central Michigan University (CMU). Kimberly educated me on private scholarships and Betty filled me in on university-specific awards. They both gave great tips on winning college scholarships.

. . . .

1. Start early

. . . .

Kimberly recommends exploring scholarship opportunities at least by the summer before your senior year of high school. Betty recommends visiting college campuses and narrowing your choices in the summer before your junior year based on factors such as admission criteria, cost, and programs of study.

. . . .

2. Take advanced-level English classes

. . . .

This can help boost your high school transcript and equip you with the writing skills you'll need to create stellar essays. You should also take advanced-level courses in other core subjects.

3. Log community service hours

Many scholarships require a certain number of service hours; and time serving the community can help you become a more experienced and compassionate person.

4. Go to summer camp

Many colleges and universities offer pre-college programs or specialty camps in areas such as music, art, theater, media, and computers. Not only do these programs allow campers to explore interests and improve skills, but they also allow department heads to identify rising stars (and potential scholarship winners).

5. Apply for as many as possible

More money is (nearly always) better. The more money you can bring in from outside sources, the less you or your parents will have to pay. Scholarships can reduce financial aid packages, but since this aid is often in the form of self-help or student loans,

it is wise to offset your needs with free money as much as possible.

6. Be organized

Kimberly indicated that the process is time-consuming, and that the students who win scholarships tend to be entrepreneurial (they consider finding scholarship money similar to running a business). They are well-organized, meet deadlines, quick to respond, and persistent.

7. Know your competition

Call scholarship providers and ask how many students apply and how many awards are given each year. This can help you prioritize and tailor your applications.

8. Compile and gather information

If the applications require documents such as transcripts or letters of recommendation, make sure to get those ahead of time. Going to your favorite teacher to ask for a letter of recommendation one day before your application is due is not a sign of a responsible student. Also start brainstorming for essay ideas early— you'll probably have to write several of them.

9. Follow the 1-2-3 process

Rather than blasting out all applications at one time, send out 1, then 2, then 3 applications; it will give you time to reflect on the process, rethink your essay, and make adjustments.

10. Keep trying

Don't stop after you have won your first scholarship. Your credentials are now validated and looked on more favorably by subsequent scholarship committees. (Some scholarships, though, may be reserved for those who have not yet won awards.)

Kimberly also gave a little advice on what judges look for. Primarily, they look for differentiation. Consider and explain how you are different from your peers. Though you may have a similar academic record as another applicant, you may have a vastly different personal life and may have faced unique challenges. They are also looking at your writing skills. There's a reason an essay is usually involved.

A $500 award that may seem small now could double in value if used to offset student loans (based on 8% interest rate, capitalization of interest while earning your degree, and 10-year loan payback).

After you have begun college, you can pursue new scholarships, scholarship renewals, and scholarships pertaining to specific majors. But remember to make good grades so you can keep any scholarships that are dependent on maintaining a certain GPA. — **Julie Rains**

10 Ways to Eat for Free in College

Eating seems to be a major expense for college students not on some sort of meal plan. How will you survive the next few weeks until you go home to Mom and Dad with a car full of laundry and a scheme to get them to help you out until the end of the semester? Here are a few tricks of the trade I learned. Take notes, my students, and swallow your pride.

1. Professors

Make friends with your professors and get invited over for dinner. My friend Jennifer and I survived countless poor Friday nights by getting invited over for dinner. We stuck together and would make sure we could bring a friend; since there are lecherous professors out there, bringing a friend helps keep everything on the up and up and you get a free meal and possibly wine or beer too.

. . . .

2. Art show openings

. . . .

You are in a college town! There are bound to be a few art show openings. Find out when they are and attend. Many times galleries in an area will team up and have a bunch of openings on the same night. This way you can walk a few blocks and hit wine, bottled water, cheese, fruit, and veggies dipped in dressing at a few places so you won't look like you are hovering over the food necessarily.

. . . .

3. Collect recycling

. . . .

Honestly. One of my college apartments was next to a grocery store and I saved all my family's recycling to put in the machine out front which would spit out coupons to use in the grocery store. Even today when my husband and I take in recycling we sometimes collect about $9–$11 dollars' worth of free groceries for our troubles.

. . . .

4. Bake sales

. . . .

Work that bake sale for that cause you kind of care about. There will be left-overs, and if you sample beforehand, you can make recommendations.

. . . .

5. Raid meetings

. . . .

Check out conferences and meetings on campus. Nine times out of ten your college will put out a little catered spread at various functions on campus for people who are attending to have a snack. Dress a little nicer than usual.

. . . .

6. Realtor open houses

. . . .

Hungry on Saturday and campus options all closed? Head into the community. Granted, the food will be similar to the art openings, but beggars can't be choosers and it'll at least be fresh. Dress nicely, talk about being pre-law or pre-med and how that house will make a great starter home.

. . . .

7. Befriend someone in culinary school

. . . .

They work in some pretty nice kitchens, and that'll be a great switch from eating wine, cheese, and grapes from the open houses and art shows. My sister befriended and dated a lot of culinary academy students. In the first four years she lived in San Francisco I don't think she ever paid for a meal. Ever. In every kitchen in town she seemed to know someone who would at least get her and her date a complimentary appetizer.

....

8. Flirt

You can always scrounge up a few pennies for coffee at a coffee shop. Go in late at night. Be kind to the waiter or waitress. Smile. You might see a free piece of pie. I am forever grateful to the guys at the Apple Pan in Westwood down the road from UCLA. Thanks for feeding me!

....

9. Work it

Think about getting a part-time café job. You can survive well on just about day-old anything. Your café won't be able to sell those day-old bagels or quiche, but there isn't anything wrong with them.

....

10. Get help

Tell your grandparents to buy you gift cards to grocery stores that are near your school or to put money on your meal card for the next semester. They don't know what to buy you for your birthday anymore—this is a great solution for them to help with college and for you not to have to wear that ugly sweater they were going to buy you.

Just look at all those solutions; you didn't even have to dumpster dive! Mom and Dad would be so proud of you. — **Margaret Garcia-Couoh**

10 Ways to Homeschool for Less

In a recent cost-study I completed, I found that it is possible for American families to spend between $300 and $4,325 per year to homeschool a single child. While this is as varied a figure as the child it represents, there are some very simple, smart ways to keep your costs on the low side. Here are my top picks for keeping curriculum expenses low and how each has worked for our family.

1. eBay

I'll be the first to admit that my top pick for cheap textbooks and student materials is going to fall behind other resources. Now that eBay (www.ebay. com) has a strictly enforced rule that prevents the buying and selling of teachers' editions (even those clearly labeled as home educator editions), it has left many loyal eBayers in the lurch. While still a great resource for buying student copies and readers at pennies on the dollar, I predict it going the way of the dinosaur for most parents.

2. Wagglepop

A whooey what? This up-and-coming auction site (www.wagglepop.com) has been making a modest comeback for some time. With only a handful of sellers offering homeschool curriculum, it isn't for everyone. There are some fantastic deals to be had, however, and I personally purchased over a dozen books from one seller with superb results. Given some more time, this could be the solution to eBay's teacher edition conundrum.

3. Amazon

Taking over as my personal #1 resource for buying student and teacher materials, Amazon (www.amazon. com) offers copies of textbooks that range anywhere from a penny to very close to retail value. Older editions of textbooks can be identical to newer ones in content, so do your research to find out if buying that newest release for 50% more will only net you a shinier cover. (How much has algebra changed in the last 10 years, anyway?) The only drawback to using the Amazon sellers' marketplace for finding textbooks is that you purchase sight unseen. Book descriptions are vague, and shipping is not usually able to be combined. I have had great experience, nonetheless.

4. Homeschool forums

With many parents fed up with auction sites, they have turned to each other for their cheap materials. The best sites for forum-based curriculum listings include Homeschool World (www.home-school.com/forums) and Homeschool.com (http://forum. homeschool.com). You may also be able to search around some Yahoo forums to get a more local set of listings. I have been successful finding curriculum for my children at reasonable value, and the materials have been in great condition. Most parents on these forums aren't resellers looking to profit; they just want to get enough money from last year's curriculum to buy next year's.

....

5. Local library

....

It doesn't get any cheaper than this. While not usually offering textbooks, your library will have some excellent resources for the homeschooling family. This is especially useful for those families following a Charlotte Mason model or who just want to interject some classical reading into their educational diet. By buddying up to your librarian, you may find them consulting you on what types of books they should order, and this could be a huge opportunity for you and other homeschool families.

....

6. Internet resources

....

If you are a worksheet kind of instructor, you'll be pleased to find many printables online for all grade levels. Some Web sites may charge an annual fee in exchange for high-quality worksheets and lesson plans. Others can give you the same kind of access for free, if you're willing to put up with a few ads and limited ownership rights.

....

7. Scholastic book clubs

....

I will always remember getting the book order forms at school, looking them over with big plans for acquiring paperbacks, and then having my parents tell me "no." Homeschool parents can sign up for the same ordering info from Scholastic's Web site (www.scholastic.com) and get order forms for as many grade levels as you teach. They have some great deals throughout the year, and there are no minimum ordering levels. If you do purchase above $20, however, you get free shipping and some fine promotional perks. With each dollar spent, you will accumulate "points" that can be redeemed for future purchases. In addition to getting some nice classic paperbacks at school pricing, we have been able to get a few Nintendo DS games for my daughter well below retail. The Scholastic teachers' site also has a good selection of seasonal printables, including answer keys.

....

8. Craigslist.org

....

No resource list would be complete without my current shopping addiction. Granted, you will need to weed through listings for mint condition Playboys and tattered boxed lots of V. C. Andrews, but if you check early and often, there are deals to be had at Craigslist (www.craigslist.org).

9. Garage sales

Those parents especially dependent on concrete plans and tight deadlines might not appreciate the beauty of a surprise curriculum find at a garage sale. There are no guarantees that homeschool curriculum will even be mentioned in the sale ad. You just go, dig through books, and see what you find. I have gotten boxes and boxes of books for quarters, just by asking. If the family seems to be the type that might homeschool, ask! (Usually the lab equipment, early childhood education software, and huge blackboards will give them away.)

10. Homeschool support group

If you are homeschooling and haven't joined a local support group, you are missing out! In addition to access to cheap and fun activities, discounts, conferences, and educational programs, there is often a forum or e-mail list for trading and selling used curriculum. The best deals come from those you know!

One of the biggest expenses you will bear as a home-educating parent is the curriculum. Get out there and get informed about what you will need and what it will cost so that you are prepared to barter your way to a cheaper school year. If you make a mistake, just resell it. It's all about learning, anyway. — **Linsey Knerl**

8 Endurance Principles for Staying the Frugal Course

Frugality is a lifestyle choice that allows you to live within your means, resist impulsive consumer habits, and enjoy the things you have debt-free. But don't be fooled: As frugal days turn into frugal years and frugal decades, bag lunches can become boring; smallish houses, confining; thrift-shop clothing, unfashionable. And though you may not care what people think of your "voluntary simplicity," it can become tiresome to always live outside of an acquisition-oriented, size-counts-the-most social norm. When frugality starts feeling like a sacrifice, you're in danger of falling off the wagon. Here are eight endurance tips for staying the frugal course.

1. Don't let frugality inhibit your ambition.

Just because you can live on less doesn't mean that you have to make less money. While money or the opportunity to earn more doesn't need to drive every career and life decision, getting better at what you do, making greater and greater contributions to your employer or community, building a reputation for excellence, setting and meeting aggressive goals are worthy apart from a merit raise or bonus.

2. Take excellent care of yourself.

Being frugal should not be hazardous to your well-being, but rather improve your mental outlook and physical health. Cooking at home, a frugality mainstay, is typically less expensive and healthier than the often high-calorie, high-fat, and high-sodium meals from restaurants. But don't stop there. Make sure you get regular health screenings (physicals, blood work, and cancer checks) and push the exercise as much as possible to control weight, and build stamina and strength. You don't have to look frumpy just because you are frugal.

3. Go on adventures.

Adventures allow you to 1) have pure fun and 2) give you intriguing stories to tell, further separating you from things-based social status. Whether a backpacking trip on the Appalachian Trail or a theater- and museum-hopping visit to London, if your experience involves what you love, do it; who doesn't respect someone who dares to live his/her dreams? Frugality just means spending wisely—it doesn't mean never allowing yourself to splurge on trips you can afford.

4. Take excellent care of things you own.

Being neither materialistic nor visually attuned to artistic details made it difficult for me to understand the value that society places on appearances. But I finally realized that stewardship should be aligned with ownership, which meant taking care of my possessions: polishing my shoes; getting machines repaired; clearing up water stains; and replacing dented vinyl floors. Making overdue renovations to my home in the past few years made me understand that I can afford nice things though not necessarily super-sized ones of everything.

Friends and guests are charmed at fine finishes, not just large structures.

5. Stay on top of technology.

You don't have to be an early adopter, but years of eschewing new technology can make you seem like a dinosaur, or worse, just plain slow to grasp new things. These days, technology isn't just a luxury. Many items are functional and helpful, and don't have to be expensive.

6. Become an expert in something.

If you don't already have an expertise, get one. Having a hobby and devoting yourself to an interest can distract you from the marketing messages pushing your consumer buttons.

7. Forgive yourself for frugal lapses.

Stay upbeat even when you take a frugal misstep or just feel like paying for convenience. You may not lead in every stretch of the race but you'll be a winner of the marathon.

8. Be nice to the wealthy.

There are people who can reside in 3,000+-square-feet homes, drive upscale cars, take luxury vacations, *and* give to charity, build wealth, and enjoy honorable lives. They have much in common with the frugal: They want to be admired for *who they are* rather than their net worth. Make friends and don't worry about spending differences.

Frugality is more than saving a few pennies and becoming debt-free. It's about pursuing your dreams and not letting someone else define your success. — **Julie Rains**

PART TWO

Personal Finance

Personal finance is . . . well, personal. It's something that you probably don't discuss with your mailman or announce to family members in your annual holiday newsletter.

We're okay with that, and we'll never ask you to tell us a thing about where you keep your paychecks or who you owe money to. We will request that you listen to our stories, however. We've learned a whole lot about what works (and what doesn't). We also know that what doesn't kill us only makes us stronger if we're wise enough to remember the lessons we've learned and if we're willing to change our habits.

If you're uneasy about your financial situation and unsure where to start, a budget may well be the very best thing you'll ever create. We will help you get on the right track, with tips for making it realistic, and encouraging goals that will tell you how you're doing.

When you're ready to move on to bigger, better topics, you'll find it here, too. Financial planning only *seems* intimidating until you start learning the basics. Once you get involved, you'll see a world filled with excitement and opportunities.

FINANCIAL PLANNING & BUDGETING

I s your budget working for you? You'll know if it isn't: Bills can't get paid, money isn't accounted for, and there's an overall feeling of financial failure. We'll show you what a successful budget plan looks like and how a few easy assessments can get you started right away. When you've mastered the first steps, you can read more about keeping your money safe and what dangers you can avoid to make sure every penny remains yours. After all, you've earned it!

Everything You Need to Know about Personal Finance

A few days ago, I had lunch with an individual who is considering hiring me to give a multi-hour seminar to a business convention on personal finance. This person knows me from the local community and is a reader of TheSimpleDollar.com, and he felt that I might be the right person to give such a presentation.

During the lunch, out of the blue, he asked me to give a five-minute nutshell version of what I would present to the group. I thought for a minute, pulled a pen out of my pocket, and

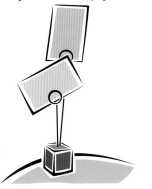

asked him for five business cards. In those next five minutes, I summarized everything I know about personal finance in the following pocket-friendly presentation.

1. The most important thing

In the end, this is the fundamental rule of personal finance: Spend less than you earn. It's the one point that comes up time and time again in almost every personal finance book you read or presentation that you hear. Why? Because it's true.

There are two avenues to achieving this goal: spending less and earning more. By working on either (or both) of these areas, you can increase the gap between those two numbers—and that gap is your ticket to freedom. The harder you work on either spending less or earning more, the bigger that gap will become and the quicker that train to your dreams will arrive at the station.

2. Earn more

So how does one *earn more*? Many people will argue that there is no universal way for people to earn more money, and they're right: While some people are born entrepreneurs, others function much better in an office environment. Some people are endlessly creative; others are masters at completing long lists of tasks. Once you dig past that, though, there are some common things that anyone can do, regardless of their financial state, to earn more money.

Get educated

This doesn't mean drop out and go back to school. It merely means to keep learning new things. If something interests you, read a book about it. Take evening classes to get certification in a certain area or get a master's degree. No matter what you're doing, there's some way you can learn more and improve yourself.

More income streams

Always be on the lookout for ways to have money rolling into your pocket from a lot of different places. Maybe you're a good writer and can sell a short story or an online e-book. Maybe you've got a little piece of land somewhere that you can lease to a farmer or a developer. Maybe you spend your free time managing a flower bed in the park—why not put a little wooden freewill donation box out there for people to drop a coin in? Maybe you have some extra cash laying around with which you can buy a long-term treasury note that will keep issuing you a check every six months. Having more in-

come streams merely means that losing one of them (like your job) is less devastating in your life *and* it also means your overall income for now will go up.

Start a side business

Instead of burning a few hours in front of the telly each evening, how about investing at least part of that time into starting a side business? You can try starting a blog with a few ads on it, or maybe you're good with woodworking and can make deck furniture. Maybe you're good at baking bread and can take loaves to the farmer's market, or maybe you deeply enjoy gardening and can sell vegetables. There are lots of possibilities out there for starting a business that will supplement your current income and perhaps eventually grow into your main income.

Move toward your passions

Whenever the opportunity presents itself, gravitate toward the things that really excite you, because passion is what will make you successful. For me, my passion is writing, so I've made an effort to gravitate toward it by working on TheSimpleDollar.com in my spare time. For others, it could be anything—maybe it's leading a team, or perhaps it's writing beautiful computer code. Whatever really excites you and makes you want to do *more and more and more* and *better and better and better*, that's what you need to move toward at all times.

Don't burn bridges

You never know when a relationship you've forged in your past might come in handy later on, even the ones you completely don't expect. Thus, even if you feel wronged in a situation or want "revenge" on some people—or even if you just feel an urge to spread negative gossip—resist it. As you get older, you'll find yourself time and time again bumping into people that you forged relationships with earlier on; if you burned those bridges, you'll find that eventually you'll have burnt the very bridge that you need to cross to get ahead. My advice? Never spread a negative word about anyone, because it never helps.

Keep in touch!

When you do build a bridge with someone, don't let it get old and worn-out; spend the time to keep in touch with that person. Shoot them an e-mail or a phone call every once in a while just to see what they're up to. When it's clear they need help and you can easily provide it, *always* provide it. I found the book *Never Eat Alone* by Keith Ferrazzi to be particularly powerful in this regard. I'm rather introverted, and it's often a challenge for me to initiate and then keep communication going with someone, and this book provided tons of tips on how (and why) to keep in contact with people.

. . . .

3. Live frugal!

. . . .

For a lot of people, frugality is a nine-letter word for cheap. They think of people doing stuff like buying cartloads of generic products, using 40 coupons in the checkout aisle, wearing patched clothing, driving a rusted-out old vehicle, and other such things that it's easy to look down your nose at.

Here's a secret, something that I've witnessed several times in my own life and read about many more: Those frugal people that you look down your nose at often have a mountain of cash in the bank (not always, of course, but more often than you think). They're not drowning in a mortgage, they're not making payments on a five-figure credit card debt. They're not working to death on the weekends or drowning an ulcer in Pepto-Bismol. They're living their life according to their own rules.

The best part is that we can all apply some of those same rules in our own life. Here's what you can do to start reducing that spending.

Maximize every dollar

Every time you spend money, you make a decision. You decide that whatever you're giving that dollar for is worth it, and thus you make the exchange. The real key to spending less is to raise that definition of what a dollar is worth. You know those times when you buy something, but you realize you don't really need it and you're also not convinced that it's a very good deal? Make the choice to not buy it, or buy a cheap version and see how much you actually use it. Don't be afraid to shop around a bit.

Food is a great example of this. Quite often, people will eat out at places like Applebee's and drop $20 or $30 on a meal that they could have made at home for $3. "But it saves time and is convenient," you say? Just for fun, try making an equivalent meal at home sometime. You might be surprised to find out how easy it is and how much you'll save.

Habits of all kinds are dangerous!

Most people have some sort of routine in their day where they buy a morning latte or a bagel, or they drink six cans of soda, or they eat out at the same place each day for lunch. What these routines add up to is a lot of money. Spending $5 every day in a workweek adds up to $1,300 over a year—that's a mortgage payment for a lot of people. Spend some time looking at the stuff you do every day, especially the ones that require you to spend money, and ask yourself if they're really necessary or could be replaced.

The 10-second rule

Every time you go to make any purchase, even when you pay a bill, stop for 10 seconds and ask yourself if this is really something you want to spend your money on. Do you really need this item? Do you really need to be paying $14.95 a month for un-limited text messages when you use maybe 10? Could you reduce that electricity bill by putting in a lot of compact fluorescent lightbulbs? This one simple technique will often point you in the direction of spending less money.

Don't make yourself miserable!

Most of the time, when you cut a bit of spending from your life, you'll find that you never miss it. However, there are times when you find yourself really regretting it. If that's the case, then it's probably a worthwhile expense for you. Saving money doesn't have to equate to misery; it just means that you cut down on the unnecessary.

But don't forget the big picture

That, of course, doesn't mean that you should justify every purchase with a basic "I want it and I have money in my account." That shouldn't ever be enough to motivate a purchase. I find that using a visual reminder in my wallet of what I'm financially working toward does a great job of keeping my mind on the big picture and helping me filter out what's really needed and what's just a fleeting desire.

. . . .
4. Manage money
. . . .

Whenever you increase your income or decrease your spending, you'll find yourself with more cash at the end of the month. That cash is your ticket to financial freedom, and the more you can get each month, the better off you are. The trick, though, is to not spend it, but to do things that will build a stable future for you. Here's the game plan.

Pay off all high-interest debt, such as credit cards

Anything with an interest rate over 9% needs to go as soon as possible. Use the extra money to make double or triple payments on these debts, focusing first on the one with the highest interest rate. When that one's gone, keep going with each successively lower interest rate debt. This is akin to Dave Ramsey's popular "debt snowball" technique.

Build an emergency fund

An emergency fund is an amount of money you keep in a savings account that's intended to be used in the event of a major crisis, such as a job loss, a medical emergency, major car damage, and so on. I usually suggest to people that they measure their emergency fund in terms of months' worth of living expenses—you should have a month and a half worth of living expenses for each person you claim as a dependent. So, for me in a house with two children and my wife, I have a six-month emergency fund.

Max out retirement

By this, I mean you should go to one of those retirement meetings at work, ask exactly how much you should be putting away to ensure that your living expenses are well covered in retirement, and put that much away. This varies a lot depending on how much you have in right now, how much your employer matches, and so on, so you should talk to your retirement planner at work about the specifics.

College savings

College savings are next. If you have kids, set up a 529 college savings plan for them and start automatically putting a certain amount into this account each month. The plan I use for my own children is College Savings Iowa, which is managed by Vanguard. I currently put in $100 a month for each child.

Pay off all debts

If all of these are covered and you still have cash left over (which you will, given some time), the next step is to pay off all of your debts. Get rid of your car loans, your student loans, and your mortgage. This is actually the step I'm focusing on right now, as

I have already taken care of steps one through four.

Invest

You might also want to start investing at this point. My recommendation is to buy low-cost broad-based index funds because they don't have many fees and grow very nicely over long periods of time. I personally invest with Vanguard directly through Vanguard. com.

....

5. Control your own destiny!
....

Most people see the goal of all of this as being rich. That's why you see so many books about millionaires on bookstore shelves—being a millionaire is something many of us aspire to, right?

Here's the secret: It's not about being rich. Having a big net worth is just an indicator of what this whole process is really about.

It's all about freedom. Freedom from debt. Freedom from supervisors telling us what to do. Freedom to spend the time to do things right. Freedom to try out new things and follow our interests. Freedom to sleep until eleven one day, then stay up until two in the morning working on what we're passionate about.

That's what most people really want. I know that's certainly what

I want. Having a big bank account just means that I'm not beholden to others. I can follow my passions and dreams wherever they take me. If my job is not satisfying to me, I'm no longer tied to that paycheck; I can just get up and walk away. I can do whatever makes me happy and avoid most of what makes me sad, without regrets or worries.

It's a lot of hard work to climb that mountain, but the air up there is the sweetest thing there is.

Want to know more?

You can check out the five business cards I drew up online (tinyurl.com/simple-dollar). If you liked the information here, take the time to dig into TheSimpleDollar.com, or my new book, *365 Ways to Live Cheap.* Also check out some of the other excellent personal finance blogs out there—they do a far better job of humanizing and explaining money and personal development than many of the "big" corporate sites.

Most importantly, remember that you *can* do this. Two years ago, I was almost bankrupt and in deep despair because I didn't believe this stuff, either. It took a lot of learning and a lot of honest soul-searching, but I began to realize what was really important and I turned the ship around. Trust me: You can do it, too. **— Trent Hamm**

10 Ways to Simplify Your Budget

I'm always looking for ways to simplify my finances (I'm weird like that, I know), and recently I've been scrutinizing my already-simple budget to make it even simpler. I thought it would be helpful to share some of the ways to make your budget as simple as possible.

The goal is to reduce headaches, eliminate the need for complicated tracking schemes, and reduce the time you spend on your budget and finances to about 15–20 minutes per week. I can't claim these ideas are original, or that I haven't discussed them in various places before, but in my experience, they work. They're simple and powerful.

Let's first look at setting up a budget. If you haven't done it yet, it's probably because budgets seem intimidating to you, or they are too much hassle to set up and maintain. Those are both valid points—which is why you should follow this simplified plan if these things apply to you. Now, there's plenty of fancy software out there for setting up budgets, but I don't think they're necessary. A simple spreadsheet will do—and if you can create a SUM formula to add up the total of a column of numbers, you have all the spreadsheet knowledge necessary.

Create a simple spreadsheet for your budget, if you haven't already, and start by listing your income and your monthly expenses. Estimate, in round numbers, how much you spend on each expense every month. You can adjust later, but it's better to err on the side of too high a number, rather than putting a low number and breaking your budget.

Now let's look at ways to create a simple budget:

....

1. 60% solution.

....

There are many ways to structure your budget, but the simplest I've found is the 60% solution. Basically, this budget asks you to fit your regular monthly expenses within 60% of your gross income, so that you have room for savings (long-term and short-term), retirement, and spending money ("fun money"). These are the things that most often break a budget, because most people don't budget for them. Now, your percentage will vary, but the percentages given here are just rough guidelines:

60 percent: **Monthly expenses.** —This includes housing, food, utili-

ties, insurance, Internet, transportation, and so on. This is the part most commonly thought of as a budget.

10 percent: **Retirement.** If you're doing it right, this is being automatically deducted from your paycheck for a 401(k) investment.

10 percent: **Long-term savings or debt reduction.** It's best to invest this in something such as stocks or an index fund, and this can serve as your emergency fund. But if you are in debt (not including a home mortgage), I would advise that you use this portion of the budget to pay off your debts, and even draw some from the other categories such as retirement to increase this to about 20% for now. Once your debts are paid off, you can switch this to long-term savings. You still need to have an emergency fund, but while you're in debt-reduction mode you can either create a small, temporary emergency fund out of the money from this category or the next.

10 percent: **Short-term savings.** This is for periodic expenses, such as auto maintenance or repairs, medical expenses (not including insurance premiums), appliances, home maintenance, birthday and Christmas gifts. For this savings account, be sure to spend the money when you need it—that's what it's for. When these expenses come up, you will have the money for them, instead of

trying to pull them from other budget categories.

10 percent: **Fun money**—you can spend this on eating out, movies, comic books—whatever you want. Guilt free.

2. Fewer categories

A lot of budget software asks you to fill in a million categories and subcategories. Those can be useful if you want to track all that stuff, but I don't. I recommend simplifying: just use broad categories like food and gas and spending and utilities. Use what works.

3. Pay bills online

As much as possible, pay your bills online. These would be most of the bills in the first category above —utilities, rent or mortgage, cell phone, Internet, etc. If you can't pay electronically, have your bank send out a check to the vendor. Make these payments automatic so you don't need to worry about them.

4. Automatic savings

Make your savings automatic as well. Every time your paycheck is deposited, have a scheduled transaction transfer a set amount from checking to savings. Use a high-yield online savings account such as Emigrant Direct, HSBC, or ING Direct.

5. Cash

For everything else, use cash. If you're doing automatic bill payments and savings deductions, the only things you'll likely need cash for are gas, groceries, and fun money. Withdraw these amounts in cash twice a month, rather than using checks or credit cards. The reason is that it's simpler—with cash, you don't need to worry about overspending, or tracking how much is left in that category. You can see how much is left. Leave the credit cards for when you absolutely need them—traveling, for example.

6. Envelopes

If you use cash for three categories, for example, use three envelopes. This is an old-fashioned system, but I use it because it works. I have an envelope for groceries, gas, and fun money. If I'm going grocery shopping, I bring the groceries envelope. I know how much is left in the envelope before I go grocery shopping. I spend the cash for groceries, and then can easily see how much is left now. Simple, and no tracking necessary. When the money is gone, you've spent your budgeted amount. If necessary, you could transfer cash from one envelope to another, and there's no need to adjust your budget.

. . . .

7. 15–20 minutes a week

Now, the budget and spending plan I've outlined above is fairly simple and headache-free—but you shouldn't assume that it doesn't need any maintenance. You should devote 15–20 minutes a week to ensuring that your finances are in order. Just this little amount of time each week will greatly simplify your financial life, reduce headaches, and prevent any messes from occurring later. Set a day and time when you take a look at your finances each week. Set aside 30 minutes, just to be safe. Now take 5–10 minutes to enter your transactions into your financial software (I use MS Money, because it came with my computer, but a spreadsheet or other financial software will do fine). If you're following the plan above, all you'll need to do is go online, look at your bank account, and enter your deposits, bills paid, ATM withdrawals (only do this twice a month!), and any other fees. It shouldn't take long. Now spend another 5–10 minutes to review your budget and make sure that all bills have been paid that should be

paid. If not, pay them. It's that simple. You're done. Now go back to reading your blogs.

. . . .

8. Fewer accounts

Some people have complicated systems set up with lots of different accounts. I say simplify. You don't want to be checking a million different accounts. You should have one checking account and one or two savings accounts (one for emergency fund and one for periodic expenses). You could have a bunch of investment accounts if you want, but I've found it simpler to just have one. I lose diversity, but my fund is already pretty diversified.

. . . .

9. Dump credit cards

Multiple credit cards are also a headache. Simplify by just having one. Or do what I do—have none. This will draw the usual outraged or preachy reaction from those who really love their credit cards, but I don't care. I don't like credit cards. Call me old-fashioned. They charge high interest and they're potentially dangerous (if you run up a high bill and an expense comes up that you need to pay for which means you can't pay your credit card bill on time, you now are stuck with high-interest credit card debt). Use a debit card if you need to.

10. Pay all bills at the same time

It often just takes a simple call to get a vendor or creditor to change the due date on your bills. If you can get all your bills to be due on, let's say, the 10th of the month, you can do all your bill paying at once. For some people, this will mean they will need to do a bit of scrimping to get ahead enough so that they can afford to make all their month's payments at the beginning of the month, but it's worth it. You can pay all your bills and be done with it. For more ways to simplify your life, check out my new book, *The Power of Less*, or visit www.zenhabits.net. **— Leo Babauta**

6 Tips for Following a Budget Without Breaking Down in Tears

Budgeting can be difficult. For some people (like me!), it brings up things that they may not want to see. For others, it's a necessary but frustrating tool to curtail spending, or a painful reminder of how much they overspent, yet again.

But there are a few people who live well on a budget. These few manage to record their spending and yet aren't overwhelmed by that. They see where they spend too much and yet don't give up the budget. Month after month they take the time to collect their receipts, enter them, and evaluate based on the results. They aren't overwhelmed or discouraged, and they don't give up. Instead, they plug away at it until they get their spending under control, and then they often keep at it to have a record of where their money goes. Slowly, slowly, I'm becoming one of them, and here is what I've learned along the way.

1. Give yourself some space

Your budget is not going to work perfectly from the beginning, unless you're a financial genius. It's just not. Gas will cost more than you expected, or your phone will get stolen and the company will charge you for the extra minutes, throwing off your careful planning. Things happen. Life happens. Particularly in the early stages of budgeting, where you're working with unsure numbers. You'll get better at estimating as you go along. You'll also get better at knowing what you need. A friend might only need to spend $50 a month on gas, but your visits to Grandma Sue push that up to $100 for you. It's okay.

Also, part of what a budget is intended to do is to track money *over time.* So if your cell bill is high one month, it might be lower the next. Maybe you'll change plans in six months and pay a lower monthly fee. Your budget will show you your average spending, which will both cancel out some extra costs you might pay along the way and help you make a better average next time.

....

2. Budget for yourself
....

You have needs and desires that others don't have. I, for instance, really want to take a pottery class next fall. So right now I'm starting to budget for it. It shouldn't be too expensive, but I want to be sure those recreational costs are covered. These are costs that others

won't have, but they're important to me and that's okay.

Many budget programs come with a list of categories, and it's easy to feel like you need to fit your spending into those. Instead, wipe the memory clean of categories and start from the beginning. Make *your* budget reflect *your* life, or it won't help *you* save. It might help Joe Generic save, or the couple two doors down, but it won't help you.

....

3. It's okay to overspend sometimes
....

Money isn't the highest priority. When something else is more important than keeping to your budget or saving money, and you make the decision, it's okay to overspend. For Valentine's Day, my husband and I went out to dinner. It wasn't anything particularly fancy, but it cost us a little extra in our "eating out" category.

For us, that was okay because we decided to overspend. We were intentional about it and evaluated it in light of the other categories in the budget. Since we didn't spend nearly our full amount in other categories, and we really needed a break, we decided to splurge a little. It's hard to see the numbers at the bottom of our column turn red (that means we overspent) and not feel like I'm somehow a bad, irresponsible person, but I do know better.

4. Your money is only yours

You earned it so it's yours to spend. However you like. Whenever you like. Wherever you like. End of story. You can publish your budget on the Internet, but you don't have to. If others are going to be critical, keep them out. You're also the one trying to be responsible with your money here, which means that it's fine to ask for help if you want it. But don't ask from someone who isn't going to approve your categories, your amounts, or anything else about your budget. You make it, you keep it.

5. Work with a group

If you're trying to learn to budget, find some friends who are in the same boat, or who have been budgeting for a while. Agree to meet and talk about how your budget is going, whether you're keeping it up, etc. If you're worried that they might not approve of your choices or understand your categories, agree beforehand that they can help you keep to what you budget, but can't set your categories or criticize the decisions you've made unless you ask them for that kind of advice.

6. Give it at least six months before you give up

If you haven't done it before, budgeting is a new habit. It takes a while to feel natural, not kludgy, and not binding. Give it at least six months before you decide to throw in the towel. Stick with your decision to record your spending and you may just find that it fits you after all. It's like switching to shoes when you've worn sandals for years—they feel tight, but they're really the right size.

While budgeting is difficult, it's not impossible, and it does get better with time. Stick with it. Have courage. Face down the evil checkbook. Eventually, you can be triumphant.

— **Sarah Winfrey**

How to Choose a Financial Planner

I don't care who you are. (Well, actually I do, otherwise I wouldn't be writing this.) What I mean is, I don't care about your background, education, financial prowess, or absolute lack thereof.

You need a financial planner!

There are a number of different credentials, titles, creeds, and pay-scales that flood the financial services industry, and can confuse the heck out of the average bear.

In fact, even the idea of seeing a financial planner may be so daunting (or embarrassing?) that you find ways and excuses to avoid it altogether. Here are a few things to think about in your search, or to compel you to search, depending on your current position.

1. Everybody needs a financial planner

I feel very strongly about this one. I don't care if you have $70,000 in debts and $5 to your name (I actually had a client like this once), or the other way around. A financial planner is more than a money manager, and everybody can benefit from their services. And the younger you are when you start to take control of your finances with the help of a planner, the better off you will be in the long run.

2. Call them what you will

I'm calling them financial planners here, but they can be financial advisors, investment advisors, personal bankers, etc. Technically anybody can hang a shingle out tomorrow calling themselves a financial planner. The trick is . . .

3. What are their credentials?

There are any number of letters and credentials and titles that people can carry. The hallmark for financial planning is the CFP (Certified Financial Planner) designation, which is internationally recognized. The requirements of becoming a CFP entail years of education in addition to extensive work experience.

4. Where do they work?

Check out the company the planner in front of you is representing. Are they a major player in the industry, or a ma-and-pa shop? Some people don't mind ma-and-pa, some do. Are they limited to proprietary investments, or can they recommend what is truly best for you? A large firm generally lends some credibility to the planner, although this isn't a hard-and-fast rule. *Ask your friends and family who they use;* most often referrals work wonderfully.

5. What can I expect?

True financial planning isn't investment management. It isn't banking or loan services. It isn't insurance. And it isn't taxes. It's everything. A real financial planner is going to take a personal approach to your financial situation. They should sit down with you and analyze your entire financial situation. Income, expenses, assets, liabilities, insurance, and even some of the intangibles like your personal approach and attitudes toward money. They should be interested in what you want to accomplish with your life, what major purchases you have in your future, what sorts of vacations you like to take, and how you envision your retirement years. They also need to know your personal tolerance for risk and fluctuation in your investments, and should coach you on it. If they don't do all these things, they can't properly advise you!

6. Won't this cost a ton?

Financial planning actually doesn't have to cost you a penny out of your pocket, depending on the planner and where you go for your services. Many banks have a team of financial planners who are available to help the bank's clients. They are paid a salary by the bank, and often don't cost you a thing. You can also choose asset-based advisors who again, you won't have to pay for out of pocket, but who are only compensated by their employer based on the money you invest with them. Believe it or not, this doesn't mean that you necessarily need a ton of money to invest; many of these advisors want long-term relationships and believe they can help you over the long run and will ultimately be compensated for it. And of course, there are also fee-based planners and those with other methods of compensation.

7. Who is best for me?

What you need to look for in a planner first and foremost is somebody you like. If you're going to share details about your financial life and dreams and expectations, you need to feel comfortable opening up to them and establishing a relationship of trust.

8. Can't I do all this on my own?

There are a ton of solutions out there on the Internet. My response to that is: Do you have a life? The job of a financial planner is a full-time gig. They know a lot and need to stay up-to-date in the ever-changing world of finance. If you keep up with all the latest tax legislation, investment regulations, and insurance opportunities and lingo, then be my guest and give it a whirl. What you'll still be missing is a third-party perspective, and possibly some creative strategies that you (or your research) didn't come up with.

In addition, I believe in delegation, and the fact that time is money. You defer your legal matters to your lawyer, and tax matters to your accountant. You defer your medical matters to your doctor. You don't perform surgery based on an Internet program's recommendation, do you? And if you are still asking why you can't just do it on your own, please refer to point 5 again. I've yet to find a financial planning program that is intuitive enough to do all that.

Your time outside of work is better spent enjoying life, spending time with your family, and chasing down dreams—not toiling over your finances in a haphazard way. — **Nora Dunn**

9 Signs You Need to Fire Your Financial Planner

In tough economic times, financial planners are on the front lines. They are the gateway to investment returns when the markets are good,

and are the buffer against financial disaster when the markets are bad.

When I was in the financial planning business and markets experienced corrections of sorts, my colleagues and I would brace ourselves for something called "statement shock." Clients would receive and open their quarterly or monthly statements, and regardless of whether they were keeping up with the news of market performance and understood the circumstances, they would experience a certain degree of shock when they realized how their own dollars and cents were affected.

There were three possible outcomes from this onset of statement shock:

1) They would realize that it is a function of the markets and not the planner and stay the course.
2) They would call their financial planner for some reassuring words of encouragement and possibly ask for a meeting to devise a new action plan.
3) They would look for a new financial planner.

I was lucky. Most of my clients fell into categories one and two. I worked hard to educate them, work within their tolerances for risk, and was there to hold their hands when they needed it. This also usually put me on the receiving end of new clients who were in category three and displeased with their old financial planners.

But in times like these, when terms like "Meltdown Monday" and (ssshhh . . . the "r" word) are being tossed around, financial planners around the world are waking up in the middle of the night in cold sweats. Try as they may to buffer their clients against market down-turns, statements will look bad. And they will be sure to hear about it. And ultimately, through no fault of their own, they will lose clients.

Some planners, though, will lose clients, and arguably deserve to. They will not have performed the proper amount of due diligence with their clients by assessing their investment personalities and time frames, and in-stead of facing the music when their clients call, they may instead choose to hide under their desks as a way to weather the storm. They will not have addressed their clients' larger finan-cial situation and dealt with issues like taxation, short- and long-term savings, and estate planning, and will instead have simply focused on re-turns—something which can never be promised and will never be predictable (unless you are invested solely in term deposits, in which case again I would suggest the advisor's incompetence).

If you are experiencing state-ment shock, or are wondering if your financial planner is up to snuff, here are nine signs you may need to fire your financial planner.

1. They never asked you about your personal goals and time frames before recommending investments.

There is no such thing as a one-size-fits-all investment plan. Although having a standard set of investment recommendations according to your stated time frame and tolerance for risk is acceptable, they must do the initial groundwork to determine who you are and what you want from your money.

2. Only one company's products are recommended.

As good as that company's products are, true diversification includes not only a range of asset classes, but also a range of investment managers. Recommending only one type of company-labeled product indicates that the advisor is not providing truly unbiased advice.

....

3. You received no written financial plan, prospectus, or documentation.

....

Every investment product should be accompanied by a detailed written description of the investment, including its composition, historical performance, and inherent risks and rewards. This is generally covered in the prospectus, which is a bare minimum of what you should receive. Better yet, you should also be given a *written financial plan*, which addresses your personal financial situation and outlines a financial road map to reaching your short- and long-term goals.

....

4. You are pressured into making investments.

....

Although sitting on the fence forever is an advisor's nightmare, and sometimes clients need a little extra push, undue pressure into doing something you are uncomfortable with is not right. Even if the recommendations are sound, if you get bad vibes from high-pressure sales tactics, your ability to communicate with this advisor and for them to listen to your needs

is going to be problematic going forward.

....

5. Your planner's recommendations don't match your financial goals.

....

You say you want to save up to buy a house, and your advisor recommends high-risk long-term investments Something is not jiving here, and it is likely that they are either not listening to your needs, or are not acting in your best interest.

....

6. You can never reach your advisor when you want to, and they don't return your phone calls.

....

With an onset of statement shock, you need to talk to somebody. Often big problems and feelings of discomfort can be alleviated with a simple phone call and a reassurance that staying the course is the best thing to do. But if you can never reach your advisor, if they pawn you off on an assistant, or if they don't return your phone calls promptly, they are not doing their job.

....

7. They constantly change your investments.

....

Seeing a regular list of transactions coming through may lead you to believe your portfolio is being actively managed. However, a true financial planner (and not a broker, who is transaction-oriented) should be focused more on the game plan and less on making money by moving it around. It's a "slow and steady wins the race" approach. Too many transactions may also mean that they are making commissions on each move—a sign that they are not truly working for you.

. . . .

8. The plan given to you seems too good to be true.

. . . .

If it seems too good to be true, it probably is. If that tax strategy seems a little lofty, or you are introduced to a strategy that you've never heard of that flies in the face of everything you know to be true and legal, then you may eventually find yourself in hot water. Although the advisor may be liable, you are ultimately the one who will have to clean up the mess if your financial actions were unruly.

. . . .

9. They tell you they can time the market.

. . . .

I don't care who your financial planner is—they can't time the market. If they call you wanting to make drastic changes based on what they *think* the market is going to do, run. What they

should really be focused on is *you, your goals, and a plan* (and portfolio) that will weather the good times and the bad. Sure, small adjustments here and there may be prudent, but moving everything in and out of different asset classes is a losing game. They may get it right a few times, but all it takes is one bad calculation to lose everything you have gained.

IF IT'S TIME TO FIRE YOUR FINANCIAL PLANNER

Please do them a favor and give them a call. Sometimes things are lost in translation, or a breakdown in communication is accidental. In my experience, people can be shortsighted, focusing on returns and setting unrealistic expectations based on short-term performance. When the markets are booming, people expect consistent double-digit returns and forget not-so-distant times when that wasn't the case. And vice versa: After a stretch of poor performance, the same person may be convinced that the bad times will never end and want to stash all their money under the bed, forgetting to take the bad times with the good to achieve an overall rate of return that will help them attain their goals.

By calling your financial planner and giving them a chance to explain their actions, you may be able to save the hassle of moving your accounts and starting from scratch with a new planner.

Then again, don't stick with a planner because it is the easy thing to do. If your financial planner is the culprit of any combination of the abovementioned blunders, it is a problem that needs to be addressed and fixed—either by finding another planner or by being honest with your existing planner.

Statement shock sucks, through and through. But don't take your eye off the ball because of the initial shock of seeing your investments lose value. If the markets are down overall, don't blame your financial planner; they don't have a crystal ball. And if they pass the acid test above, then keep communicating with them; together you will weather this market downturn, as with every other downturn. The media will sensationalize every market correction and somehow identify that this is the worst, the most dramatic, or the hardest whatever

since whenever. But time and time again, slow and steady is what wins the race. — **Nora Dunn**

6 Horrible Financial Products You Should Avoid

Dealing with financial products can be very confusing and stressful, but there are some products that you should absolutely stay away from for the sake of your financial health. Here are six of them.

1. The 401(k) debit card

This is a fairly new product that is designed to let people under age 59.5 raid their retirement funds at an ATM. This is a horrible idea because it makes it easy for people to destroy their nest eggs. Early withdrawals carry a 10% penalty plus tax expenses, so $10 withdrawn from a 401(k) becomes only $6–$7.

In the past it took at least a few forms to do an early withdrawal from a 401(k), so it was not worth the

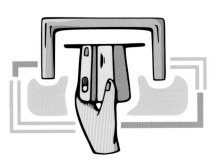

effort for every $5. However, a debit card just makes the process of withdrawing small amounts so easy that I could see people spending their entire 401(k)s without even feeling it.

2. Credit cards that charge maintenance fees

There is absolutely no need to get a credit card with a maintenance fee these days. When credit cards were a new product most of them had maintenance fees, but now very few charge them. I am surprised that companies still issue ridiculously bad cards. I've even seen a credit card that charges a $150 yearly fee plus a $6.95 monthly fee!

3. Store-specific credit cards

Store-specific credit cards are those that can be used only at the store where you signed up. Do not be enticed to sign up for these cards even if the store gives you 30% off everything you buy on the day you sign up. The reason is that they generally have very high interest rates and could lower your credit score.

These are different from a cobranded credit card that can be used anywhere. An example of a cobranded credit card is the Box Store American Express Card, which can be used out-side of said Box Store. Cobranded cards generally have better rates and better internal controls than store-specific cards.

4. Payment protection insurance

These are insurance policies marketed by credit card companies or mortgage companies that insure you against debt payments if you become ill or lose your job. It sounds good, right? The truth is that they are usually quite overpriced, and the policies have so many exclusions that very few benefit. You are probably better off taking the money you would have paid for this insurance and saved it in an emergency fund. These insurance policies were investigated by the UK government, and the consensus is that these products are highly lucrative for the lenders and rarely benefit the consumer.

5. Payday loans

These are loans given for the amount of your future paychecks, and they carry ridiculously high interest rates disguised as a fixed cost. If you calculate the interest rate, it is often hundreds to thousands of percentage points. I think if you really need the money, a low-interest credit card is usually better than these loans because you can pay a credit card at the next statement date and your rate would be lower. Another horrible product in a similar vein is the tax refund anticipation loan.

....

6. Any financial product you do not fully understand

....

Any financial product could be a potential disaster if you do not understand how it works and how it benefits you. For example, a lot of the current sob stories relating to foreclosures involve borrowers who did not understand how their mortgages worked. All they saw was their initial mortgage payment and did not understand how the payments would adjust.

The lesson here is that before you lay your money on the line for any financial product, you must research it and read the fine print. If you do not do your due diligence, a product that is potentially beneficial to others could be a nightmare to you. — **Xin Lu**

The Best and Worst Places to Stash Cash in Your Home

The current economy has many people considering a simpler method of financial security—cold, hard cash. And while we all agree that a buck has value, it is also a bit vulnerable when not hidden properly. Forget the $3,000 high-tech safe, and stick with these affordable tricks I picked up. You'll never guess which way I'm using to hide my money!

TAMPON BOX

I'm not kidding. Walletpop.com recently mentioned this gem of a tip, and I was instantly intrigued. By leaving a little "product" in the box for authenticity, and taping a wad of cash to the inside, you can be sure a robber won't think to look in there. (Ladies can be certain that a husband or boyfriend won't find it, either.)

FAKE DRAIN

Another beauty from walletpop.com, this one involves a little more handi-work. By constructing a false drain in the floor of your garage or base-ment, you can place a pipe full of money where no one can see. (Just make sure your cash is stored in a wa-terproof container or baggie, in case an unknowing person tries to use the drain!)

THE YARD

Digging holes and hiding money is an age-old practice. The key is to re-member where you put the cash and keeping it safe from the elements. Most experts recommend using some kind of PVC piping to keep dirt away from the stash, and to discourage the ground from caving in. This will also prevent a pesky underground burrow-ing creature from discovering your se-cret. (Be sure to bury deep, and don't forget where you hid it!)

RETURN-AIR VENT

To see this one in detail, you'd have to snag a recent issue of *The Fam-ily Handyman* magazine (November 2008). It offers step-by-step direc-tions for using the faceplate of an air vent to conceal a cubby you can stash valuables in. The best part is that it is held in place by magnets (to give you fast access to your own cash), and the sawed-off screw heads give the whole thing a look of really being secured to your wall. If you use your imagina-tion, you could probably rig one up without the directions.

FROZEN FOOD

I wouldn't put your bling in a box of Pizza Rolls, but if you have some ag-ing frozen haggis or a box of hominy you're not overly attached to, you can use it as a covert hiding place for a wad of twenties.

TENNIS BALL

I like this idea of cutting open a ten-nis ball, stashing your valuables in-side, and then placing the ball back between two others in their original tube container. Just make sure that the goods don't rattle when you shake them. (You can stuff some tissue pa-per in with jewelry or coins to hide their sound.)

ELECTRICAL OUTLET

Please don't take this to mean a "real" outlet. You can use a method similar to the return-air-vent technique to create your own wall cubby that most smart burglars won't attempt to touch. You can also skip the work of the DIY method, and buy one premade.

These are places you *shouldn't* hide cash:

UNDER THE MATTRESS

This is one of the first places thieves are going to check, and it is hardly conducive to a good night's sleep.

TOILET TANK

Several Web sites still list this as a good place to hide money. (Too bad every mob movie I've seen with home invasion as a pervasive theme directs the goons toward this niche first.) The only thing going into my toilet tank is a freshening tab (or possibly a brick to save on water usage).

PURSE

Yep, it's been said that a lady with a large purse collection should pick some random handbag and stick it in there. Chances are good, however, that this totally-out-in-the-open hiding place is a little too available for many thieves. Don't you want them to have to at least work for it? (And what if the thief has a penchant for Prada, Kate Spade, or Jaclyn Smith?)

A few other pointers for those who want to conceal cash in their home include:

Be aware that many homemade safes (including those I mentioned) won't make your valuables immune from fire damage. If you are concerned about the possibility of your nest egg going up in flames, consider a fireproof case or bag.

Leave a clue to where you keep it. If you should happen to die or disappear for a really, really long time, would your loved ones know where you keep your cash? Unless you want your valuables to be of no use to anyone else in your passing, let a few close relatives or a trusted friend know your plans. You may also want to have it clearly explained in your "top-secret" will.

Make sure you have the value of your cash added to your home owner's or rental insurance, if at all possible. Some companies will have specific regulations as to what they can and can't cover. If you have large amounts of cash on the premises, however, see how you can best minimize loss in a bad situation using your insurance plan. — **Linsey Knerl**

11 Ways to Be Generous on a Budget

Love to be generous with your friends and family? Tired of having the gift-giving and "chipping in" budget be out of control when you are scrimping and saving in every other area? Following are some ideas to continue the tradition of generosity that don't necessarily involve cash or driving your budget into the ditch.

1. Reach out and touch someone

Find a great unlimited calling plan and a super communications package. There are plenty of landline calling plans out there that offer unlimited North American calling for a nominal fee. Some even include a few European countries. Pair that with a slamming cell phone plan and great Internet options like instant messaging, Internet calling, and of course, e-mail. There are plenty of ways to offer support that don't involve writing a check. E-cards, calling to brainstorm ideas or offer condolences, or just touching base with your friends and family on a regular basis to share the love are all more than worthy.

2. DIY gifts

Dry mixes in a jar, building a picnic table, planting a flower garden, a car tune-up, mending, making someone's favorite dinner, dropping off a casserole during a sickness or family crisis . . . it's not all homemade placemats in this category.

3. Bartering

This may seem like an odd item to include in a list of generosity ideas, but bear with me. What if you have a friend or colleague whom you respect who is trying to get their business off its feet? Rather than charging them, or giving something valuable from your service list away that will leave you feeling out of balance, consider letting them swap services. A custom paint job on their storefront sign for a full-body hot stone massage for example. Then you also get to be one of the people that can give a testimonial on their brochure, and they get to feel professional rather than like a charity case.

4. The gift of time

This relates a bit to the first one, but could also involve stopping by to hold someone's hand during a chemo treatment, sitting with them while they wait for someone to come out of surgery, consulting with them in an area where they may need some assistance with business, investing, etc. Even exercising a little patience with someone you find challenging can be a huge gift in certain circumstances. Volunteering opportunities abound for this item.

. . . .

5. Kiva.org

. . . .

Kiva.org is only one of many options to help those on the other side of the world from you. For an initial modest donation, you can have an account that keeps on giving long-term.

. . . .

6. Thoughtful purchases

. . . .

By making careful choices about which items a person will truly need or love, you can make sure the gift does not go to waste. Don't buy a gift just for the sake of gifting.

. . . .

7. Be there

. . . .

Honestly. Just be there. During a major family crisis, if you've flown thousands of miles to be there and paid countless dollars in travel costs to offer support, should anybody give a damn if you have flowers in your hand? It's

nice if you do, of course. But if you can't, and they don't understand . . . maybe you need to rethink your relationship with that person or group of people.

. . . .

8. Stick to your guns

. . . .

Again, this is another item that may seem odd to include on a list of generosity ideas. However, I'm struck by something I heard Suze Orman say once on the *Oprah* show. By giving in when your conscience is telling you not to, what you are really sharing is the poverty cycle. Think about what funds you'll have available if you keep giving frivolous high-cost items and then a crisis comes up that you feel it's mandatory to write a check for. A funeral, the surgery of a child in the family, the winter coat for a niece or nephew whose parents might have hit a financial roadblock . . . you get the picture. Your friends will understand if you let them know you just can't afford to buy a nice gift for them.

. . . .

9. Set a dollar amount for incidental gifts

. . . .

This of course will be a personal decision based on where you are financially and what your goals are. But there are lots of ideas out there for affordable gift giving, whether you are looking for hostess gifts, just-because presents, political contributions, birthday ideas for children, or a romantic anniversary. The important thing is to stick to your agreed-upon range, whether it's $5, $50, or more.

10. Pick a pet charity

Or two. Or three. The point is, having a set location where you channel your charitable gifting monies can not only help you determine a specific amount to contribute according to your budget, but it also gives you a framework to refer to and rely on when those unexpected solicitation calls come in. Politely declining yet stating that you've already given to a charity you've chosen to consistently support can often get them off the line. If they ask for your support as well and you really feel you want to but can't afford to write a check, consider other efforts you can contribute to for their cause. Offer to write about them on your blog or reach out to others you think may be able to donate. If they don't appreciate your efforts, then you've at least made an effort you can be proud of.

11. Have some fun at it

If you are looking for a budget option to go out on a dinner date with your partner, and someone is hosting one of the fund-raising variety, why not get a two-fer? Other options are out there for this as well, including shopping for items you were going to need anyway that give proceeds to a particular worthy cause. If it's within your budget, and you were going to anyway, why not? — **Myscha Theriault**

10 Easy Ways to Find Money for Charity

When my husband and I both worked, I was into instant-gratification charity. I remember reading the newspaper at my desk one morning and seeing a child the same age as my daughter on the front page. My daughter was a healthy toddler, but this little girl was emaciated, no bigger than an infant, and could not lift her head.

She was in Sudan, so I logged right onto www.UNICEF.org from my office computer and made a credit card donation. If I donated my take-home pay from that one day, I could then go about my work without feeling too bad about the horrible inequity of a world that allowed my child to enjoy a nice lunch with her even nicer nanny while this other kid went hungry and suffered. Never mind that random small gifts are not the most effective way to support the charity of your choice.

Now that we are a family of four living on just one income, it takes more planning to find a little extra to share. Here are 10 ways to find at least one charitable donation for the year:

1. Pay on the installment plan

Lots of charities, such as Chicago Public Radio, will take an annual gift in regular payroll deductions. A $120 gift then becomes 12 barely noticeable payments of $10.

2. Add an extra "person" to your holiday gift list

If a new person joins your family, there is no question that you will somehow find the cash to give them a holiday gift. Either you add a little more to your budget, or everyone else gets a slightly smaller gift, and no one suffers in the end. You can add your favorite charity to your list in the same way. This technique is most intuitive when participating in Toys for Tots

or some other children's gift program, but you can use it for anything.

3. Gift donations

Now, this is tricky. Since most Americans already have too much stuff in their houses, and so many Christmas presents end up in the back of the closet, giving donations can be a good gifting strategy. But you can actually be selfish even while giving if you announce to everyone on your list that you've donated to your own favorite charity in each of their names. Charitable donations as gifts go over best if you:

Take time to choose a cause that will resonate with the recipient. For instance, my husband would be delighted if someone donated to the Electronic Frontier Foundation in his honor, but if your uncle's an executive at one of the companies sued by this organization, he'd likely be unenchanted by the same gift.

Find out if your recipient is going to get deluged with requests for more money after your gift, and try to prevent this from happening.

Consider whether your gift will honestly be appreciated. A fresh-out-of-college niece who really needs cookware or a child may not feel so merry if all they get is a slip of paper.

Pairing a modest gift with a donation could solve this problem.

. . . .

4. Start a new holiday tradition

. . . .

This year I'm going to help my older daughter choose a recipient of a charitable gift, something I'd like to continue with my kids as they grow. I think we'll appreciate these memories as fondly as we'd remember an annual holiday tea at Chicago's Drake Hotel ($29.95) or tickets to *The Nutcracker.*

For your extended family, if everyone's into it, you could even replace the annual gift exchange with charitable donations.

. . . .

5. Make rules

. . . .

At our house, anytime we win money, it goes into our daughters' college fund. Not the best educational planning, I admit, but it's better than nothing. You could apply the same rule to charity. Or, if you receive an annual bonus at the end of the year, earmark a portion of it for philanthropy.

. . . .

6. Clean house

. . . .

Prosperous families need to streamline annually anyway to avoid turning their home into a junk warehouse. A good way to kick off the holiday season is a clean-out day where everyone—including and especially the kids—chooses items to either donate directly to a charity shop or to sell to raise money for a donation.

My husband practices a version of this strategy throughout the year. Whenever he sells something online, the money goes to his PayPal account. Rather than bothering to have PayPal cut him a check, he transfers the proceeds at the end of the year to his favorite charity.

. . . .

7. Develop a just-for-charity income stream

. . . .

So you put ads on your blog and—if you're like me—are depressed by the rate at which the proceeds trickle in. The whole thing might turn from a downer to a source of cheer if you watch your earnings oh-so-gradually grow over the course of the year, and then donate it all to a worthy charity.

Kids, too, can find ways to earn a little money for charity through crafts or other business endeavors.

. . . .

8. Take advantage of matching gifts

. . . .

Whatever you can scrape together can go farther if your employer matches employee donations.

9. Donate something other than money

Gift cards, frequent flyer miles, food from your cupboard, even your newspaper subscription while you're on vacation—you might have more untapped value sitting around than you realize. If you're thinking about donating a car, make sure you thoroughly investigate the organization first.

10. The pickle jar

Maybe you've been lucky enough to get forwarded that chestnut of a dad who saves his quarters in a pickle jar for his son's college education. When I was growing up, my dad saved his quarters for Vegas. At any rate, the same strategy can be used to gather an annual donation. When you're cleaning out the pickle jar, don't forget to also look for coins in your couch cushions, laundry area, car, pockets, etc.

Knowing that you're helping someone live a much better life makes all that scrounging seem worthwhile, no? — **Carrie Kirby**

CREDIT CARDS & DEBT

Consumer debt is at an all-time high and can lead to ruin for many families. However, credit cards and loans can be a blessing when used as tools for increasing your financial reputation, and when payments are made in a responsible manner. We share the dirty secrets that credit card companies don't want you to know about and offer proven tips on how to escape the burden of debt. By learning from someone else's mistakes, you can get the upper hand on credit and gain a lifetime of financial freedom and security.

6 Steps to Eliminating Your Debt Painlessly

Eliminating debt painlessly. Rarely do you see these words fit together in a neat little sentence. The very act of putting your hard-earned money toward the stack of debts you've accrued is painful. The good news is you can snowball your progress against mounting debts if you use this high-interest-first debt-reduction plan.

....

1. **First things first: Write down each debt vehicle you have, the amount of the debt, and the rate of interest charged.**

....

Department store cards are inevitably the worst culprits, charging interest rates that border on criminal. Next in line are usually the credit cards, student loans, then lines of credit, and your parents (unfortunately, they usually come last).

Let's say you are juggling a number of debts, from student loans to credit cards to that loan your parents don't expect to ever see repaid but won't let

you forget about either. For example, your accounting of what you owe might look like the chart found on page 231.

....

2. **Determine how much money you have available each month to put toward all your debts.**

....

If you're like most people on a tight budget, you probably haphazardly throw the minimum payment plus a bit at each debt every month, hoping that eventually it will all magically disappear. Unfortunately, making minimum payments on most credit cards is a sentence to upward of 15 years of paying off that debt, and paying at least double the original balance in interest only.

Let's say the total amount you can put toward your debt each month is $450.

Your minimum payments due each month add up to $347. You have $103 left over to allocate. Should you spread the $103 "surplus" across all your debt or choose one to pay off first? Which one?

....

3. **Choose the highest-interest debt on your list.**

....

I don't care if it's the highest or lowest balance, just look at the interest rate.

Balance	Owing	Interest	Minimum Payment
Dept. Store	$500	28%	$16
Visa	$2,000	18%	$66
Mastercard	$1,000	16%	$25
Student Loan	$6,000	10%	$150
Line of Credit	$5,000	8%	$90
Mum & Dad	$1,500	0%	$0
Total	**$16,000**		**$347**

With the money you have designated toward all your debts, make *only* minimum payments on all your debts, except your chosen highest-interest debt, to which you put all the rest of your monthly allocation. Hopefully this is a fair bit more than the minimum payment.

Back to our example. Looking at the table of debts, the highest-interest rate is the department store card with a 28% interest rate. If you have $450 to spend toward your debt, and it costs only $347 to pay the minimum balance on all your debt, apply the extra $103 to your store card. So instead of paying just the $16 minimum payment on the store card, you would pay $119 per month ($103 + $16).

. . . .

4. Continue until your first debt is paid off.

. . . .

Now you have one less debt to juggle each month. Yay! It may have taken a while to get here, but now you can cut up one card. No, really. Cut it up. (Especially if it's a department store card. They're pure evil.) The reason you got in this place to begin with is that you had too many cards, so let's reduce the number you have.

In our example, the $119 per month payment to the department store means the debt is paid off in five months. Card is destroyed.

. . . .

5. Choose the next-highest interest debt on your list.

. . . .

Repeat the process in steps three and four. You'll notice now, though, that you have more money to contribute toward your next debt of choice, since you now have one less debt payment nagging at your pocketbook.

In our example, Visa is next. Now you have an extra $119 per month since the store card is paid off. Add that to the minimum Visa payments you were making, and your total Visa payments are now $185 ($119 + $66).

....

6. And so on.

....

Each time you systematically pay off one of your debts, you'll have more and more money to pay off the next debt on your list, effectively snowballing the process of paying off your debts. It picks up momentum quickly, and by the end you're blasting through your debts and even your parents get paid.

Here's how our example would play out:

After the Visa is paid off, you have $210/month for your Mastercard.

After the Mastercard is paid off, you have $360 for your student loan.

After the student loan is paid off, you have the full $450 for your line of credit.

After that, pay off your parents! It will only take you three months, and will get you in their good books for sure.

The total amount of time required to pay off this laundry list of debts: under five years.

This is a long time, but think of it this way: now you're debt-free! You didn't have to toil every month over how much extra cash you can throw at the never-ending debt load, and

you minimized every single dollar of interest you possibly could.

The trick is, you need to continue to allocate the same amount of money (or more) toward your overall debt every month until all your debts are paid off. If after tackling one or two cards you decide you can decrease your monthly allocation toward your debts, you'll only prolong the process and end up paying a ton of interest. A little bit of short-term pain makes for lots of long-term gain. You deserve it!

HIGH-INTEREST FIRST VS. LOW-BALANCE FIRST DEBT REDUCTION

There are other debt elimination plans that would have you pay off the lowest balance first, instead of the highest-interest debt. The reason for this is the feeling of satisfaction you get from knocking off a debt from the pile, even though you may be doling out more interest dollars on a higher balance elsewhere.

The wrong person without enough dedication to the plan outlined in this article might give up if the first few debts were slow to be paid off. For example, if your department store card had the $6,000 balance, it would take you over three years just to pay off your first debt. That's a long time to wait for tangible progress, even if it is the most efficient.

So take a look at your debts and ask yourself if you have the discipline to stick to the high-interest-first plan. If not, try paying off a few smaller debts to get your legs under you and then reevaluate. — **Nora Dunn**

10 Dirty Secrets Credit Card Companies Don't Want You to Know

The average American has around eight credit cards and is carrying roughly $9,000 in credit card debt. If that's not bad enough, the credit card companies are involved in what can only be described as a conspiracy to keep Americans in debt, permanently.

I watched an incredible PBS documentary online recently called *Secret History of Credit Cards*. If you don't

have an hour to spare, here are some of the biggest dirty secrets for you. You may want to sit down for these.

. . . .

1. Minimum payments can take more than 35 years to repay.

. . . .

The minimum monthly payment used to be 5%. That caused a problem for the credit card issuers. Folks were being forced to pay off their balance too quickly. *Plus* the cost of that 5% minimum made people wary of running up high bills. The solution was genius. Institute a 2% minimum payment. Not only will people splurge more because they have to pay less back each month, but it adds thousands of dollars in interest and increases the repayment time by *decades*. Sneaky doesn't even cover it.

. . . .

2. A late payment to any creditor can skyrocket your APR.

. . . .

I'm not talking here about just your credit card payment being late. If you miss a car payment, mortgage payment, cell phone bill—in fact, any payment, your APR can automatically increase to the massive default APR, which is usually 25–35%. Even if you're *on time* with your credit card payments, a late payment anywhere else can instigate this penalty. It's known as the "Universal Default

Clause." Supposedly, it protects the credit card issuers from folks who are credit risks. Like these multibillion-dollar companies need protection from the little people.

3. There is NO LIMIT put on late payment charges.

This is something no other industry could get away with. You'd think there would be some kind of law preventing the banks from charging loan shark penalties, but there isn't. Be just one hour late for a payment and instead of a $5 or $10 fee (which, prior to the 1996 *Smiley vs. Citibank* case, was the limit), you're looking at $30, at least. My credit card charges $36. Many financial analysts believe that with no cap on these fees, they will easily rise to $50–$60 in the next year. And remember, when you're late they also kill you with a huge APR. Double whammy.

4. There is also no federal limit on interest rates.

Don't you find it odd that in a time of very low interest on anything from car loans to mortgages, credit card companies can hand out APRs that embarrass loan sharks? Well, it's not unusual to see 34.99% APRs, especially as a default rate, and the reason

is simple. Most credit card companies reside in states like South Dakota or Delaware. These states have very weak or even no "usury laws." So, there's no cap on interest. By law, there's nothing to stop them charging whatever interest they want.

5. You can often pay interest TWICE in one month.

This one's called "two-cycle billing" and it's also a completely legal loophole. Let's say you pay off the balance of your card in full at the end of one month, say April. But in May, you don't pay off your complete balance. Boom, some credit card issuers will charge you for two months' worth of interest. Aren't they lovely?

6. Grace periods are getting shorter . . . or being eliminated.

Remember the good old days, when you had 25 days to pay off your balance without incurring charges? Well, those could soon be a distant memory. Some banks have already shortened the grace period to 20 days. (Do you know what yours is? It may have changed.) And other banks are doing away with grace periods completely. That means you're paying interest on anything you buy, the second you buy it, even if you pay off your balance each month. The clock is running, folks.

7. Cash advances hit you twice in the wallet.

First, as I'm sure you know, you'll get a different, higher APR applied to your cash advances. But you also get hit with a transaction charge, around 2.5%. Even credit cards that confidently announce "no finance charges" can still bill you for transaction charges.

8. The fine print is a web of deceit.

Let's be honest—these days you need two hours and a law degree from Harvard to understand the mumbo-jumbo in the fine print. But try and read it if you can, because this is where the credit card issuer can hide a whole bunch of nasty surprises. The biggest is scarier than Godzilla on crack. Basically, the credit card issuer can change your APR at *any* time, as long as they give you 15 days' notice. No reason required. Imagine if any other industry worked that way, like your mortgage? While you're reading the fine print, also check for things like purchase protection, lifetime warranty coverage, and travel discounts. These may end when your introductory rate ends. And speaking of that, what does your introductory rate become after the teaser period? It could be more than you bargained for, especially if it's a variable APR.

9. Good payers are called deadbeats!

Deadbeats—it's what credit card companies call those folks who are responsible and pay off the balance each month. They don't like those people, not one bit. That's because they make little to no money off of them. No, credit card companies like you to carry a nice hefty balance and pay only the minimum each month. If you're one of those people, known as "revolvers," you're part of the crowd that contributes roughly 90% of the credit card company's income. What a crazy upside-down world credit is.

10. You can demand a better deal.

APR too high? Hate the annual fee? Want a longer grace period? It turns out your credit card company may just have to do your bidding. See, the fees they charge are not considered a necessary cost of doing business, so you can request, firmly, that they be reduced or eliminated. Now, imagine what would happen if we all did that?

No wonder they want that one kept secret. And remember, if all else fails, find a lower-cost APR card and transfer your balance. You have at least that going for you.

That's the scoop folks. If you happen to be in spiraling credit card debt, there are places you can go to for help. PBS.org has a great list of resources. From now on, I hope you all look a whole lot closer at that handy piece of plastic in your wallet. It's far more ominous than it first looks. Pleasant dreams, everyone. — **Paul Michael**

What Credit Counselors Do and How to Pick One

So you are up to your eyeballs, drowning in debt and expenses, and struggling to keep your head above water. You have been reduced to the life of a monk and are still making no headway. Is it time to see a credit counselor?

First, let's take a look at the typical symptoms that may require credit counseling:

1. You use credit cards to pay for groceries and other household expenses because you don't have the cash.
2. You don't even know how much debt you owe anymore.
3. You use one credit card to pay off another.
4. You use cash advances as the only way to get some cash.
5. You are denied when you ask for an increase in your credit limit.
6. You ask for a credit increase in the first place because you think it will help you manage your expenses.
7. You worry about money all the time.
8. Let's also assume that you have tried every way possible to "find money" in your current budget and are still financially suffering.

Now it may be time to see a credit counselor.

WHAT DO CREDIT COUNSEL- ORS DO?

First of all, a credit counselor will (or at least should) spend some time with you to get a handle on your situation. If it's appropriate, they will prescribe a Debt Management Program (DMP).

Basically a DMP will consolidate your debts at lower interest rates. The actual interest rates you get vary by creditors and what they can offer to credit counseling firms—it's fairly standardized. As part of the DMP, late fees and other penalties you have incurred will also be waived, which can be substantial if you're at the point of needing credit counseling.

Once you're in the DMP program, you will pay the credit counselor monthly, and they will distribute the money among the creditors you owe. You have the advantage now of not having to juggle a million debt payments, and in turn you agree not to charge anything further to your cards or apply for any credit increases.

For this service, credit counselors get paid in two ways:

1. They receive a rebate from the creditors.
2. You will also pay an up-front and monthly fee for this service.

NOT ALL CREDIT COUNSELORS ARE CREATED EQUAL

As with any business service, you need to do your research before you sign up for a DMP plan. There are some shady credit counselors out there.

Here is a checklist of things you should look for:

- Not-for-profit status.

- A good Better Business Bureau status with minimal complaints (ideally none).
- Certification with the National Foundation of Credit Counselors (NFCC) or the Independent Association of Credit Counselors (IACC).

QUESTIONS TO ASK A CREDIT COUNSELOR

Before signing on the dotted line (or even agreeing to an appointment), here are a few questions you should ask of your potential credit counselor.

....

1. How long is the initial appointment?

....

You are looking for them to say they'll spend at least half an hour with you. They need to assess your entire financial situation, which can't

be done effectively if you are shuffled in and out the door in record time.

....

2. What will you do?

....

The best answer you can get is for them to say they'll examine your situation, and only if it is appropriate, they can arrange a Debt Management Plan suited to your situation. Sometimes after a consultation, they will advise you to tackle your debts on your own because they're not bad enough yet, or conversely will advise you to see a bankruptcy attorney.

....

3. What kind of debt can you help me with?

....

You don't want a counselor who will just address your credit card debt if your student loans, mortgage, and other debts are also eating away at your finances.

....

4. How much will this cost?

....

Ideally you should not pay more than $75 up front, and no more than $35/month ongoing.

Don't be too embarrassed about your financial situation to see somebody who can help you. The best way to move forward with your life is to take ownership of your current predicament and make the right moves toward financial freedom. It is still possible. — **Nora Dunn**

7 Questions to Ask Before Buying Credit Card Insurance

So your credit card company just called offering you balance protection insurance against job loss, disability, death, or critical illness. The cost will be just pennies, calculated

monthly based on your outstanding balance.

Do you take it?

The question is: Have you performed an insurance-needs analysis, or will you just make the decision to take the insurance based on impulse and instinct?

There are typically four different types of credit card insurance:

Involuntary Job Loss: This pays your monthly minimum payment for a specified period of time after you lose your job through downsizing or layoffs.

Disability: Like above, your monthly minimum payment is covered for a specified time period upon becoming disabled and unable to work.

Critical Illness: Similar to above.

Life or AD&D (Accidental Death & Dismemberment): If you die, your entire credit card balance will be paid.

The cost may initially seem small at between $0.75 and $1.50 per $100 of outstanding credit card balance each month, but in the spirit of being frugal, is that money wisely spent?

Consider that with the exception of credit life protection, this insurance doesn't actually pay off your debt. It simply makes the minimum payments on your outstanding balance for the term of the contract. In fact, depending on the credit card

and interest charges, you may sometimes find that the balance at the end of the contract is actually higher than when the claim occurred due to compounding interest.

Are those minimum payments something that would cripple you financially in the event of an illness or job loss? The answer will be different for everybody; this is just food for thought.

Similar to individual critical illness, disability, or life insurance policies, there are seven questions to consider before buying credit card Insurance.

1. What are the terms of the policy?

For example, what are the specific definitions under which the insurance company will pay?

2. What coverage do you need?

If you lose that income or become ill, will minimum payments on your credit cards be of benefit to you, or do you have other funds that will suit the purpose?

3. What coverage do you already have?

There is no point in duplicating your insurance coverage if you already have a critical Illness policy in place.

4. In the case of job loss insurance, what are the exact terms?

You may be surprised at the restrictions of this initially appealing option.

5. Is it cost-effective?

As a case study, let's examine life insurance. On a $10,000 credit card balance, at $0.80 per $100 of outstanding balance, your monthly charge would be approximately $80/month. For $80/month, a 35-year-old nonsmoking female in good health can purchase upward of $500,000 of term life insurance.

6. Can you cancel the policy, and under what terms?

If you do decide to take it, make sure you keep all your documentation together so canceling it when the time comes is easy.

7. Are you insurable?

Many balance protection policies don't require any evidence of insurability to qualify. If you have medical issues that make you a higher risk such that individual policies would either be cost-prohibitive or unavailable

to you, then maybe this is just the protection you need.

On the flip side, one type of credit card insurance that you may not realize you might automatically have is travel insurance. Many credit cards feature automatic flight and travel coverage if you pay for a trip using that card. In fact, before you go out and purchase travel insurance, it bears calling your credit card company to find out the specific terms of their coverage. You may find that you can save a few extra bucks by not having to go out and get extra travel coverage!

As with all insurance policies, take a good hard look at what you need, what you can afford, and whether the "easy option" being offered to you over the phone is going to be easy in the long run. — **Nora Dunn**

5 Laws the Leg-Breakers Don't Want You to Know About

Gone are the days when debt collectors only hassled the lazy, financially inept, or the completely downtrodden and hopelessly unlucky. More and more consumers are being contacted by debt collectors as part of an attempt to be paid for past-due accounts, either for their own debt, debt inherited as a condition of a death in the family, or as a horrible consequence to an identity theft. Whether or not you actually owe the money, the rules are the same. Debt collectors acting as a third-party interest in past-due accounts are bound by the laws of the FDCPA. Learning what they can (and, more importantly: *can't*) do is vital to protecting your rights and preventing undue stress.

The Fair Debt Collection Practices Act, often referred to as the FDCPA, was passed by Congress in response to abusive conduct by collection agencies. Here are five actions that are considered illegal under the Act.

1. Contacting a third party not involved with the debt

This means that if your boyfriend's name is on the debt, they can call him. They cannot, however, contact Aunt Edna. They also cannot call you at work if it has been made known to them that it is a violation of a work policy. Once you tell them that they cannot call you at work anymore, they need to comply.

2. Threatening you

This includes threats to sue you, throw you in jail, garnish your wages, or kill your dog. They can inform you of an actual impending intention to refer your case to an attorney or to report your debt to a credit agency, but not with the intention of getting you to pay. Additionally, they cannot be a potty mouth by using racial slurs, insults, or profanity to make their point.

3. Letting your debt be known to others

All communications from the agency need to be private. Envelopes containing letters should not have any blatant wording of it being from a collection entity. When calling to speak to you at work, they should not inform your boss or anyone else answering the phone that the call is regarding a debt.

4. Calling outside of normal hours

Unless you have given explicit permission for 2:00 AM phone calls, agencies may not call someone before 8:00 AM and after 9:00 PM regarding debt.

5. Pretending to be someone they aren't

Letters from the agency need to be on agency or creditor letterhead. It is against the law for a notice to come from an "attorney" or "court" letterhead, unless it is an actual legal document from them directly.

Other illegal tactics include asking for you to provide checking account numbers or postdated checks with the intention of prosecuting you if they come back "insufficient" from your bank. They also may not charge interest or collection fees not stated in your original purchase contract or that may be prohibited by state law.

The FDCPA also requires that agencies send a written notice within five days of their first contact with you. This notice must include:

1. How much money you reportedly owe;
2. The name of the creditor to whom the debt is owed;
3. That unless you, within 30 days after receipt of the notice, dispute the validity of the debt or any portion thereof, the debt will be assumed valid by the debt collector;
4. That if you dispute the debt in full or in part within that 30-day period, the debt collector will obtain verification of the debt and mail it to the consumer (please note that this does not prohibit the agency from continuing with normal proceedings during the 30-day period); and
5. That upon your written request within the 30-day period, the debt collector will provide you with the name and address of the original creditor, if different from the current creditor.

A "mini Miranda warning" must be included in the notice. This is a statement letting you know that the notice is from a debt collector, and any information obtained may be used to collect the debt. Every notice or letter from the agency from this point on must also contain the warning.

While there are many reputable, law-abiding collection agencies out there, it is best to make yourself aware of the proper recourse should you encounter a stinker. If you experience any problems with an agency violating the laws of the FDCPA, please contact your state attorney general's office. If you are dealing with an out-of-state agency, you may also call the Federal Trade Commission at 1-877-382-4357 (877-FTC-HELP). Being educated is the key to being protected. Know the law, and you can keep an old debt from ruining your life!
— **Linsey Knerl**

INVESTING YOUR MONEY

Everyone tells you to start investing, but where does a newbie begin? We will introduce you to the basic investment strategies used by experts, and explain every step in plain English. Learn about the various types of investments, which ones are best for your current situation, and how to get out if you have to. Getting into the investment game doesn't have to be scary at all. We promise!

Asset Allocation: Where to Put Your Investment Dollars

Asset allocation, being the distribution of your investment portfolio across different types of assets (known as "asset classes"), is not meant to be something that changes with the markets. In fact, it's quite the opposite: A properly allocated portfolio is meant to weather both good markets and bad; to allow you to rest assured that your investments will reach your ultimate goals of what you need the money for without actively moving the money around.

The effects of proper asset allocation are not to be underestimated; the vast majority of your long-term returns are attributed to asset allocation—not market timing or selecting specific investments, as you might suspect.

But achieving the right asset allocation can be like groping around in the dark (and not in a fun kind

of way!) if you don't know where to begin. This article will help you to determine the proper asset allocation for your money. But first, here are some definitions of the different types of asset classes.

DIFFERENT TYPES OF ASSET CLASSES

1. Cash

Despite its name, this allocation is not a license to hide money under your pillow! Cash investments include high-interest savings and money market accounts—ones that won't make you a ton of money, but that are guaranteed and will likely keep pace with inflation.

2. Fixed income

These are mostly interest-bearing investments, and sometimes guaranteed (technically "cash" is a fixed-income investment too). A fixed-income investment won't generally shoot the lights out in returns, but chances of investment losses are also capped. Examples are bonds, term deposits, and even some real estate derivatives.

....

3. Equities
....

Equities can be subdivided into *Domestic* and *International* categories. All equities are stock market investments, and of course not all stocks are created equal. This is where your financial planner (or a heck of a lot of research) will come in handy, differentiating the degrees of risk within an equity portfolio and reducing unnecessary risks. Although equities historically achieve the highest long-term returns (by far) of any asset class, they will also see the most short-term fluctuation.

Large Cap (short for market capitalization) or Blue Chip equities refer to large, stable companies that have a good history, long track record, and fairly steady returns. *Medium Cap* encompass smaller or newer companies but still widely recognized ones, and *Small Cap* investments will often be higher risk investments—start-ups or smaller companies in less popular market sectors. The more risk you assume, the higher your potential return will be—within reason.

Domestic equities will generally be safer than international equities, because investing internationally subjects you to a new form of risk: currency risk. Your investment overseas may do gangbusters, but if your domestic dollar gains value comparatively in the meantime, you could actually see losses overall.

....

4. Sector
....

Sector investments refer to highly specialized equities. They entail the highest amount of risk (along with potential for the highest gains), and should be limited in any portfolio. Examples of sectors include *Natural Resources* or *Science & Technology*.

DETERMINE YOUR OWN PERSONAL ASSET ALLOCATION

Now it's time to determine your own personal asset allocation and how to diversify your portfolio across the above asset classes. Here are a few questions to ask that affect your portfolio's asset allocation.

....

1. What is your investment time frame?
....

The shorter your time frame, the safer your portfolio needs to be. The general rule is as follows:

0–3 years = short-term
3–5 years = medium-term
6+ years = long-term

You will now recognize that the asset allocation for a portfolio used to accumulate and save money for a major purchase (short-term) will look different from a retirement portfolio (long-term). Even those who are on the brink of retiring need to consider how long this portfolio needs to produce an income (count on 20–30 years), so don't set your date of retirement as the date you cash everything out; you may be cheating yourself out of some much-needed returns to keep pace with inflation over the duration of your retirement.

....

2. Do you need an income?

....

For somebody retiring as above, you may have a long investment time frame, but also the need to draw an income from the portfolio. The more income you need (as a percentage of the entire portfolio), the more conservative a portfolio you should have.

The next question to ask under this category is "How long will you draw down on the investment?" If you expect to deplete the fund in four years (as with a child's postsecondary education portfolio), then your asset allocation should be more conservative than somebody looking for 30 years of income.

....

3. What is your marginal tax rate?

....

Depending on how much income you earn, you may be looking to shelter some of the growth from taxation, or even convert highly taxable income (like interest income) to tax-efficient forms of income (like capital gains). Your marginal tax rate may determine how to invest money you don't have a specific direction for, and may influence the specific choice of investments within your portfolio.

Also, if you expect your income to change in the next few years, your asset allocation could be affected. Sheltering gains during years of high income and producing taxable investment income during lower-income years are all specialized asset allocation strategies.

....

4. How strong is your stomach?

....

This is probably one of the factors that will most influence your asset allocation choices, since you are the one who has to live with your investments. You may be young, saving for retirement, and showing all the technical signs of being a long-term aggressive investor, but if you can't handle the heat when the markets do loops, it's not worth the heartache. You will ultimately feel stressed out about money, will worry constantly, and will eventually bail—probably at the wrong time.

RECOMMENDED ASSET ALLOCATION FOR 6 COMMON INVESTMENT PERSONALITIES

So how do these factors determine your investment mix? Here are six common types of investment personalities, and the recommended asset allocation for each.

1. Cash

You need the money within a very short period of time and cannot afford to lose a cent of it. You are likely accumulating for something like a down payment on a house, or some imminent purchases.

Allocation: 100% Cash

2. Conservative

You have a short investment time frame, and a low tolerance for investment fluctuation. You may need to draw a hefty income from the portfolio now, or shortly. Hopefully you are not in a high-income tax bracket, because a conservative portfolio will generate mostly taxable income (unless it is in a special tax-sheltered account).

Average Allocation: 15% Equities (all Domestic), 85% Fixed Income

3. Moderate conservative

You either have a stronger stomach or a longer time frame than your conservative counterpart. You likely are still working within a short to medium time frame, but have the ability to expose a little more of your portfolio to fluctuation, with the hopes that you will achieve higher overall returns.

Average Allocation: 25% Equities (of which up to 10% can be International), 75% Fixed Income

4. Moderate

A true fence-sitter with a medium time frame, and/or a middle-of-the-road tolerance for risk, you are the picture of balance between fixed income and equities.

Average Allocation: 50% Equities (of which up to 25% can be International), 50% Fixed Income

5. Moderate aggressive

You likely have a long time frame and a good ability to ignore market fluctuations to achieve your long-term goals of good returns. You are interested in sheltering income from taxation, and your moderate aggressive portfolio is likely geared toward retirement.

Average Allocation: 80% Equities (of which up to 40% can be International and up to 10% can be Sector), 20% Fixed Income

6. Aggressive

You are ready to hang it all out there, and in market scenarios (like the present) when news of the sky falling is rampant, you are cool as a cucumber. In fact, you are probably investing even more money right now (which is the perfect thing to do). You are interested in tax shelters, are young, and certainly have a long time frame to ride out the bumps.

Average Allocation: 100% Equities (of which up to 50% can be International and up to 15% can be Sector)

ASSET ALLOCATION IS IMPORTANT FOR YOU

It doesn't matter what stage of your life you are in—asset allocation applies to you! If you don't have a portfolio to speak of and are looking at saving money each month, that doesn't mean you don't deserve to have a properly allocated portfolio; simply start now.

There are lots of managed funds out there that will cater to your specific investment personality and will take care of the asset allocation for you within the fund. All you have to do is worry about saving the money; your solid asset allocation plan and the investment managers will take care of the rest. — **Nora Dunn**

8 Investing Tips for Any Market

What if there was a way to invest with less worry and less emotion? Now I can't say that you can be entirely worry-free when you invest, but you can certainly mitigate concerns over your portfolio when you apply a few techniques. As an investor for over 20 years who's lived through two recessions (and going on a third), here are some tips to weather market cycles without losing sleep.

1. Look at the long-term

The idea of "long-term" varies depending on how old you are. The younger you are, the longer is your investment time horizon and the more time your investments can grow to make up for bad market cycles or to benefit from the awesome power of compounding. In this regard, investing early gives you a leg up. The flip side, of course, is that the older you are, the more conservative you should become. A good technique is to diminish your exposure to equities over time by doing portfolio reallocations on a regular basis. Rule of thumb: Subtract your age from 100 to yield a recommended percentage for your stock allocation. Though this is a simple way of arriving at a ballpark stock allocation, you'll still need to take into account your risk profile and financial goals to arrive at your final numbers.

2. Resist market timing

I learned the hard way that short-term market timing is a lousy approach. I've been whipsawed by the market via short sales and stock trades during volatile periods. These days, I resist the urge to market-time even while the market dances like a drunk sailor. My take is that if you trade, you should know what you're doing, and not just get into this because you're acting on emotion.

3. Be well diversified

Stock market diversification can be effectively realized via indexing and appropriate asset allocation strategies. You can also buy general, actively managed mutual funds and achieve some level of diversification, although this means you're entrusting the performance of your funds to its fund managers. I prefer to do it the passive way—by tracking the indexes that represent major asset classes.

4. Choose good asset allocations for your portfolio

Believe it or not, the overall total returns of your investments will depend largely on how your asset allocation is structured. Most financial literature will suggest an allocation that includes stocks, bonds, cash, real estate, and even precious metals or commodities in your portfolio since these asset classes don't behave in lockstep (the less correlated asset classes are, the better!).

5. Go automatic and invest piecemeal

Dollar cost averaging is a great way to ignore the current volatility in the markets. Invest regularly and forget about it. It'll keep you from obsessing about your losses while allowing you to accumulate battered investments at lower prices.

6. Keep an eye on your portfolio

Diversification, asset allocation, and dollar cost averaging are techniques that allow us to be more complacent about our portfolios, but don't forget about your investments for too long! You'll need to evaluate your investments on a regular basis just to make sure you're on track toward your long-term goals.

7. Rebalance your investment over time

And once you do evaluate your portfolios, you can decide whether it's a good idea to rebalance your holdings to reflect your allocations accurately. When the market goes haywire, rebalancing to keep the asset classes in the correct proportions will allow you to automatically buy those assets that have suffered price drops, while selling out of assets that may be relatively pricier (or that represent a higher weighting or concentration of your total assets).

8. Know when to hold and when to fold

You've got losers? Did you invest in speculative penny stocks, individual stocks, or REITs in the last few years? Maybe it's time to unload them now and take the loss. By doing so, you'll achieve two things—you can harvest your loss and make it benefit you during tax time, and you'll be able to move your position into hopefully better investments like index funds, where your funds can grow with a bit more predictability. — **The Digerati Life**

The Basics of Mutual Funds

A mutual fund is a "basket" of investments, managed by a fund manager (usually with the help of a team of analysts). This basket of investments can be made up of stocks, bonds, short-term securities, or even real estate among other vehicles.

As a mutual fund investor, your money is pooled with that of other people who are investing in the same fund. The fund manager, now with lots of buying power since the money is all pooled together, then buys and sells the securities and actively manages the holdings.

As a mutual fund investor, you buy shares (also known as units) of the fund, based on the amount of money you are investing. You are also able to buy fractions of shares if the money you invest doesn't divide exactly into the share value or if you are investing small amounts of money. Mutual funds are open-ended, so when you invest, you buy shares directly from the fund itself, and when you wish to sell, you sell directly back to the fund. This makes for a fairly liquid investment, as you don't have to find a buyer in order to sell (or vice versa).

Mutual funds are valued daily (and in some rare cases like real estate, semi-monthly or monthly). The daily value (known as the net asset value) is calculated as a function of the current market value of the holdings divided by the number of shares outstanding.

PERFORMANCE

Performance of a mutual fund depends entirely on two factors:

1. What the fund invests in.
2. The competence of the fund manager.

A fund that invests in small cap stocks will perform quite differently from one that invests in bonds, and differently again from a short-term money market fund. Likewise the competency of the fund manager comes into play and can drastically affect the returns. The fund managers do, however, have many incentives to perform, as they can lose their job if they underperform compared to other funds of similar mandates.

MAKING MONEY WITH MUTUAL FUNDS

Assuming your mutual fund is a winner and is making money, the fund manager passes the capital gains/dividends/interest earned by the holdings on to us, the shareholders. Thus, at the end of the year, you must report the income when you file your taxes.

I will also note that in most cases, people reinvest the income in the fund, which is a great case for compound growth and passive money management. You are still required to report the income on your taxes each year, though, even if it is reinvested.

THE EVER-PRESENT FEES

One of the biggest criticisms that the mutual fund industry battles is that of their fees. It is often expressed as a percentage of the assets of the fund and goes toward managing the fund, covering expenses such as trade fees, admin, custodian, legal/audit, accounting, and even salaries of the managers and analysts. These fees are often referred to as Management Expense Ratios (MERs). Not all funds carry the same fees either.

Please note that all reported or advertised performance figures of a mutual fund are always net of fees. What you see reported is what you get. So even if a fund carries a higher fee, if it outperforms other funds in its peer group, it still warrants consideration.

LOAD VS. NO LOAD

In addition to the MERs which are ever-present and unavoidable, you may find yourself weighing load and no-load options.

A loaded fund is one which carries an additional charge to invest in the fund, usually because you are receiving advice from a salesperson or financial planner. A front-end load entails an up-front fee for investing in the fund, and a back-end load (also known as a deferred sales charge) would charge the fee upon redemption. Both fees are often expressed as a percentage of the money invested. Some back-end fees operate on sliding scales, such that if you leave the money in the same fund or family of funds for a certain period of time (usually five to seven years), the fees decline to nothing. Thus, if you plan to invest for the long haul, these back-end loads are often the most appealing.

And although the term *no load* obviously means there is no additional charge, they can sometimes charge a higher MER than their loaded sister funds, thereby reducing your effective returns.

INDEX FUNDS

An index fund operates very much like a mutual fund, except it is not actively managed. The performance of the fund is linked to the performance of a market index, such as the S&P 500. Thus, the fees are often considerably lower than other mutual funds, since you as the shareholder aren't relying on the fund manager's expertise to pick the right investments.

Historically it has been a toss-up as to which option is better. Because of the lower fees, index funds can be harder to beat. However, indexes weren't created to be investments unto themselves; they are more of a barometer as to how certain markets are performing. They can also be heavily weighted in certain holdings, thereby reducing the diversification you might get with other funds. (A mutual fund is not allowed to invest more than 10% of its assets in any given investment, thus providing an amazing amount of diversification. If one specific investment tanks, you still have a number of others to save the day and reduce your losses). Fund managers can also make certain investment decisions and change up the holdings of a fund if there is trouble brewing, something index funds can't do as easily. If an index is sinking and you're not watching it actively, you're going down with the ship.

MORE ABOUT MUTUAL FUNDS

There is much more to mutual funds than the simple overview given here. We could talk about classes of shares, equity funds, bond funds, money market instruments, disclosure scandals, Exchange-traded funds, and the list goes on and on from there.

What I can say in favor of mutual funds is that they are a great way to invest for the long haul in a passive manner. You can create a "bomb-proof" portfolio of funds that is well balanced and diversified, and then technically forget about it. Given enough time, good fund managers, and a good financial planner keeping an eye out for you, you can reach your financial goals without having to watch the stock ticker every day.

— **Nora Dunn**

How to Start a Roth IRA (and Where to Do It)

You've heard how awesome Roth IRAs are and how starting one now can mean big bucks when you're older. You've even done some research so you have a vague idea of how a Roth IRA works. Now what? How do you actually start one yourself? It's surprisingly easy to set up a retirement account and to begin investing in your future.

BEFORE YOU INVEST

Saving for retirement is important, but there are other aspects of personal finance, and you should take care of two of them before opening a Roth IRA.

1. Tuck away at least $1,000 for emergencies.
2. Pay off your credit card debt. At the very least, make significant headway on your debt and have a plan for its elimination.

Here's one excellent way to begin your retirement savings: When you've finished paying off your debt, take the amount you were using for this each month and, instead of spending it, stick it into a retirement account. You've already developed the habit of using the money to improve your financial life; this is just another way to do it!

WHERE TO OPEN A ROTH IRA

Deciding where to open your Roth IRA is the most difficult part of the process! Many financial institutions offer IRAs. Each place has its own strengths and weaknesses. It's important to search for a company that suits *your* needs. Don't fret about finding the perfect match—find a good match and then get the IRA in motion. Questions to ask during your research include:

- Is there a minimum initial investment? Minimum contributions?
- What sorts of fees are assessed to the account?
- Does the company offer automatic contributions?
- What investment options are available? Can you invest in stocks? Mutual funds? Real estate?
- Is it possible to download statements automatically into Quicken?
- How reputable is the provider?

If you already have an investment advisor, ask her for recommendations, but look for other options, too. Some banks and credit unions offer Individual Retirement Accounts. My credit union, for example, has Roth accounts, but they're limited to certificates of deposit at 1.50%.

If you're willing to make some decisions on your own, you can open a self-directed IRA through a mutual fund company or through an online discount brokerage.

THE BIG THREE

Fidelity, Vanguard, and T. Rowe Price are three of the best places to start. As Vintek, one of my regular readers pointed out, we designate these firms as the Big Three "not only because they're enormous, but also because they have a variety of funds that cover every investment style and segment you could wish for. If you're just starting out, you should probably pick one family and stay with it. You'll be able to track all your investments more easily in one place."

I explored each company's Web site to discover what sorts of Roth IRA options they offered for beginning investors. Here's what I found.

Fidelity Investments (www.fidelity.com) offers a no-fee IRA. There's a $2,500 minimum initial deposit, but this is waived if you commit to $200/month automatic contributions. They offer 4,500 mutual funds, about a quarter of which have no transaction fee. In short, you can open a no-cost IRA at Fidelity with a $200 starting investment if you invest in mutual funds and you agree to contribute $200/month.

Vanguard Group (www.vanguard.com) also offers a no-cost Roth IRA. To do this, you must elect to receive electronic statements and start with $1,000 in the company's STAR fund. (The STAR fund is a mutual fund of mutual funds, a safe choice for beginners.) Additional contributions require a minimum of $100 unless you use their Automatic Investment Plan, in which case the minimum is $50. There are no fees to purchase the STAR fund.

T. Rowe Price (www.troweprice.com) charges $10/year for Roth IRA accounts until you have a balance above $5,000, after which there is no fee. You need $1,000 to open your IRA, but this minimum goes away if you sign up to contribute at least $50/month with the Automatic Asset Builder. There are no sales fees or commissions to invest this money in T. Rowe Price mutual funds.

The information here will get you started with the minimum investment and the lowest costs. If you have more money at your disposal, you have more options. It's possible to make much more sophisticated trades with each of these places—purchasing stocks, for example—but not for free. All the companies mentioned in this article update their plans frequently. Therefore I encourage you to look more closely at each company's Web site, and to read the literature for each investment you consider.

DISCOUNT BROKERS

Discount brokers appeal to many people because they have a low barrier to entry. They offer lower fees than traditional brokers because they don't have research departments and they don't offer investment advice. They only act as middlemen for trading in the market.

I opened my Roth IRA at Sharebuilder.com after reading David Bach's *The Automatic Millionaire.* It felt great to finally open a retirement account. (Seriously—I was stoked.) Now, though, I fret about the costs. Sharebuilder charges a $25 annual custodial fee for a Roth IRA, plus $4 every time I make an automatic investment. (Other transactions cost $15.95!) Because I'm careful, I'm not hit with a lot of fees. Though I love how easy it is to automate investing through Sharebuilder, my research for this article revealed two other discount brokers that look appealing.

People have all sorts of good things to say about Firstrade.com. This company offers a no-fee Roth IRA, but requires a $500 minimum initial investment and $100 subsequent investments. Firstrade charges $6.95 per transaction, though they do offer a wide range of mutual funds that one can purchase for no charge. Firstrade looks good for somebody who wants to invest in mutual funds, but doesn't want to (or can't afford to) sign on with a larger mutual fund company.

Zecco.com, the new kid on the block, charges $30 a year to carry a Roth IRA. That's it. There are no other commissions or fees unless you're a very heavy trader. There are no minimum balances or contributions. From what I can tell, the Zecco investment universe includes most stocks and Exchange-traded funds, including some tasty Vanguard index funds.

Discount brokers are a good option if you're primarily interested in purchasing individual stocks instead of mutual funds. They're also a fine choice if you want to get started *now*, but can't afford a program with one of the mutual fund companies. Another option if you're short on cash is to open a CD-based IRA at a bank until you've saved enough for the minimum initial deposit at one of the Big Three.

HOW TO OPEN A ROTH IRA

Here's a secret: Opening a Roth IRA is *easy*. Have you ever filled out a job application? Have you ever applied for a credit card? Have you ever opened a bank account? Of course you have. That's exactly what the process is like to start an individual retirement account.

Some firms require that you download the forms and then mail or fax them to the company. Most places, however, provide online applications. Before you begin the application, you will need the following:

1. Your social security number.
2. Your bank account information.
3. Your employment information.
4. Some money. (Depending on where you choose to open your IRA, you may need $25 or you may need $3,000.)
5. About an hour of uninterrupted time. (Actually, you probably only need fifteen minutes, but allocate more time just to be safe.)

Gather items 1–4 in one location when you're ready to begin. (If you're opening an IRA through a brick-and-mortar bank or broker, take this info with you.) From this point, it's simply a matter of answering simple questions.

Once you've completed the application process, you will be asked to transfer money to your account. This money will probably earn interest in a money market fund until you choose an investment.

I'm a big fan of automatic investment plans. Most of the companies I mentioned earlier in this article offer some sort of program that will pull money from your bank account every month to invest in stocks or mutual funds that you designate. By setting aside $50 or $100 or $500 in this way, saving becomes a habit. You don't notice the money is missing. It's a regular expense that becomes incorporated into your budget.

NOW WHAT?

That's all there is to it. Really. The most difficult part of this process is deciding where to open an account. Set aside an hour or two some Saturday morning to explore your options over a cup of coffee. With some research, you should be able to find a company and program that fits your place in life.

I always believed opening a retirement account is difficult. "Besides," I thought, "I don't have money to invest." Last year I forced myself to find the time and the cash to open a Roth IRA, and it has been one of the best financial decisions I've ever made. My account balance is small, but I love to watch it grow! For more great ideas on how to grow your retirement fund, check out GetRichSlowly.org.

— **J. D. Roth**

How (and Why) to Start an Investment Club

Would you like to be on the same financial page with a group of people? Meet regularly with like-minded and fun individuals, and collectively learn about and discuss new financial concepts? Are you tired of labored conversation at dinner parties, where any topic that touches on money is frowned upon?

Then joining or starting an investment club may be just what the doctor ordered!

Investment clubs take on many forms, from those who pool their money and invest collectively, to more social meeting forums where guest speakers are regularly invited to entertain and enlighten. Some

clubs focus on each member's individual financial plan with an eye toward putting everybody's head together and suggesting ideas for improvement, and yet others allow members to maintain relative financial anonymity, focusing instead on broader financial concepts.

Given the wide range of clubs and activities available, here are a few guidelines if you want to start an investment club of your own.

1. Find some friends

The underlying tone of all investment clubs is a social one, so it is imperative that you enjoy the company of the other members! You don't necessarily need to know them all well—having friends recruit new members and accepting referrals can be quite effective—but you have to start somewhere.

Are you a new mom? Getting together with other new moms to form an investment club is a great way to socialize, and to learn about financial concepts that apply to your specific demographic.

Or maybe over drinks you and some other business owners in your association tend to chat about money matters. Here is another like-minded group of people you could formalize the process with.

There is something to be said for attracting members with different backgrounds, too. The more diverse your club membership is, the more each person can bring to the table. So although everybody may have the common bond of being a new mom, colleague, or fellow business owner, hopefully there are also elements of diversity built in.

The way in which members must be on the same page, though, is with regard to financial philosophy. If one or two members only want to discuss short-term trading, and others want to discuss retirement plans or insurance, there will only be friction and disappointment on somebody's part.

2. Plan the meeting, and stick to an agenda

Ideally somebody can offer up their home or has a line on a quiet place to meet, where interruptions will be minimal and people can linger. Planning a meeting around food is always a great icebreaker, and sharing food tends to open people up to new ideas and conversation. Depending on the group size and dynamic, you can reserve a private room in a restaurant and all pitch in to have it catered, or everybody can simply bring a dish of something over to a member's house for sharing.

Even though you may be well-versed friends, this is a social gathering with a purpose, and that precedent must be set right from the beginning. Formalize the meeting process, and you will be less likely to get off track, both during each meeting, and on the whole.

Here is how the first meeting could look:

- Open the meeting.
- Discuss what investment topics the club wants to focus on, and the format each meeting will have. For example, will you invite knowledgeable guest speakers to present to the club each week, or invite each member to research and discuss a topic, or collectively focus on a certain type of investment or style of investing? Also, are you interested in the same financial topics?
- Query each member as to what they hope to get out of the club.
- Vote on all decisions with a show of hands.
- Elect club officers. This may be unnecessary if you want nothing more than an informal social gathering, but will be required if you take legal steps to lodge investments together.
- Define each member's responsibilities. When electing club

officers this is especially important, but even in an informal setting, saddling everybody with some form of responsibility will increase the club's overall chances of success.

- Set regular meeting times, locations, and miscellaneous details.
- Choose a club name.
- Vote on any necessary decisions with a show of hands.
- Close the meeting.

Subsequent meeting agendas will hinge on the results of the first meeting, and it is equally important that an agenda be set forth for each meeting, and ideally that it remain the same every time. Formalizing a meeting doesn't have to make it dull. It simply keeps things moving and creates a set of expectations that each member can rely on.

This is just enough information to get your club off its feet and into infancy. Where you go from here varies according to the membership, desired outcome, and the format decided upon.

Here are a few Web resources for you to research investment club topics and formats, or even to find an existing club to join: Investment Club Central (iclub.com) and The National Association of Investors Corporation (betterinvesting.org). — **Nora Dunn**

HOUSING & HOME IMPROVEMENT

$

Renters, owners, and couch-crashers all have one thing in common: They need a place to put their feet up at the end of the day. With mortgage concerns and the rising costs of keeping a home safe and comfortable, it may seem like too large of a responsibility for some. We feel that with the right guidance and a little inspiration, anyone can contribute positively to the household budget. This chapter will give you the straight talk about living large in any housing market.

12 Ways to Become Rent- or Mortgage- Free

Trying to reduce your monthly overhead? One of the most significant line items for anyone (in addition to groceries and transportation) is the cost of physically having a roof over your head. Following are a dozen suggestions for making this recurring monthly expense virtually disappear.

Some are immediate, others require more time and discipline. All require compromise and responsibility. But . . . and here's the important thing—they all work. If you are willing to do some work, being rent- or mortgage-free can happen for you . . . probably faster than you might think.

. . . .

1. House-sitting

. . . .

This is probably the most immediate method with the least amount of cash outlay. Normally, you are required to pay utilities, provide your own transportation (although depending on the location, this is not always necessary to have), and pay the cost of actually getting yourself there if you are not already in the neighborhood. Aside from a possible ticket or distance-driving cost, the costs you are expected to pay are ones you'd be incurring anyway. This is a good idea for responsible people who have experience being completely in charge of pet and home care. If you are looking to find a cool pad in Paris for 24/7 partying, keep looking. You won't find it on this circuit. Authors and people whose income is not dependent on a particular location are also ideal house-sitting candidates, as are retirees and mature, responsible travelers.

. . . .

2. House swap

. . . .

This option is more for those who already own a home outright, and would like the benefit of having another place to visit that they do not have to take out a mortgage for. Retired or semiretired individuals are very well suited to this option. Again, responsible individuals only need apply. You wouldn't want your house trashed by a group of derelicts, and nobody else wants their home abused either. Be considerate.

3. Buy a multiple-unit dwelling

There's a reason this strategy is popular . . . someone else is paying your mortgage. It doesn't get any better than that. Ideally, you'll want a positive cash flow with the building so that the loss of a job or family health crisis does not have to mean the loss of a roof over your head. However, even if you only break even, you are still not paying rent. Of course, upkeep is still yours, as are any insurance considerations. This is a great way for young people with good credit but lower income to get into the game and start moving ahead. Word to the wise: Whenever we have looked into these income buildings in the past the rule of thumb we were given was that anything up to a four-plex was considered residential, which means that you'll get the residential rate when borrowing money. Five units and above fall into the commercial category, so you'll get charged higher interest rates.

4. Use your job's housing allowance

If your job comes with a housing allowance (and many do), purchase a house in a price range that will cause the payments to fall within your monthly allotment. If possible, try to purchase in an area with great annual value increases. When the time comes, sell the house. If you have a profit (and most likely you will if you shopped wisely to begin with), great. If not, and you just break even, at least you'll get a retroactive reimbursement of your living expenses. Yes, you have to wait for the return on this. And yes, you have to shop wisely up front. But how many landlords have you rented from who will refund your rent after you move out?

5. Pay cash

Yes, this can be done. Granted, for those without a trust fund (which is most of us), it requires the advance use of strategies such as numbers 1–4, but it *is* achievable. If you've been saving for a while and your income is not dependent on a particular location, consider purchasing a more rural property. You can oftentimes get more bang for your real estate buck this way, and actually have a shot at things you want early on in the game. Maybe not the first purchase of a home, but certainly by the second it is possible to get things like more acreage, waterfront, or a small hobby farm type of property for the kids to enjoy.

6. Live in a yurt

Contrary to the belief of uninformed individuals, these structures are *way* above tepee status, and there are modern versions that you can use in all climates, however extreme. They aren't all pitch dark and made out of goat hair, either. We're talking French doors, roll up walls, lots of windows, insulated enough to work in extreme northern climates or open enough to be plunked in the tropics. I've seen them with baby grand pianos, full bathrooms, fireplaces, full kitchens, Internet, electricity—the works. The Cadillac versions might run closer to twenty-five grand, but there are many ways to get started for much less than that. This would enable you to pay it off very quickly and start saving for a home. These structures leave a very low ecological footprint as well. Many people choose to live in them permanently, while others use them after the home is up as a studio or guest house. A bonus is you can pack the whole darn thing up and ship it to another location if you find things aren't working out well for you where you are. You'll just need to find a new parking spot for your home.

7. Consider a Quonset hut

These will cost you a bit more than an actual yurt, and they are far from a traditional form of housing. That being said, I have seen them done on the interior in a style that those comfortable with the loft look could probably go for. You could also consider it a place to have an apartment in a loft section of the building and a garage underneath. Then you could plan to have this as a garage with a rental once a larger structure went up. Although, some people dig these things enough to make their permanent home.

8. Stay in a shipping container

There has been much talk on the news lately about using these things to create alternative, eco-friendly housing. Some of them, however, cost closer to half a million dollars. If that is your budget, good for you. If not, there are much more affordable ideas out there that even include a shaded carport.

9. Part time caretaking

There are many options available for this. Searching the newspapers in your area for people in need of a little handyman work in exchange for rent is a place to start. International housesitting organizations are another. In addition to the house-sitting option listed first, many places need people to tend their lodge or working guesthouse while they travel abroad or tend to family issues. There are even people who love their remote larger estates yet have to travel and need people to stay there and make sure the pool guy can get in and that their dogs receive all the affection they need. Rough, right? As with the other home-sharing and -sitting options, though, responsible individuals only need apply.

10. Pay-as-you-go construction

This can be a long, time-consuming process depending on your current income level. Be prepared to suck it up with some seriously extreme frugality options when it comes to your lifestyle, but there's no reason all the renovation and remodeling needs to be done all in one shot.

11. Buy small, pay off early

The smaller the mortgage, the more rapidly you have a chance to pay it off. Go with a shorter mortgage, making extra payments at least once a year. This can happen very quickly if you are disciplined. After the payoff, you can enjoy where you are without overhead, or take any profit from the sale to pay cash for your next place if the market affords you that option.

12. Anchors away

For those of you who haven't explored the living-on-a-boat option—

it's come a long way. Go with a small houseboat, or purchase a larger out-of-service barge from a ship broker and have the whole thing converted into a floating loft. This is a great way to get waterfront living ability in places a young professional might not otherwise be able to afford. Think of every posh waterfront city you might want to live in and thought you could only drool over the possibility. You'll need a bit of cash up front for this option, but that amount can flex depending on the type of vessel you buy. I've also seen time-shares of these living spaces sold for certain times of year when the owners travel. It's a way to get back your cost fairly quickly if you are moored in an expensive location. If you are willing to think outside of the box, you can get a really cool place this way. You can also have these towed to a new location if you get sick of your current one.

So there you have it—twelve ways to gain independence from the traditional rent and mortgage scene. Some may seem extreme. Some may take a tiny bit longer than you had hoped. Let me say this: I never promised you a rose garden. Financial independence does not come without serious self-discipline and at least certain periods of self-sacrifice. Be prepared to "suck it up" financially. That being said, financial independence in many cases can be achieved in less than 10 years, and in some, less than 5.

It all boils down to personal choice and priorities. Would you rather live large in small bursts for the rest of your life (or at least until old age), or have the power to completely check out of societal expectations and live large full-time at a younger age? Only you can answer that question, and the answer is different for all of us, as is the financial path and method. But if you are serious about removing rent and mortgage overhead, the twelve methods mentioned above should give you some ideas for where and how to start. — **Myscha Theriault**

20 Tips for Getting Your Security Deposit Back

Although most of my landlords have been really great, I did have one a couple of years back who pulled the security deposit trick on all her tenants.

Before moving out, I cleaned that apartment from top to bottom, bleaching the mold that formed in the closets (it was there when I moved in, and I battled it monthly), relining the cupboards with that stick-on liner so they were clean and fresh-looking. My boyfriend helped me to repair a shelf that had completely collapsed in the closet. I never wear shoes in the house, so the carpet was spotless.

When I left, I somehow managed to forget a bicycle tire on my balcony, a spare tire that I had been meaning to patch. The balcony was so moldy and terrifying that I rarely stepped out on it, and simply forgot that the tire was there.

I was charged $75 for its disposal. And that's *on top of* the nonrefundable cleaning service.

This wasn't exactly a swanky neighborhood in which tire disposal services run at a premium. We're talking about a musty apartment only one block from the area of town known as Crack Whore Row. And it was a *bicycle* tire, not a car tire complete with wheel and hubcap. I was pissed off that I forgot it, because I could have used it, but I didn't have the energy to fight the landlord over the charge. I wish I had, because it was completely bogus. But I didn't fight the charge, even though I now know I should have raised a stink over it.

Since then, though, I've learned a few things. Here are 20 tips for getting your security deposit back.

BEFORE YOU MOVE IN:

1. Google the leasing company, landlord's name, property name, whatever. See if you are dealing with people who are on the up and up. Check the Better Business Bureau's online business listings (BBB.org) for the leasing company's name (ask the landlord if they have a relationship with the BBB). The landlord that charged me $75 to throw away a bicycle tire had an awful Web reputation—had I known that, I might never have rented the place to begin with.

WHEN YOU MOVE IN:

2. Read your lease carefully. Understand everything that is contained therein. Note that *leases are not set in stone.* You can actually make alterations to them—nothing ridiculous—but if you find something in the lease that you find unreasonable (like being required to give two months' notice when you plan to leave), you can alter it, cross it out, or make additions to it.

3. Your landlord *should* give you a checklist of rooms and ask you to detail the condition of each one. If they don't, make one up yourself. Notice any damage that exists already (*dings in wood, cupboards that don't close properly*). This can be extremely tedious, so make an evening of it. Invite some friends over for a few bottles of wine (or beer) and walk around the apartment, critiquing the hell out of it.

4. If you have a digital camera, take pictures of every room, every blemish.

5. When you have gathered all of this info, written and photographic, do a walk-through with the landlord and make sure that they sign off on the list. Mail them printouts of the photos and the

room-by-room description (make sure to send the letter certified mail), and let them know that if they don't do the walk-through with you within two weeks of receiving the info, you will assume that they have signed off on your assessment.

WHILE YOU LIVE THERE:

6. For goodness' sake, try to be clean. Get to stains before they set. Bug-bomb the apartment if you get some kind of nasty bug infestation. If you have pets, clean the place constantly, get an air filter, open the windows, and clean up any mess as soon as you find it. Nothing is more terrifying for a landlord than walking into an apartment and seeing that your 13 cats have made the place damn near unlivable.

7. If you have a problem with any part of the apartment, if something breaks from normal wear and tear, the landlord is obliged to pay for it. If they don't, and you opt to fix it yourself (I had to replace a broken toilet seat and the bathtub caulking), take a picture of the before and after and add it to your notes, including the cost of replacing the item.

Bill the landlord for the item ASAP. If the landlord tries to bilk you later, you have more evidence of what a responsible tenant you were.

WHEN YOU LEAVE:

8. Whether or not you clean the place really depends on if you already paid a nonrefundable cleaning deposit. I have never lived anywhere that didn't require me to pay a cleaning deposit. So I'll clean up anything egregious, but the rest of the place, I leave broom-clean. If you haven't already paid a nonrefundable cleaning deposit, clean the bejesus out of the place.

9. Do the whole picture thing again. Make sure that the landlord does a walk-through with you, and have them sign an agreement that you have left the apartment in fair condition. Don't feel like a jerk for doing this. You have the right to protect your money and yourself.

10. Don't assume that a super-nice landlord equals a returned security deposit. Be wary of everyone and don't let something slip just because you think the landlord really likes you.

IF A LANDLORD TRIES TO BILK YOU:

11. If a landlord tries to hold on to your money, demand an itemized list of the withheld money. Scrutinize it for redundancy. For instance, a landlord can't charge you to clean a carpet and then replace a carpet.

12. Also, when it comes to replacing things, you probably aren't responsible for the entire cost of replacement, unless whatever needs replacing is brand-new and you completely destroyed it.

   For example, the useful life of carpeting is generally considered to be seven years. So, if the carpet was brand-new when you moved in, and you ruined it, you're liable for new carpet. On the other hand, if the carpet was five years old when you moved in, and six years old when you moved out, you should only be liable for the amortized value of the carpet. Assuming you *are* responsible for damaging the carpet and it only had one year of useful life left, you should only be on the hook for about 15% of the replacement cost.

   Same goes with paint: Was the paint brand-new when you moved in? If not, you shouldn't be paying the full cost of a new paint job.

13. Let's say you get a bill from the landlord, and they are withholding most of your deposit for made-up charges. What do you do? Know your rights. Every state has different laws regarding just how much leeway both renters and landlords are given. Do check your state Attorney General Web site (naag.org) to see what kinds of protections are afforded to you.

14. If you think that the charges are bogus, raise a (polite) fuss. A crooked landlord is going to hope that you simply roll over and let them take your money because so many people do just that. Let them know that you believe the charges to be bogus.

15. Write your complaints down in the form of letters and send copies to an attorney, even if you don't plan to hire an attorney. Send them to your uncle the tax attorney, if you have to. I have a friend who works as an office manager in a law firm that I can send CCs to, if I need to. I address them to her, and she tears them up. Seeing a law firm's name is often enough to get people to back down, because no one wants to deal with a lawyer.

16. Don't let the landlord make you feel petty. If they try say some-

thing like, "It's only $100!" ask them why it's so important for them to take such a small sum away from you.

17. Keep as much of the communication in writing as possible. Oral agreements (and disagreements) simply don't offer enough proof.

18. Be respectful in all of your communication. You might want to say "You cheap, cheap bastard! I lived in this ratty @#*$ for two years and never complained about the @#$* conditions!" but you always come off better if you are polite and well-mannered. If you do have to go to small claims court, judges will look askance at written proof of your rudeness.

19. If you do decide to take a landlord to small claims court, if only to fight what you see as injustice (and keep in mind that if you win, you might be able to get your court fees paid for), do let them know ahead of time. This might avoid the hassle of actually going to court. However, don't make empty threats. Be prepared to litigate if you threaten to do so.

20. If you don't get your money back, do make sure to publicize your experience. Be reasonable, but if you truly believe that you were screwed over, let other people know. Use a site like Citysearch.com or Yelp.com to enter information about the property to warn other potential renters. Make sure that you don't exaggerate or do anything that could be construed as libel.

— **Andrea Dickson**

How to Avoid 10 Costly DIY Mistakes

I love DIY. I'm completely awful at it, but as I'm thrifty I'd much rather do something myself than pay someone else three times as much to do it. But here's the rub: You can end up costing yourself more in the long run by doing it yourself. So, I scoured the Web looking for the obvious and not-so-obvious mistakes DIY addicts make and compiled this list.

. . . .

1. Cheap tools, no tools, the wrong tools

. . . .

You can start a job thinking you have all the right equipment, but hammering a nail in with the back of your shoe ain't gonna cut it. Neither is that nifty saw you got in the $1 store with less teeth than your granny. Do yourself a favor: If you're going to DIY, buy quality tools like the pros, and research your job fully so you have all the right tools for the particular job at hand.

2. The Superman (or Wonder Woman) syndrome

You ever meet one of those people who could do everything better than you? They're the same people who think they can build an entire house in one weekend with no help from anyone else. This is known as working beyond your scope. If you can't do plumbing, don't do plumbing. If you're rotten with heights, avoid the roof. Don't think that you can stand on tiptoes on the top rung of a rickety old ladder and think you'll always be safe. One day you'll be telling your DIY story in the ER. According to the U.S. Consumer Product Safety Commission, ladder mishaps land over 164,000 people in the emergency room each year. So, if electrical work happens to be your Kryptonite, steer clear.

3. Permits? What permits?

Permits aren't there to just be a pain in your butt. They have a real purpose, and it's in your best interest. Those folks in the permit office are there to make sure the job is done right and that you don't go hurting yourself or anyone else. They also ensure that when you do an improvement, your insurance carrier has the necessary paperwork to keep you covered. Don't quite know if you need one? Well, unless you're just giving a lick of paint or new layer of paper to the guest room, chances are you'll need one. If in any doubt, call your local building department.

4. Saving a few too many bucks on materials

I love a bargain, too. But make sure you know where to draw the line. Quarter-inch inch drywall may save you a fortune, but it's about as effective as a pair of curtains for soundproofing. You'll need ¾-inch for a good sound barrier. And flooring is the same story; ¾ plywood is your best friend when it comes to keeping the noise down and giving you a strong foundation. So, crack open the piggy bank. Do the job once, do it right, and do it with quality materials. (Of course, if you can haggle over the cost of those materials, you're being a true Wise Bread shopper . . . go for it.)

5. Ummmmm, that's close enough

My pop is a great DIY dude. He told me something that was not exactly original, but I never forgot it. "Measure twice, cut once." And you know what I'm talking about if you've ever cut anything to length only to realize that you measured at 18¼ instead of 18¾. Bang. Your money is down the drain. So, always, always err on the side of making something a bit too long. It's much easier to cut down than build up. So, remember—Measure twice, cut once on anything from drywall to plumbing pipes and crown molding.

6. Duct tape for life

In my short DIY career, I've done the occasional plumbing repair with duct tape. It's handy stuff. But it's not a repair—it merely buys you a little time. If you're walking out of the door to catch a flight for your two weeks

in Hawaii, duct tape could very well save your bacon. But it's *not* permanent. It *will* leak, as sure as night follows day. So, get it fixed as soon as you possibly can. And if plumbing is not your thing, get a pro to do it. Water damage can cost thousands and thousands of dollars in repairs.

7. Rushing the prep work before painting

When I first started painting my house, I jumped straight in. Yippee. But I spent more time cleaning up my many mistakes, spills, drips, runs, and shoddy lines than I did painting. Do yourself a favor; do the prep. Clean your walls, patch up holes with good filler, and use a good painter's tape for windows, doors, ceiling lines, and anything else that you don't want paint on. Lay down a good-quality tarp that you can use again, and set a primer on oil-based paint or dark walls you're painting a lighter color. You'll thank yourself later.

8. Any paint will do

Sorry, it won't. You don't want a flat paint on anything other than a ceiling (put it in a kid's room and watch what happens when you try scrubbing off the crayon and marker pen). Go for eggshell or satin finishes on interior walls, as they can resist a lot of washing. Exterior paint is clearly marked and weatherproof. And for your deck, use a linseed-oil-based stain. Unlike clear sealers (which don't block UV rays), the linseed stains drive the pigment deep into the wood and preserve it.

9. What could possibly go wrong?

How about everything? Safety is essential when working on any DIY project, and even if you look like a dope, you need to wear the right equipment. Safety goggles are vital when operating power tools, and hard hats are equally as important when working under scaffolding. If you're painting or using harsh chemicals, open a window or two to keep the area well ventilated. If you're a big fan of those baggy carpenter jeans and old, loose T-shirts, you may want to rethink them. Loose clothing can get caught up in power tools and machinery and the results are none too pretty. Of course, wear a good pair of gloves for carrying wood, metal, rock, or anything else sharp or abrasive. If you're in the basement, follow the safety rules regarding spiders and other dangerous critters (black widows and brown recluses love basements…and one bite can do major damage).

10. A little knowledge is a dangerous thing

A lot of folks just dive right in on home projects. They've seen a *Bob Vila* show or two, they borrowed a book from the library, and they think they're good to go. That is, until the new addition collapses under their feet. Don't start on your own projects by yourself, and don't start big. If you know someone who happens to be good at this stuff, tag along. They'll be happy for the extra pair of hands on their own project and you're getting valuable experience. Places like Lowe's and Home Depot offer workshops. Take them—they're fun and educational. And when you eventually do start your own little remodeling project, listen to the voice of reason. If you really don't feel 100% sure about what you're doing, step back. You don't want to knock through a supporting wall and end up in traction. — **Paul Michael**

12 Small-Space Survival Strategies

While living in a smaller space can be a great way to simplify your life and reduce overhead costs, the process of reducing and cramming our worldly possessions into drastically reduced square-footage allotments can be frustrating to say the least. Here are a dozen ways to survive in a small space without completely losing your mind.

1. Under-shelf storage space use

You can really get some storage mileage here by hanging things underneath every available shelf with extra space on the bottom side. In the kitchen, this means more room for coffee mugs, cooking utensils, and the odd gravy boat. In the bathroom, it can mean moving hair dryers and curling irons out of storage space better used for bulk tissue and shampoo purchases.

2. Closet organizers

Lots of products are out there on the market now. Pick ones that work for your space and budget. You'll be amazed how much more you can cram into a small closet with a few extra organizational tools.

3. Ceiling racks

The most dramatic difference I've ever found with ceiling storage (in addition to the extra pots and pans storage in the kitchen) is in the garage or workshop-type rooms. Cruise your local home improvement box store. You'll find all sorts of support racks to hold holiday decorations, bicycles, lawn tools, and more.

4. Group containers in larger containers

This can mean large freezer bags, giant jars, or clear plastic storage bins with snap-on lids. How much easier is it if all the extra cord adapters, for example, are in one clear bag in a drawer rather than all tumbling about mixed in with other things? This also works for such items as flavored baking extracts, nail polish bottles, twist ties and bread tabs, etc. One thing we've been using for the first time this year is those galvanized steel rectangular bins that look like the old-fashioned pullout locker drawers. You can find them in the organizational aisle at your home improvement store. Following the container principle can help you feel organized instead of cluttered.

5. Wall storage

You can use anything from peg board and hooks to specialized hanging racks from the home and garden store. DIY shelving is another great idea to use up wall space to its maximum. Wall storage is extra efficient because it incorporates the "go vertical" strategy, which leaves you way more room to actually move around.

6. Pare down

It's amazing how many things we have that we don't actually need. Sell, give away, or just throw out things that do nothing but take up space.

7. Use even small spaces

There may not seem to be a lot of space between your countertop and the bottom of the cupboards, but there's room enough for a towel bar and S-hooks to hang necessary kitchen items within easy reach.

8. Like in, like out principle

If a new item comes into the house, like a sweater or souvenir coffee mug, make sure something similar goes out. Take it to the recycling center, Goodwill, a friend, or if necessary to the dump. This will keep you from reestablishing clutter after you have put forth the effort to downsize.

9. Under the bed

This storage real estate is underused much of the time. It's no place to push aside junk you don't know what to do with, but it works very well as an efficient and useful storage space.

10. Corner organizational tools

There are many options to maximize corner spaces. Corners are often not used to their maximum efficiency, and any affordable organizing tools can be worth their weight in gold for the small-space dweller.

11. Small-space furniture

There are tons of items out there that are multifunctional when it comes to storage. Ottomans, chairs, coffee tables with lift-off tops and storage compartments, end tables and day beds with rolling storage baskets underneath—these are all items that get you more bang for each square foot.

....
12. Open up . . . your floor
plan, that is
....

Extra rooms can really result in a great deal of unused space. While this is of no concern to most people anyway, it's of particular note when dealing with small homes. Poorly planned closets and pass-through halls can seriously cut down on your usable square feet.

— **Myscha Theriault**

How to Get Rid of Your Junk

Are you barely able to breathe in your cluttered household? Have tons of stuff that you need to get rid of? Many times the process of uncluttering is stopped short for emotional reasons. Here are some popular ones:

I PAID SO MUCH FOR IT!

Yes, but are you getting your money's worth from it? If you are not using that antique dresser, and it's just collecting dust and spiderwebs, sell it. Ignore the *Antiques Roadshow* fantasies.

I HAVE SENTIMENTAL ATTACHMENT TO IT.

This is my biggest problem. See step 4 on page 276.

SOMEONE ELSE WILL BE ANGRY IF I SELL IT / GIVE IT AWAY.

The best way to deal with gifts that are no longer providing you with use or pleasure is to contact the giver. Let the giver know that you are trying to simplify your life, and that although you appreciate the thought that went into the gift they gave you, you simply aren't using it. You can ask if they would like it back, or if they have any input as to what you should do with it. This can be a difficult proposition, but many people appreciate the honesty. The other option is to get rid of it and just tell them that you broke it if they ever ask, but it's easier in the long run to be up-front when dealing with friends and family.

MY CHILDREN WILL EVENTUALLY WANT IT.

Keep in mind that what you like now isn't necessarily going to coincide with what your children will want 20 years from now. Ask your children if they will eventually want that set of brandy glasses, and check back every couple of years to see if they are still interested. I am the not-so-proud owner of a monstrous set of big, fake plastic grapes glued to a piece of driftwood that I *loved* as a child. They belonged to my grandmother, and I used to think they were magical. Now, I can't think of anything to do with them, short of launching them into the ocean using a homemade trebuchet.

BUT THIS IS A POTENTIAL HEIRLOOM!

So you may think. If you believe you are the owner of an object of heirloom quality, get it appraised and store it properly. Many of the things that you consider heirloom quality might not be, although an heirloom doesn't necessarily have to have monetary value. Also, you might want to consider the possibility that you may have a potential heirloom that nobody wants. My grandmother left me a gigantic, gaudy 1970s gold ring with a giant amethyst in the middle, knobs of twisted gold, and lots of little diamonds around the sides. I appreciated the value of the gift,

if not the aesthetic, and so I had a jeweler melt it down and make three different pieces of classical, timeless jewelry out of it. That way, one ugly item became three different pieces of jewelry that I can hand down to my children.

IT'LL BE WORTH SO MUCH MONEY SOMEDAY!

This might be true. But although collections can be fun to keep, if your entire house is consumed by boxed action figures a la *The 40-Year-Old Virgin*, you may want to consider paring down. If collectibles are getting in the way of your everyday living, selling some of them off now will save you years of annoyance, which is worth a bit of money. You can invest that money and watch it grow, and it will grow faster than the value of the baseball card / action figure / porcelain doll, without a doubt.

Once you've broken down the mental wall of letting go of junk, here are some tactics to actually help you sort through it.

....

1. Start small, with one closet or one corner of a room.

....

Set realistic goals and pace yourself. Try using an egg timer to set 15-min-

ute intervals. If this is the first time in many, many years you will be going through your things, you may need to schedule an hour or two once a week. Parting with junk you've had for years can be tough, so don't overtax yourself. It's not just about the time and effort. It can be an emotional journey.

2. Label three boxes *KEEP, UNDECIDED,* and *TOSS.*

Divide your junk into these boxes. This isn't just for the once-every-few-years major clearing. Keep these boxes accessible so that you are constantly maintaining your clutter-free lifestyle. I actually use KEEP, DONATE, and TOSS, because I like to make my decisions straight away.

3. Resist the urge to walk through memory lane.

Don't look through the photo albums, yearbooks, and memory boxes of old letters and postcards during the first round. Put them in the *KEEP* box and go through them at a later date.

4. Deciding what to get rid of is hard, but it must be done.

We often hold on to things that simply *remind* us of a nice memory. If you bought a useless trinket from your wonderful trip to Paris, take a picture of it to put with the other photos you must have taken on that trip. You don't need to keep the trinket.

Here are some guidelines for determining how to get rid of something:

1. Does this item bring you joy or serve a useful purpose in your life?

Yes = Keep, but decide how to use it more effectively. No = See step 2.

2. Would a photo of the item be sufficient to help you recall fond memories of a person, place, or time?

Yes = Take picture, get rid of item. No = Get rid of item.

Now that you've gone through the process of deciding what you want to get rid of, what are your disposing options?

- Give it to a friend or relative.
- If it's a large object, put it outside with a FREE sign (some cities have laws against this).
- Post it on freecycle.org.

- Recycle it (there are many places you can drop off your old electronics for recycling).
- Call a junk removal firm.
- Sell or trade it (have a yard sale or sell online).
- Take it to Goodwill.
- If nothing else, toss it.

You'll probably be surprised how much stress is relieved by parting with your junk. It can be hard to part with things that you've owned for a while, but frankly, any potential monetary sacrifice can be compensated for by having a clean, livable abode. When they say that you can't take it with you, they aren't kidding.

— **Andrea Dickson**

Biggest Money-Saving Tip: Move Far Away from the Joneses

I have to admit that while many people in the U.S. talk about "keeping up with the Joneses," I spent the first 20 years of my life never knowing what that meant. My rural lifestyle kept me somewhat content with the things I had. I quickly learned, however, that being "well-off" has a lot to do with "location, location, location."

My first abrupt introduction into material desire came when I moved to the city. Living there the first two years, I never really felt I needed more. My friends and I all had clean apartments, enough food to eat, and extra cash for the occasional concert or party. I bought CDs when I wanted to, kept a pager, and wouldn't hesitate to buy a sweater on clearance at the outlet mall. I felt like I was really living the life, and my friends in the restaurant business felt the same.

After landing a very nice job at an insurance-related company, I was slowly seeing the world in a new way. Sweaters became suits, my pager was traded up for a cell phone, and $2 taco dinners at the dive down the street gave way to $9 wings at the upscale brewery. Even my car (which I adored) was feeling the pressure of this faster, more expensive social circle. (I remember telling my new coworkers about my Dodge Charger. They ran outside to see it, envisioning some souped-up *Dukes of Hazzard* lookalike to be waiting there. Their disappointed faces told me that 1982 was *not* the year for that particular model. We took my friend's pre-owned, two-year-old Lexus to lunch after that.)

My new coworkers were not shallow. They just had grown up differently than I had. I grew up wearing the same pair of jeans for as many years as it took to wear out the knees. When they became too worn or outdated to wear in public, I threw them on to work in the garden or do farm chores (which consumed much of our time). Nothing was done away with simply because there was a newer, slicker alternative on the market. My new coworkers, on the other hand, had always lived or worked in the city, came from homes with double incomes, and spent more time traveling than at home. While neither way was better, I was reeling from the new pressures.

I managed to appear on the outside that I was keeping up. I parked my car far away from the office building, made friends with the mailroom employees (who were younger and more easygoing), and planned my road back to a simpler lifestyle. Seven years after I moved away from my tiny rural town, I've moved back again.

Right away, I noticed that nothing much had changed. I recognized my neighbors right away, because they were still driving the car they drove when I was in junior high. *If it ain't broke, don't fix it.* Since it was largely still a farming community, no one gave me a second look when I popped into town with muddy tennis shoes and a tore-up baseball cap. I wondered what my old friends from work would have said.

And while I still keep in touch with my dearest pals from the city, the gap gets wider every year. They talk Mommy-and-Me classes and shoes, while I talk 0-point turning mowers and how much my kids enjoy pulling weeds. Do I see farmers in my community go overboard, being consumed by materialism and competing with their neighbors for a faster boat, bigger truck, and greener yard? Sure. But it is far easier to avoid the rat race when there's eight acres between myself and the next rat.

For some, it may be easy to keep your focus on just what you need, and moving away from temptation and pressure could seem like a cop-out. For me, it just made sense. There's a freedom in finding your geographical place in the world. Whether you're a city mouse, a country mouse, or an everywhere mouse, finding a place to settle in and be content for the moment is still the very best way to save money. — **Linsey Knerl**

Finding Your Home's Value the Quick and Dirty Way

I've learned how to divine home values by looking at public records and applying the methodology used by professional appraisers. I'll show you how to do your own public-records search, and explain why online home-valuation sites may or may not get the home-value number right.

Here are some ways of judging value:

- *Tax value* (which may be based on the price paid for the house 15 years ago, the home's replacement cost, or other factors)
- *Market value* based on the sales comparable approach (that is, comparing your house to homes that are comparable to yours in geography and construction, and then adding or subtracting value based on features and amenities, similar to the approach taken in HGTV's *My House is Worth What?*)
- *Replacement cost* less depreciation plus land value
- *Combination* of all of the above

Information can be gleaned from the following sources:

- Public records
- Aggregated public records mixed with mapping technology
- Site inspections combined with general knowledge of construction costs and market conditions

PUBLIC RECORDS

Public records are a gold mine of free information regarding tax values of individual homes as well as sales histories, privacy concerns notwithstanding. Your city or county will typically have these records, which are often accessible and searchable online. The most recent sales price, year of construction, square footage, number of bathrooms and bedrooms, zoning information, and more are often contained in these records. (Call your local government or do a search on real property or tax administration to find the records.)

Is there a political component to tax values? I think so. Higher home values can mean higher property taxes (depending on assessment rates) and more money in the public treasury. Except when, perhaps, there is a public disincentive to increasing property values, say in a neighborhood where the state or municipality intends to acquire properties (or has in the past) by exercising eminent domain. For example, when I reported over $40,000 in home improvements made by a licensed general contractor to my home (such as bringing the bathroom up to new building code, replacing vinyl flooring with ceramic tile, and ripping out pressed wood and installing maple cabinets), the tax assessor increased its value by $0.

I haven't complained, of course, and plan to resist asking for a revaluation until I put my house on the market; for now, there is a 60+% differential between my home's tax-assessed value and Zillow.com's.

REAL (CERTIFIED) APPRAISALS

Real appraisals are performed by licensed or certified appraisers, regulated at the state level. To get an idea of the information they gather and analyze (either through full-home inspections or drive-by inspections of single-family homes), check out the Uniform Residential Appraisal Report.

Appraisers should have an understanding of housing market trends, including sales activity relating to specific neighborhoods. Knowing the value of certain features and amenities (number of bedrooms and full baths, in-ground pools, decks, patios, two-car garages) is especially useful for calculating replacement costs and figuring out adjustments based on differences for sales comparables, which is often the focus of the appraisal.

SALES COMPARABLES

Appraisers find residential properties that are comparable to your house (the subject property). In a large suburban development, that's usually pretty easy because several houses of similar size and construction type will often sell each year; in a rural area, it's trickier because fewer houses may sell, and those that do sell will often differ greatly in size and amenities.

Next, the appraiser compares your house's features (age, condition, number of bedrooms, etc.) to the comps and calculates an adjusted sales price for each of the comps; from that information, he/she can develop a market value.

Appraisers may also consider the replacement cost of the home or use the income approach: estimated monthly rent x GRM (gross rent multiplier) to develop market values.

ONLINE HOME-VALUATION SITES

Sites such as Zillow.com, Eppraisal. com, and RealEstateABC.com aggregate public records and, with the help of mapping technology, develop a home value (or rather, a range of values) based on recent sale prices of nearby homes (but not necessarily ones that are comparable to yours). However, Real Estate ABC has an interactive feature that allows site users to select and deselect sales comparables (comps). In my case, I could keep the comps that were in my neighborhood of single-family homes and deselect the large homes with significant acreage and the condos less than a mile away. This approach, though

simplified, is most similar to methods used in a real appraisal.

APPRAISER BULLYING

When I was in the market for the house I own now, in the 1990s, a licensed real estate agent explained the appraisal process to me like this: The appraiser starts figuring the value of the house but stops when he/she gets to the contract (sales) price. I found her comments disturbing; technically, she was wrong, but she did reveal to me some gaps in the real estate sales-lending system. According to the Appraisal Standards Board, potential clients have made requests that are contrary to industry standards for real estate appraisal, such as:

"We need comps for (property description) that will support a loan of $_____; can you provide them?"

"Approximate (or minimum) value needed: _____."

"If this property will not appraise for at least _____, stop and call us immediately."

Making the appraisal = the sales price or loan amount is not a good idea, as the State of New York, First American, and Washington Mutual confirmed last year.

In regard to the pending nightmare awhile back, my husband and

I found ourselves selling a house that we had owned for less than six months due to a corporate relocation; we had bought the house at a moderate bargain because it had been on the market a while and sat a couple of doors down from a foreclosed home owned by a bank. But when our first pick for a real estate agent included our house in her sales comps (for a market analysis, not an appraisal), she saw a downward market trend and panicked. We quickly found a more enthusiastic and clear-thinking agent, who helped us to sell the home at a reasonable price within 30 days. Housing prices can rise and fall, but one transaction doesn't make a trend.

These tips should give you a good indication of your home's value until you are ready to get a certified appraisal. — **Julie Rains**

How to Find Savings in Every Room

I recently walked through the entire house with a pencil and paper, finding, quite literally, savings in ev-

ery room. Where I've found most of the savings opportunities are in the areas of consumable products and hard infrastructure. Here's a breakdown of where I found the savings opportunities, room by room.

THE BEDROOM
Overstock Sheets

Since we have relocated to the land of reasonable shopping opportunities, this was a bit easier to do. With access to Ross, Marshall's, and other discount overstock stores, we found great high-quality sheets that usually go for over $100 for under $40. Having three sets of sheets per bed is more than enough. It allows you to have one set in the laundry, one on the bed, and one clean backup set for an unexpected need.

Universal Bed Frames
They don't get much cheaper than this. We got one delivered with the

mattress set for under $50. What I love about these things is that they collapse down to a very transportable size for moving, and they save you the entire cost of a more elaborate bed frame. Throw on a bed skirt and toss up a hanging tapestry or some sort of DIY headboard.

DIY Linen Spray

While I love the idea of having a freshening spray for bed linens, curtains, and pillows, I don't see any reason to pay big bucks for this stuff. Pick up a spray bottle, add water, rubbing alcohol, and scented oil of your choice to create your own version of this product.

Custom Candle Containers

The super-large designer candles aren't cheap, and if you like to enjoy candles in your personal space as much as we do, they can be expensive to keep replacing. Create your own luminaries using tea lights and votive holders. Get a few reasonably large clear containers and fill with something decorative and affordable, such as beach sand and shells, glass beads, river rocks, or potpourri. Arrange the smaller glass votive holders inside the larger container. They will be supported by the filler you choose. Go nuts with your tea lights (which you can buy in bulk from places like Ikea).

THE BATHROOM
Multipurpose Dish Soap

You don't need to spend extra just to get a bottle labeled "toilet bowl cleaner" with a fancy nozzle to clean your toilet—that's what the brush is for. By switching from various different cleaning products to dish soap only, you can buy the dish soap in bulk, saving more per bottle.

Refillable Containers

One way I keep my sanity is to have certain things we use regularly at every single workstation where I might need them. For example, with lotions I like one by the kitchen sink, every bathroom sink, and a couple of other places like by the couch where I read and next to my side of the bed. While I'm definitely a buy-in-bulk girl, dishing out for that many giant bottles of lotion is simply unnecessary, not to mention space-hogging. Keep products in small containers around the house where you use them, and refill when necessary.

Multipurpose Shampoo

Like dish soap, shampoo is not a one-purpose item. In addition to its primary use, I use it as a shower gel, detergent for hand-washing delicate items, gentle face cleanser, bubble bath, and an add-in for homemade cleaning sprays.

THE LIVING ROOM / FAMILY ROOM

Skip the Facial Tissue

Sure, it's in a larger, more pleasant shape, but when you need something to handle a sneeze or running nose, a standard roll of toilet paper does the job just as well. If you think your inner decorating diva can't quite handle this, consider a decorative container, or keep it in a drawer in your end table.

Lose the Cable

It's never been as easy to live without cable. Between Netflix and free online viewing of most TV shows, there's no longer a strong case to drop $50 to $100 each month for cable. You don't even need a TV to watch television anymore—just a computer and Internet connection.

Budget Decorating

The living and family areas really do have a ton of potential for budget and DIY decorating integration. Upholstery scraps for new bar-stool seats, homemade throw pillows and stapled-on throw covers for stained yet comfortably stuffed sofas and love seats. A few small touches can make it look like you have brand-new furniture.

THE KITCHEN

DIY Dishrags

Got an old T-shirt or pair of sport socks that have seen better days? Sanitize them in the laundry and sacrifice them to the cause for a great way to keep it cheap and go green at the same time.

Multipurpose Homemade Spray Cleaner

Mix water with witch hazel, add a few drops of grapefruit seed extract and earth-friendly dish soap. You can also make other versions with vinegar or rubbing alcohol. You can find a variety of recipes online.

Go Generic

Don't have time to clip coupons or price-compare? Picking up generic store-brand items can easily shave 25% off your regular grocery total.

Keep Empty Bottles

When our juice bottles are empty, we keep them around for a bunch of things—to mix frozen juice in; use the bottom to make a toilet brush holder; use the top for a funnel. Why spend extra to purchase containers, when most things you buy come in one?

THE HOME OFFICE

Creative Desk Options

A funky old farm table with a comfy chair, a core door on top of some old filing cabinets, or a piece of plywood attached to a couple of sawhorses and painted black are all ways I've seen work-at-home desks done on the cheap.

Rubber Stamps

Skip the special-order address labels and save yourself the individual addressing time by picking up a return-address rubber stamp for your home office. Reusable, affordable, and simple.

Supplies

It's easy to go overboard on nice office supplies. Turn boxes inside out and re-tape for shipping. Wait for deals and rebates from the larger box office stores (and check their clearance boxes). When it comes to reusable items, you may have better luck at the thrift store than you think. Binders, clipboards, and desk organizers are all items I've found through those sources before.

THE YARD, PATIO, AND GARDEN

Composting

Save on potting soil and create your own "green gold" by trying your hand at composting. There are many options depending on the size of your yard, amount of trash you can use for composting, and your level of comfort. By reusing your trash, you reduce the amount you're contributing to the landfills.

Consider Rustic or Artsy

I'm referring to your landscaping style here. Twig arbors or DIY mosaic stepping-stones are all fun projects the entire family can enjoy participating in. It's also much easier to take your time with these designs and still have your yard looking kept up with a simple mow. Think rock accents and mossy walkways with wildflower accents.

Plant Functionally

A large tree will not only provide you with a comfortable shady spot to sit, but it can also lower energy costs inside the home. Plant greens that you like to eat, like herbs, fruit, and nuts. You'll have one less thing on your grocery list. — **Myscha Theriault**

11 Penny-Pinching Ways to Pimp Your Garage

When you open your garage door, does it look more like the room of doom than a place to park your car? Are holiday decorations taking up the corner where you can only dream of a humble workbench? It's time to put your garage back into good use. Here are 11 frugal garage-pimping tips.

. . . .

1. Ceiling racks

. . . .

These are a huge help and perfect for those items you only access seasonally, such as holiday decorations. They come in a variety of styles and save your wall space for those items you need access to on a more frequent basis.

. . . .

2. Peg board

. . . .

Available for cheap at your local home hardware store, this stuff is easily attached to wall studs, and can be loaded with hooks to keep your handy items in plain sight. Want to make sure the tools get placed back in the right place? Trace hammers and other tools in black marker exactly where they hang on the peg board. The outline will serve as a reminder to return the tool to its precisely allocated spot.

. . . .

3. Wall organizers

. . . .

Wire baskets, wall hanging units, and vertical bike racks all come to mind here. Basically, you just want all the precision storage you can get for those tougher-to-streamline storage categories.

. . . .

4. Rolling industrial shelves

. . . .

Industrial shelving is particularly well suited to the garage because of the abuse that anything in that room

is generally required to take. This is the kind of storage infrastructure that can take a licking and keep on ticking. Bonus? The wired version allows the bulk of the dust and debris to float directly down to the floor, making it easy to vacuum up.

. . . .

5. Keep everything off the floor

If you are following the tips above, this should be easy. Keeping everything off the floor via wired storage items and wall units makes routine pushbroom sweeping and power-vacuuming a breeze.

. . . .

6. Bins

For durability, pick up the galvanized steel ones. They are rectangular, can be stored easily, and are very affordable. Some ways to use them? Storing jump ropes, baseball, gloves, soccer balls, and sports equipment in general. Gardening paraphernalia would also be a good candidate for bin storage.

. . . .

7. Zones

One of the easiest ways to keep things from getting chaotic again is to keep all categories of items in their assigned zone. For example, all sports equipment, from volleyball nets to croquet to soccer balls should be stored in the same general area. Ditto for lawn and garden items, as well as workshop items and general tools. Having a zone system keeps frustration levels low and success rates high during retrieval and return. Side perk? No more volleyball nets on your soldering table or hammers tossed in with the football pads.

. . . .

8. Hang a neon Ping-Pong ball

If you are tired of having the car nick a work bench, use this marker to prevent a misjudgment in space. Pull the car in exactly where you want it parked. Then hang a bright-colored plastic Ping-Pong ball from a string attached to the ceiling. The trick is to hang the ball so it touches your windshield in a particular spot, like the center spot behind the rearview mirror or behind the inspection sticker. Your accidental paint dings from opening the vehicle door into the side of the lawn mower are a thing of the past.

. . . .

9. Padded workstations

If you have one or two workstations in your garage where you need to stand for extended periods of time, consider giving your joints a break with padded floor tiles. You don't need to do the entire room, just a rectangular space large enough to step around on a bit. Your back will thank you.

10. Power shopping for the man's man

Stocking a garage or workshop for home use can easily cost a small fortune. But by using simple power-shopping strategies and demonstrating a little patience, you can have what you need for much less. Cruise moving and estate sales, as well as flea markets and store models for things like shop vacuums, generators, snowblowers, air compressors, and more. It might take a bit longer, but so does saving up for the full-price version.

11. Customized drawer liners

I know we're focusing on the frugal alternatives for garage pimping, but if you do have a set or two of rolling tool cabinets (and they can be affordable from time to time), consider custom-cutting holes in a foam liner to keep expensive precision items in place and protected. This also serves the same purpose as outlining items on the peg board. You can also use the rubberized rolls of kitchen shelf lining material. It's affordable and ideal for those shallow drawers of items you don't want to have rolling around.

— **Myscha Theriault**

CAREER & MONEY-MAKING IDEAS

$

Unless you're an heir to a large, tax-free fortune, we know that you've probably had to work at least once in your lifetime. First jobs, part-time gigs, and lengthy careers are all options for the path to self-reliance, and we want to help you wherever you are. This chapter is designed to inspire ideas for earning cash, recovering from unemployment, scouting out that perfect new job, and having fun (yes, fun) in the process.

20 Signs that a Pink Slip Is Coming

There are two types of employees: One has a good idea of what they do, who they are, and what position they play in the company. They are savvy. They know the score. They are under no delusions, and will no doubt leave for another job long before they are ever considered as cannon fodder.

And then there's the other kind. The guy who could get Gandhi to hate him. The woman who spends most of her day chatting on the phone to friends or doing online shopping. Or the nice chap in Sales who is completely oblivious that the recent merger means his job is now obsolete. They all have Ostrich Syndrome. They couldn't see a pink slip coming if it was eight feet tall and glowing in the dark, screaming "You're fired!"

You want to avoid being in that second category at all costs, so I've compiled a handy list. If you can answer yes to three or more of these questions, you may want to think about sprucing up your résumé and dry-cleaning your best interview attire.

1. Are you no longer in the loop about, well, anything?

This is a huge telltale sign. Suddenly you're finding out about company news from the cleaning lady or the new girl in Accounting. If you were formerly in the know about all things business-related, but now suffer from "The company's doing what??!" disease, the writing is probably on the wall.

2. Did you recently screw up big-time?

We're not talking a minor faux pas here. Did you lose money on an account that was previously bullet-proof? Oh dear. Were you caught having sex on the boss's desk with the boss's spouse? That's probably not a career-enhancing move. Unless you're a real dope, you know if you have screwed up. And if you know, HR knows. It may not be the final nail in your coffin, but it's a nail in the coffin nonetheless.

3. Are people avoiding you at all costs?

Eye contact is difficult to make with someone if you know his or her head's on the chopping block. Small talk is just as tough. It's best just to avoid that person altogether. So if people are no longer doing that fun "stop 'n' chat" in the hall, or the coffee room empties when you arrive, then guess what—you may be a marked man or woman.

. . . .

4. Did your last performance review read like a train wreck?

. . . .

Most of the time, a performance review is a whole bunch of niceties. The boss really doesn't want to say anything *too* good, because everyone has room for improvement. But generally, they praise within reason and avoid anything too negative. So if your review paints you as a stupid version of Homer Simpson with less talent than a Backstreet Boy, well, that tap on the shoulder is coming.

. . . .

5. Has your company recently been sold or merged?

. . . .

This is rarely good news for about 90% of the staff. Sure, management is fine. After all, they negotiated the deal. But whether you were sold or merged, the outcome is the same . . . changes will be made across the board. A merger means duplication of many jobs. Duplication = redundancy. Being sold means new management, and they always have new plans for the company. New plans that include

cutbacks and layoffs. Basically, watch your back if there's a new name on the front door.

. . . .

6. Are you being given impossible jobs with no chance of success?

. . . .

This one is underhanded, which is why it's so popular. The company may need a big reason to give you the boot, especially if you've done everything right and are the life and soul of your department. Enter the impossible task. "Ahh, Wilkins, we need you to expand our new line of warm, alcohol-free beers to construction workers." "Johnson, how's that line of umbrellas doing in the new LA store?" You get the picture. If you've been given a thankless task, at least be thankful for the blatant tip-off that you're about to be let go.

. . . .

7. Do you now have less responsibility than the intern?

. . . .

Ouch. Being stripped of your responsibilities is a surefire sign that there's something unpleasant on the horizon. After all, you don't fire someone who's got a ton of important work to do, with loads of people underneath him/her. So, over time the poor sucker in management's sights will be given a new job title, less work, less people (or no people), and will eventually have a hard time finding anything of any real value to do all day. Not long after this, that same employee will be out on the street. In fact, if you're at work and have enough time to read this article, you may very well be in the firing line.

. . . .

8. Has your office, cubicle, or space been downsized?

. . . .

Remember poor old Milton in *Office Space* being moved from one small space to another, until he eventually sat in the dark, in the basement, dealing with pest problems? Well, this is not so far from the truth. When employees are in the firing line, it's a lot easier to move them around and downsize their environment without worrying about their morale. If you are reading this in your new 6 x 6-feet cubicle with no lights on a 1999 PC with a 200MB hard drive, you're not exactly a valued employee anymore.

. . . .

9. Do people whisper more, or does the conversation change as you approach?

. . . .

If you're marked for termination, you'll be the last one to know about it. And being the grown-up responsible people that they are, your coworkers will be quite happy to whisper about your impending doom in a dark corner of the coffee room. Until you show up, when suddenly the conversation will change abruptly to something really original . . . like the weather.

. . . .

10. Did you recently receive a pay freeze or cut?

. . . .

There are a few reasons this could happen; none of them are good. Either the company is in trouble and they need to cut costs, or you're in trouble and they don't want to pay you. If it's the first one, you may not necessarily be in immediate danger, but no one wants to work for a company that's going down the tubes (read *Who Moved My Cheese?* for more on that one). If it's the latter, well, your boss is basically telling you that you're about as welcome as a fart in an astronaut suit. Begin the job hunt immediately.

. . . .

11. Have you seen a job posting for your company that matches your job description?

. . . .

Human Resources can be crafty. They don't want to fire you without having someone waiting in the wings to immediately fill your shoes. That's why it's not uncommon to see your own job out on the Internet months before you actually get canned. Worse still (and this has happened to someone I know), they hire your replacement before you're fired and get *you* to teach the newbie how to do your job. Nice. Then they fire you.

....

12. Does everyone hate you? I mean, really dislike you with a passion?

....

If you're one of those people who are oblivious to this kind of question, please skip to #13. If you have a thread of common sense, read on. It's not an easy thing to face up to, but you can at least spot the telltale signs. Do you eat alone at lunchtime? Do people never laugh at your jokes? Can you clear a room faster than a pack of rabid pit bulls? If you're okay at your job but are just not popular, that will be seen as affecting morale. And morale is not something to mess with. Either shape up your attitude, or find a new job that maybe doesn't require you to work with people on a day-to-day basis.

....

13. Have you recently been asked to take some time off?

....

Let's face it. Companies in America are not prone to encouraging vacation time (compared to Europe, where they get oodles of time off). If it's not to use up vacation you're about to lose, or for a genuine reward for a huge project you've just finished, then you are in trouble. When the boss tells you to take a break, they're more than likely telling you that they'd rather not have you in the office. Maybe they'd like to talk about you behind your back (which is a lot easier when your back is in Tahiti). Maybe they need time to figure out how to can you. Either way, it's all a lot easier with you out of the picture. Time off = firing scenario.

....

14. Are you noticing paper trails between yourself and your superiors?

....

A quick word in your ear used to be just fine. A phone call was great. A stop 'n' chat in the hall was a regular occurrence. But now everything is happening via memos and e-mails. There's a reason for that. HR requires written/printed evidence of everything if there's to be a firing. A paper trail is necessary to determine that your boss did everything by the book, and to record every single one of your screwups. So, if you've gone from getting a few memos and e-mails a week, to a daily deluge of paper and a full in-box, these are warning signs that you're being watched very closely.

15. Are you finding it almost impossible to get approval or "buy-in" on projects?

Think back. A long time ago, people would green-light your projects faster than the Road Runner on amphetamines. But that's no longer the case. The boss is suddenly silent when it comes to approval. You're being passed around from middle manager to middle manager. You get voicemail 99% of the time you call someone for an opinion, and the other 1% it's their secretary . . . who then puts you through to voicemail. No one is going to green-light a project from someone whose time is up at that company. They don't want to associate themselves with the kiss of death that is your idea. If it happens to be a great idea, no worries—they'll take credit for it once you're gone. The silent treatment is a sure sign of pink-slip disease.

16. Have you recently been asked to work on a "special project"?

This could have many other names. "New company initiative" or "Confidential research assignment" are other known terms for this. But it basically comes down to one role: The project takes you away from *real* work and puts you on something that's either mildly important, not important at all, is going nowhere, or is just plain useless.

"Hey, Smith, how is that special project on frozen concentrated orange juice coming along?"

"Fine, sir. Can I ask what this has to do with the IT department?"

"Oh, you'll find out, Smith. You'll find out."

Rule of thumb: The second you are asked to leave a project you know is important for one that sounds like a bunch of bologna, your career is heading south quickly.

17. Are your successes and accomplishments being glossed over?

This one's tricky to work out, because most bosses and coworkers are weasels who will happily play down your role in order to make themselves look good. But, judge this one by looking to the past. Did your boss used to praise you up to management? Were you a golden boy or girl? That's great. But if it's now impossible to get praise for doing something spectacular, like doubling company profits, then you're being disrespected and probably have a large FIRE ME target printed on your forehead. If you're not getting kudos, you may be getting fired.

18. Are you currently being "retrained" or are taking coaching sessions?

Again, a tricky one. Retraining or coaching is often a way to try and save an employee who has lost his or her way. It shows that the company or your boss still gives a crap. But it also has a darker side. It's another one of those "cover the company's butt" scenarios, in which HR demonstrates they did everything they possibly could to make things work. And alas, it didn't, so they had to let you go. Not a major warning sign on its own, but combined with a few others, this has danger written all over it.

19. Has your immediate boss or mentor gone bye-bye?

If someone you trusted and respected, like a boss or mentor, is no longer around for whatever reason (promotion, fired, quit), this could spell trouble. This person may have been the only one keeping the wolf from your door. And there's an easy way to find out. Is it now impossible to get projects approved? Are you being left out of meetings? Does nothing run smoothly now that this person is no longer on the scene? If this is the case, that's cause for concern.

20. Have you recently been promoted to a position of less responsibility?

What a cunning ruse this one is. It's quite simple but efficient. In your old position, it may have been very difficult or almost impossible to get rid of you. But if the company promotes you into a newly created role, with less responsibility and no direct reports, then you have a new scenario: position elimination. It's hard to fire someone. It's easy to eliminate a position. You can get rid of anyone, even protected classes (older folks, pregnant ladies, etc.) if you simply eliminate a position. So, be afraid. Be very afraid. If you were formerly "Account Manager" and are now "Director in Charge of Special Project Development," you may as well clear out your desk right now. Remember, three or more of these, and you're more than likely heading for the unemployment line. Take a long hard look at your working life, and do something about it. After all, if you're not good enough for them, then they're not good enough for you. — **Paul Michael**

5 New Ways to Hack Your Boss (Without a Machete)

When I started my first "real job," I didn't realize how many situations I'd find myself in that were utterly different from most of what I'd encountered before. On top of learning the tasks specific to the job, I had to navigate office politics and figure out what it meant to be "professional." I had to make decisions about these things on the fly, without any experience and with only my intuition to guide me. I made a few mistakes while I figured it out, but eventually I learned to survive and thrive. While I'm still no expert, what I offer here are hacks to common problems that have worked for me and for those I know.

Note: These hacks will be particularly relevant to entry-level positions, but could be useful at other times, as well.

WHEN YOU'VE JUST FINISHED A PROJECT:

Let him know you're thinking about the future. Either ask him, "So, what's next?" or let him know you'll be needing some time to get things together before he approaches you with the next project. Something like, "I'm getting ready for the next project. Could we talk about it in an hour / this afternoon / tomorrow / next week after I tie up some loose ends? I've been focusing on getting this done but want to make sure I haven't let anything fall through the cracks." Both approaches let him know that you're focused on what is best for the company. The second allows you to look this way but gives you the break you need when the project you've been working your butt off to finish is finally done.

WHEN SHE'S POINTING OUT YOUR LITTLE MISTAKES (AGAIN!):

Remember that this is part of her job, and may be as distasteful to her as it is to you (or may not, depending on the boss). If the criticism is particularly difficult for you to hear, remember to breathe before you say anything. A deep breath or so, when done surreptiously, can give you the strength to respond calmly. Then, if it's appropriate, defend yourself. If her criticism is just, nod as she speaks. Tell her, "Thank you for showing me how you would prefer this to be done / how this should be done / how to add a column of numbers / whatever." If she persists, or is talking to you about something for the Nth time, say, "This seems to be something that you want me to work on / I should work on. Are there any resources available to help me improve?" Whether you need to be on time, make the Web page load faster, or something else, it's hard for a boss to fault an employee who wants to change. If she points you in a direction, follow through!

WHEN YOU'RE SWAMPED AND HE WANTS YOU TO DO MORE:

Be honest about what you can do. Most supervisors appreciate hearing when their people are overworked and stressed. If he likes up-front, honest people, say, "You know, I'd be happy to take that on, but realistically I won't be able to get to it until I finish with X, Y, and Z. Will that work for you?" He may take it to someone else, or he may give it to you, but either way he knows what he's looking at. If he's going to lay it on you no matter what you say, try, "I'll take that on. Right now, I'm working on

P, D, and Q. Where does this fall in priority relative to those?" With this, he knows where he stands and what you have on your plate, and he can determine when you get to it.

WHEN YOU KNOW YOU'VE MADE A BIG MISTAKE:

If you can't fix it in time, be the first to let her know. Swallow the butterflies and make your weak knees walk to her office (or write that e-mail). Most of the time she's going to find out anyway, so you're only prolonging the agony and creating a ton of anxiety for yourself if you don't tell her. Your poise and honesty will also make an impression, even if she's upset and there are consequences. At the very least, she'll have a positive sense of your integrity for any future recommendations. At best? You might save your job.

WHEN YOU'RE INTERVIEWING FOR A DIFFERENT JOB:

In a few companies, this is considered tantamount to treason. If you work for one of them, keep it under the table but don't lie if you're asked directly. You might be asked to leave, but they won't be able to fault your integrity in a recommendation. But if you work for most companies (or, at least, most of the ones I've experienced heard about), be honest. Tell her what you're doing. If you're valuable where you are, you would be surprised how many times she will do all she can to get you a counteroffer. If she can't or if she has some other motivation to not re-hire you, she will appreciate not being blindsided when you turn in your notice. — **Sarah Winfrey**

9 Things to Do When You Are Laid Off

Your company has announced a soon-to-come layoff, or you've been escorted out of the door. What's next? Before you panic and jump headfirst into job hunting, take a few moments to regroup. Looking at your current situation from a big-picture point of view will give you a better sense of where best to go from here.

1. Review your financial status.

Check in on your accounts and figure out how much money you have.

2. Add up your fixed expenses.

How many months can you survive before your personal financial situation moves from good to bearable to desperate.

3. Evaluate your severance package.

Consider your options, which may involve a lump-sum payment or salary continuation.

If you are offered consideration (extra cash or some other benefit) for signing a non-compete agreement, think about the implications for locating a new job. If you signed a non-compete upon your hire or for consideration after being hired, see if you can get a clear definition of what companies or industries are considered competitors, or if the agreement is enforceable in your state.

4. Look at your benefits package.

Determine your life, health, and disability insurance coverage as well as your retirement plans. When will your benefits end? Do you need to replace your insurance coverage? If you are eligible for COBRA (Consolidated Omnibus Budget Reconciliation Act), do you know its monthly cost? How much would it be to get short-term health insurance elsewhere?

....

5. Analyze your 401(k) plan options and obligations.

....

Do you have a loan associated with a 401(k) that you will need to pay off immediately? Should you leave the 401(k) with your employer's administrator while you decide where to transfer the funds? Do you need to transfer the assets immediately upon your separation from the company?

....

6. Learn the rules of unemployment insurance.

....

See if and when you are eligible for benefits (you should be eligible unless you were terminated for cause) and what the requirements are to receive payments. If you have been displaced as a result of increase in imports or offshore business, look into Trade Adjustment Assistance.

....

7. Set your professional and personal priorities.

....

Will you stay in the same town or will you relocate? Are you looking for a similar job in the same industry? Do you want to take a step forward and advance in responsibility or do you want to move laterally, or take a step back in order to spend more time with your family or developing a business idea?

....

8. Investigate a new career.

....

You might decide that you really love the industry you've been working in, but this a very good opportunity to consider other paths you might be interested in. Consider the time and resources it might take to change fields.

....

9. Check salary.com or payscale.com.

....

Determine if your professional goals, personal desires, and financial needs are synchronized with your expected compensation.

Why pause before making the job-search plunge? If you take a breath and do some financial assessments, you'll be more focused and more likely to get what you really want.

— **Julie Rains**

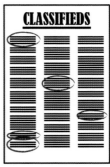

How to Answer 23 of the Most Common Interview Questions

Let's face it; no one likes the interview process. Well, certainly not the people being interviewed anyway. You have to be on your best behavior, you only get one chance to get it right, and it's like taking your driving test all over again. Over the years I've been to countless interviews. To get my first job out of college I attended some 15–20 interviews a week. Whether it was in Britain or over here in the States, the questions never really seemed to change from job to job. Not only that, but the answers to them are usually the same, with your own personal interpretation, of course. Here I present 23 questions you're likely to be asked, and how I have learned to answer them. Remember, being interviewed is a skill, and if you do the preparation, you should ace it every time.

1. So, tell me a little about yourself.

I'd be very surprised if you haven't been asked this one at every interview. It's probably the most-asked question because it sets the stage for the interview and it gets you talking. Be careful not to give the interviewer your life story here. You don't need to explain everything from birth to present day. This is your chance to tell the potential employer why you're best for the job, so include relevant job experience as well as your interests to show your personality.

2. Why are you looking (or why did you leave your last job)?

This should be a straightforward question to answer, but it can trip you up. Presumably you are looking for a new job (or any job) because you want to advance your career and get a position that allows you to grow as a person and an employee. It's not a good idea to mention money here— it can make you sound mercenary. And if you are in the unfortunate situation of having been downsized, stay positive and be as brief as possible about it. If you were fired, you'll need a good explanation. But once again, stay positive.

3. Tell me what you know about this company.

Do your homework before you go to any interview. Whether it's being the VP of Marketing or the mailroom clerk, you should know about the company or business you're going to work for. Has this company been in the news lately? Who are the people in the company you should know about? Do the background work; it will make you stand out as someone who comes prepared, and is genuinely interested in the company and the job.

4. Why do you want to work here?

This should be directly related to question 3. Any research you've done on the company should have led you to the conclusion that you'd want to work there. After all, you're at the interview; right? Put some thought into this answer before you have your interview; mention your career goals and highlight forward-thinking goals and career plans. Talk about the aspects and achievements of the company that you admire.

5. What relevant experience do you have?

Hopefully, if you're applying for this position, you have bags of related experience, and if that's the case you should mention it all. But if you're switching careers or trying something a little different, your experience may initially not look like it's matching up. That's when you need a little honest creativity to match the experiences required with the ones you have. People skills are people skills, after all; you just need to show how customer service skills can apply to internal management positions, and so on.

6. If your previous coworkers were here, what would they say about you?

Okay, this is not the time for full disclosure. If some people from your past are going to say you're a boring a-hole, you don't need to bring that up. Stay positive, always, and maybe have a few specific quotes in mind. "They'd say I was a hard worker" or even better, "John Doe has always said I was the most reliable, creative problem solver he'd ever met."

7. Have you done anything to further your experience?

This could include anything from night classes to hobbies and sports. If it's related, it's worth mentioning. Obviously anything to do with further education is great, but maybe you're spending time on a home improvement project to work on skills such as self-sufficiency, time management, and motivation.

....

8. Where else have you applied?

This is a good way to hint that you're in demand, without sounding like you're whoring yourself all over town. So, be honest and mention a few other companies but don't go into detail. The fact that you're seriously looking and keeping your options open is what the interviewer is driving at.

....

9. How are you when you're working under pressure?

Once again, there are a few ways to answer this, but they should all be positive. You may work well under pressure, you may thrive under pressure, and you may actually *prefer* working under pressure. If you say you crumble like aged blue cheese, this is not going to help you get your foot in the door.

....

10. What motivates you to do a good job?

The answer to this one is not money, even if it is. You should be motivated by life's noble pursuits. You want recognition for a job well done. You want to become better at your job.

You want to help others or be a leader in your field.

....

11. What's your greatest strength?

This is your chance to shine. You're being asked to explain why you are a great employee, so don't hold back and do stay positive. You could be someone who thrives under pressure, a great motivator, an amazing problem solver, or someone with extraordinary attention to detail. If your greatest strength, however, is to drink anyone under the table or get a top score on Mario Kart, keep it to yourself. The interviewer is looking for work-related strengths.

....

12. What's your biggest weakness?

If you're completely honest, you may be kicking yourself in the butt. If you say you don't have one, you're obviously lying. This is a horrible question and one that politicians have become masters at answering. They say things like "I'm perhaps too committed to my work and don't spend enough time with my family." Oh, there's a fireable offense. I've even heard "I think I'm too good at my job; it can often make people jealous." Please, let's keep our feet on the ground. If you're asked this question, give a small, work-related flaw that you're working hard to improve. Example: "I've been told I occasionally focus on details and miss the bigger picture, so I've been spending time laying out the complete project every day to see my overall progress."

13. Let's talk about salary. What are you looking for?

Run for cover! This is one tricky game to play in an interview. Even if you know the salary range for the job, if you answer first you're already showing all your cards. You want as much as possible; the employer wants you for as little as you're willing to take. Before you apply, take a look at salary.com for a good idea of what someone with your specific experience should be paid. You may want to say, "Well, that's something I've thought long and hard about, and I think someone with my experience should get between X and Y." Or, you could be sly and say, "Right now, I'm more interested in talking more about what the position can offer my career." That could at least buy you a little time to scope out the situation. But if you do have a specific figure in mind and you are confident that you can get it, I'd say go for it. I have on many occasions, and every time I got very close to that figure (both below and sometimes above).

14. Are you good at working in a team?

Unless you have the IQ of a houseplant, you'll always answer *yes* to this one. It's the only answer. How can anyone function inside an organization if they are a loner? You may want to mention what part you like to play in a team, though; it's a great chance to explain that you're a natural leader.

15. Tell me a suggestion you have made that was implemented.

It's important here to focus on the word "implemented." There's nothing wrong with having a thousand great ideas, but if the only place they live is on your notepad, what's the point? Better still, you need a good ending. If your previous company took your advice and ended up going bankrupt, that's not such a great example either. Be prepared with a story about an idea of yours that was taken from idea to implementation, and considered successful.

16. Has anything ever irritated you about people you've worked with?

Of course, you have a list as long as your arm. But you can't say that; it shows you as being negative and difficult to work with. The best way to answer this one is to think for a while and then say something like, "I've always got on just fine with my coworkers, actually."

17. Is there anyone you just could not work with?

No. Well, unless you're talking about murderers, racists, rapists, thieves, or other dastardly characters, you can work with anyone. Otherwise you could be flagged as someone who's picky and difficult if you say, "I can't work with anyone who's a Broncos fan. Sorry."

18. Tell me about any issues you've had with a previous boss.

Arrgh! If you fall for this one you shouldn't be hired anyway. The interviewer is testing you to see if you'll speak badly about your previous supervisor. Simply answer this question with extreme tact, diplomacy, and, if necessary, a big fat loss of memory. In short, you've never had any issues.

19. Would you rather work for money or job satisfaction?

It's not a very fair question, is it? We'd all love to get paid a Trump-like sal-

ary doing a job we love, but that's rare indeed. It's fine to say money is important, but remember that *nothing* is more important to you than the job. Otherwise, you're just someone looking for a bigger paycheck.

20. Would you rather be liked or feared?

I have been asked this a lot, in various incarnations. The first time I just drew a blank and said, "I don't know." That went over badly, but it was right at the start of my career when I had little to no experience. Since then I've realized that my genuine answer is "Neither; I'd rather be respected." You don't want to be feared because fear is no way to motivate a team. You may get the job done, but at what cost? Similarly, if you're everyone's best friend, you'll find it difficult to make tough decisions or hit deadlines. But when you're respected, you don't have to be a complete bastard or a lame duck to get the job done.

21. Are you willing to put the interests of the company ahead of your own?

Again, another nasty question. If you say yes, you're a corporate whore who doesn't care about family. If you say no, you're disloyal to the company.

I'm afraid that you'll probably have to say yes to this one, though, because you're trying to be the perfect employee at this point, and perfect employees don't cut out early for Jimmy's baseball game.

....

22. So, explain why I should hire you.

....

As I'm sure you know, "Because I'm great" or "I really need a job" are not good answers here. This is a time to give the employer a laundry list of your greatest talents that just so happens to match the job description. It's also good to avoid taking potshots at other potential candidates here. Focus on yourself and your talents, not other people's flaws.

....

23. Finally, do you have any questions to ask me?

....

I'll finish the way I started, with one of the most common questions asked in interviews. This directly relates to the research you've done on the company and also gives you a chance to show how eager and prepared you are. You'll probably want to ask about benefits if they haven't been covered already. A good generic one is "How soon could I start—if I were offered the job, of course." You may also ask what you'd be working on, specifically, in the role you're applying for, and how that affects the rest of the company. Always have questions ready; greeting this one with a blank stare is a rotten way to finish your interview. Good luck, and happy job hunting.

— **Paul Michael**

6 Warning Signs that You Shouldn't Take that Job

You're scouting around for a decent job. While you realize that great jobs are hard to find, you're avoiding getting into a position that really stinks. Here are six telltale characteristics of generally lousy jobs, and why it may be best to cut and run.

....

1. They run vague ads

....

While you can't always expect potential employers to give a detailed bio in a three-inch ad space, there are subtle ways to let you know who you may be working for. Classifieds that don't even let you know what industry you'll be working in are difficult to prepare for, and worse yet, they can often be bait for MLM (multi level marketing) or scams. In short, you should at least know if you'll be working in a restaurant, as compared to filing copies of credit applications. These are very different ball games, indeed.

....

2. They accept anyone

....

I once answered a job ad that replied with an interview appointment the same day. Since it was for a mid-level management position, I showed up in my best "interview suit" and brought extra résumés on linen paper. Looking around the reception area, I saw many other "prospects" for the same job I was interviewing for. Many were wearing sweats, and one guy didn't even speak English. I should have walked then, as they were obviously *not* looking for a mid-level manager, but door-to-door salesmen. Tricky.

....

3. They have no known address

....

This one seems obvious, but it took me by surprise. That same job I mentioned earlier with the vague address and a waiting room full of unqualified applicants didn't show up in my local phone book. The interview took place in an unmarked office building,

and there was no corporate branding anywhere inside or out. So I shouldn't have been shocked to find that it was a front for a door-to-door promotions company. When they told me I was hired, and asked if I would like to see the "operations side" of the manager position, I was taken by company car to the dumpy side of town to try to sell pizza coupons. *Yikes!*

....

4. They run the same job ad week after week (and the week after that)

....

Did you ever notice that some big companies run the exact same ad (with slightly different wording) almost regularly? There may not even be a job opening, but the high rate of turnover at these jobs almost guarantees they will be needing someone soon. Keeping a constant supply of new hires in the pipeline secures their chances of having someone trained and ready to work these jobs at any given time—if only for a few months.

....

5. A Google search turns up trash

....

I don't believe everything I read on the Web, but I am inclined to seriously reconsider working for any company with their own "this company sucks dot com" Web site. More than 150 similar complaints by previous employees should be a sign that things aren't on the up-and-up. I also check out Vault.com and RipOffReport.com to see if I'm going to be working for a product or service that generally makes people mad.

6. They don't treat you well at the interview or application appointment

I know that when times are tough, it seems like just about any job should suffice. Take it from me, however: A hiring manager who can't give you common courtesy probably won't be the best person to work for. Rude receptionists, inconsiderately late HR reps, and a general feeling of frustration in a potential workplace are usually signs of an office-wide dilemma. Unless you're craving workplace drama, it might be best to go with your gut and skip a questionable opportunity.

As much time as most people spend searching, applying, and interviewing during the job hunt, you owe it to yourself to be sure your next job is a keeper. If you can't land that killer opportunity without sacrificing your most basic standards, it may be best to keep looking. **— Linsey Knerl**

4 Ways Good Writing Skills Save and Earn You Money

Here is a list of ways good writing skills could save and earn money for you.

1. You will be able to negotiate more effectively

My grandfather told me that he saved about $4,500 on his condo purchase because he wrote a nice letter about why he deserved a discount. He showed me the letter, and it was very concise and listed both personal and business reasons why he should get a price break. If he did not know how to write so clearly, he might not have gotten the discount.

My mom also did the same thing when she and my dad purchased their first home. She wrote a clear letter detailing the issues surrounding the house and got a discount of $7,500 beyond the accepted offer.

2. Good writing skills make you more desirable to employers

In many instances, the first impression you make on a potential employer is in a cover letter or résumé. An interesting and well-written cover letter could potentially lead to an interview and eventually a job.

Even when you do not have a formal cover letter, there are often many e-mail exchanges during an interview process. E-mails that are clearly written generally makes you seem more intelligent and responsible to a potential employer.

Personally, I know that my ability to write coherent e-mails has given me an edge in finding software engineering jobs, because most software engineers are not taught to write properly.

3. It is a cheap hobby

Writing is probably one of the cheapest hobbies out there. You do not need expensive materials or equipment; you can start with a plain notebook and pencil. Writing can also take up quite a bit of time, so you could be entertained for hours by your own imagination and creativity.

4. Well-written content has monetary value

Many people make a living through writing. For example, even in a soft-ware company we have copywriters and technical writers. The ability to communicate useful information is worth its weight in gold. Even if you are not a professional writer, it is possible to start a blog and earn a bit of side income because there is an endless amount of content on the Internet, and good content is rare.

Writing is a skill that can be learned and improved. You can take a class at a local college that teaches you to write, or just read articles and books about the art of writing. Another great thing is that you can practice it anywhere and any way you want.

I think it is unfortunate that proper writing is not emphasized in this highly technical world. And even though we have mainstream journalists that publish phrases like "We wuz robbed," I believe that being able to communicate effectively through language will always be valued. — **Xin Lu**

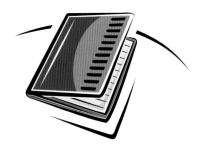

5 Ways to Squeeze Savings from Your Workplace

If you are a cube dweller like me, you may be familiar with the usual benefits of a salary and paid days off, but there are many other ways you can benefit from your workplace. I am not talking about stealing pens or embezzling large sums of money.

These are some of the practical and legal means you can use to squeeze just a little bit of extra savings for yourself.

1. Keep Tupperware or plastic bags in your cube

Not every workplace gives out free food, but if there is an instance when there is a lot of leftover food left in the break room, you should be ready to take some home. In my last company we had monthly lunches for the entire company, and every time there was tons of food left. My manager and I routinely brought home trays of food that lasted for two to three meals. He would have shopping bags readied for his haul. We only do this when everyone has eaten. My rationale is that the food would be thrown away if I didn't take any.

2. Milk the travel rewards

Do you travel a lot for your employer? If so, make sure to sign up for all the mileage and hotel programs that correspond to your travel. Generally the miles and points you rack up with business travel can be used by you personally.

Some of the people I know who work at consulting firms are able to pick up free hotel stays and flights without paying a dime of their own money. One of my coworkers from out of town told us that he is staying at six different Starwood hotels this week so that he can get platinum status under their rewards program. Once he has platinum status he can use his rewards to get highly discounted hotel rates for himself.

No matter how often you are on the go for work, it is possible to take advantage of the travel rewards.

3. Use the recycled paper

In every office I know of there is a printer room with a recycling bin full of unwanted paper. Most of the paper is perfectly fine, clean, and has only been printed on one side. This type of paper is perfect for printing online coupons and it is completely free.

....

4. Get free hardware
....

In most offices there are old computer parts that are unwanted. For example, my mom's work computer broke so they purchased a new workstation for her. The old computer's LCD panel, keyboard, and mouse were all still working but they were no longer needed. She asked if she could bring those parts home and her workplace said yes. I was able to replace my old CRT with the LCD panel for free.

It generally costs money to recycle or dispose of electronics, so you may be able to pick up some perfectly good computer parts for free at the IT department. It never hurts to ask.

....

5. Charge all your electronics at work
....

This may not save you that much money, but charging something at work does not increase your electricity bill. You can charge your phone, MP3 player, portable gaming device, and even rechargeable batteries. I think charging some small items at work is perfectly acceptable, but please do

not go crazy with this idea and charge your electric car at work.

If you take advantage of these unwritten benefits at work, you can save hundreds to thousands of dollars a year. Along the way you would have reduced waste and reused unwanted things so everyone comes out a winner. — **Xin Lu**

9 Survival Tips from Depression-Era Kids

My parents and my husband's parents were children during the Great Depression. Mine lived in large cities; my in-laws, in small towns. Their families started this era from neither a position of wealth nor desperation. Just to add perspective, though, I'll mention that their parents wouldn't have considered lack of indoor plumbing a sign of poverty, at least in their early years. Here are the basics of how they managed to survive using tactics that are still viable today.

1. Play outside

Like most kids then, my dad spent his days when not in school outside playing with his older brother and the neighborhood kids. He did have to forgo riding on his tricycle after it was repossessed, but apparently found other things to do.

Outside play is generally free or cheap, even if it means driving to the playground, and it's not just an activity for kids. When I operated on a very limited budget in a small town right out of college, I spent much of my leisure time outside, usually hiking in the nearby mountains with friends.

2. Write letters

Writing letters can be a form of entertainment or pastime, and a way to record one's history; my mother has letters from her mom, and reading them makes me feel as if she is right next to me, sharing her story.

3. Keep your government job

My mother-in-law's dad was a mail carrier with the United States Postal Service (a government job) and so had a reliable source of income, unlike many of their neighbors. Her family was able to help others in their small, rural community.

I am sure that there are many exciting and well-paying government jobs, but a key element of their attractiveness is stability. There is often a trade-off between the opportunity for higher pay in a risky environment and lower wages in a safer arena (consider looking for a new job if you have a low-paying position in a volatile environment).

4. Grow food

My grandmother raised chickens in her tiny, urban backyard; when she was ready to fix dinner, she caught a chicken and cooked it. My mother-in-law's parents had a garden on land they owned; everyone was encouraged to grow produce in order to feed themselves, and sell the excess to neighbors, as the reliability of food distribution was uncertain.

The get-closer-to-your-food movement has been gaining momentum, though many never abandoned this concept. My in-laws now have a farm on which they grow corn, potatoes, peppers, and more. My parents have always had tomato plants, and my dad is an expert farmers' market shopper, always investigating and committing to memory who is a farmer and who is a reseller only, who has the best produce and who doesn't.

5. Look for income opportunities

My grandparents took in boarders, although my dad, still young at the time, didn't really like having strangers in the house. My husband's grandparents also had boarders, but the kids, then young adults, enjoyed the company. At some point, both of my grandmothers worked outside the home to bring in money for their families.

Frugality can go only so far. Cold cash is often needed to pay for basic supplies, such as food and clothing, or simply to make payments on credit card debt.

6. Get government-sponsored training

My father-in-law's oldest brother joined the Civilian Conservation Corps. He worked and lived in a camp in Oregon, and learned job skills. Back home, he first worked as a candy salesman and then started an auto-parts store and trained his younger brother in business. Eventually, they both operated stores in small towns. My dad and father-in-law were fortunate to get college degrees on the GI Bill.

Today, taking classes at the community college is an inexpensive way to get work skills. Many community colleges also offer consultation for starting and running small businesses.

7. Stay put

My dad's parents lost their house to foreclosure. But, because no one else could afford to buy the home, they were able to stay in the house. They happened to live near the downtown area of a large city with work, schools, and stores within walking distance, so it made sense to stay where they were.

8. Move to where the jobs are

My father-in-law's family (his parents and brothers) moved to Newport News so that they could work in the shipyard (my father-in-law stayed back until he could finish high school and then joined them).

Obviously, this tactic seems to be in direct contrast to #7, and was useful only when World War II efforts began to stimulate the economy. But, having started my professional career during a recession, I'll echo that moving for work, if you can afford the start-up costs or have even a basic relocation package (mine was 30 days in a hotel, allowing me to get a first paycheck and find a roommate before putting down a deposit on an apartment), makes sense.

....

9. Share
....

Having a home and a steady job allowed my mother-in-law's parents to share with others; at some point, they gave shelter to a young woman in need. — **Julie Rains**

Everything You Need to Know About Unclaimed Property

Unclaimed property consists of cash and other personal assets that are considered lost or abandoned after an owner cannot be located within a specified period of time. This property may be cash, bonds, stocks, gift certificates, and contents of safety deposit boxes (jewelry, documents, etc). The amazing thing about unclaimed property is that it's just that—unclaimed. It still belongs to the rightful owner, and by law, all they need to do is ask for it to regain possession. But how does one go about finding out about it in the first place?

WHERE TO LOOK?

Most state treasuries in the United States each maintain their own Web sites, where users can look up any unclaimed funds by last name. The trouble with this method is that you need to go to a separate site for each state you may have property in. And who wants to Google-search for many different states that may potentially hold an unclaimed treasure? Web sites such as MissingMoney.com and Unclaimed.org, which are both maintained by the National Association of Unclaimed Property Administrators (NAUPA), can help you in your search by listing contact info for each state office and providing a search tool for several treasuries at one time.

WHAT TO DO?

Once you have found what might be unclaimed property that should be in your possession, there will be a form and some simple verification steps to follow to prove to the state that you are the rightful owner. Once this has been established, you can arrange for your property to be returned to you.

(Note: Please don't ever pay anyone to "find" property for you. This is a service that your state treasury will gladly provide you for free. It is their job, and since most unclaimed property has a value of less than $100, it does you no good to pay someone to do what you and your state treasury can accomplish on your own.)

NO PROPERTY?

Even if you don't have any property, you can still take advantage of the billions of dollars of unclaimed items left abandoned in the possession of state treasuries. Many of them are now selling this property on eBay and other online auction sites. To see a quick view of some of the items that the state of Maryland has up for auction, for example, view their seller's item list at myworld.ebay.com/mdcompfranchot. All proceeds from these auctions are held for the rightful owner or their heirs, and can be claimed at any time. It just may be a great way to get a good buy on that 1978 Krugerrand you've always wanted!

Unclaimed property is the coolest lost-and-found out there. Check it out today, and see if you don't have a little unknown treasure waiting for you!

— **Linsey Knerl**

8 Truths from a Mystery Shopper

Mystery shopping is a respectable gig for someone with some time, ambition, and a desire to do something different. As a mystery shopper, you'll visit retail stores as a casual shopper, and gather information about displays, prices, customer service and so on. You're hired and report back to a market research firm or a manufacuturer. Having mystery-shopped for dozens of companies over the past six years, I have some advice to share. These eight tips are vital to making money in this often-misunderstood profession.

1. Mystery shopping can be tough to get into

If you're okay with starting out doing $8 gigs for ordering a fast-food meal, then chances are great that you can begin right away. The higher-paying shops, however, are usually reserved for those with experience. If you want to earn a reputation for being a dependable shopper, I suggest visiting the Mystery Shopping Providers Association (MSPA) Web site (MysteryShop.org) and getting at least a silver status certification. Yes, it costs money. Think of it as a "move to the head of the line" pass for most mystery-shopping jobs. Many reputable companies will only schedule certified shoppers for their jobs.

2. You can't earn money if you don't spend it

Guess what? Mystery shopping requires you to shop. Since they don't mail you cash up front, it is your responsibility to be able to cover your purchases for the shop. It also takes between 30 and 90 days to get reimbursed. If you can't spare this money, this may not be the job for you.

3. A successful shop requires an eye for detail

I loved doing the fine dining shops. The problem was, I had a difficult time remembering all the details I needed to complete the shop. I had to covertly keep tabs on the names of every person I came in contact with, what they were wearing, what they said, what my food tasted like, etc. Needless to say, it was work! If you are looking for mystery shopping to be your free meal ticket, understand that there will not be much time for relaxing. While it is true that some shops require little work, others require much, much more.

4. Payment depends on your performance

Unlike a typical 9–5 job, you are not guaranteed payment unless your shop has been performing satisfactorily. If you forget the names of your wait staff, don't leave the right amount of tip, or accidentally reveal your shopper status, you are putting your reimbursement in danger. I have never had a shopping company not pay me, but I have also been very diligent about doing everything perfectly. If you don't take it seriously, you may not be paid—and you'll be out whatever cash you put into your shopping experience.

5. There are other costs involved

In addition to the cost of your shopping (which is usually reimbursed partially or in full), there are other costs. Gas to drive to the shop, the cost (if any) to put an item on your credit card until reimbursement, or the cost of a tip (which is often not covered) are just a few expenses that may come up during a typical shop. Obviously, the best strategy is to shop close, only take shops that reimburse in full (and with an extra shopper's fee, if possible), and turn in your reports on time.

6. You are responsible for your own taxes

As a mystery shopper, you are considered an independent contractor. While it is unlikely that you will earn over $600 a year for any one company, you will still be responsible for reporting that income on your tax returns. You can count it as self-employment, deducting expenses as needed, so keep track of the cost of your new mystery-shopping job.

7. Some mystery shopping isn't shopping or a mystery

Many shopping companies have begun scheduling work for companies that aren't even related to mystery shopping. Audits, merchandising, and other tasks (including headstone cleaning) often come up on the mystery-shopping job boards from time to time. If you don't have an interest in these types of jobs, don't feel obliged to take them. They can be a good source of income for you, however.

8. A reputable mystery-shopping company will never ask you for any kind of fee

I'll say this again: You should not have to ever pay for the "privilege" to shop. You are performing a service, and should get paid. Any fee that is guaranteed to get you a list of jobs is bogus. For a genuine listing of most every single shop service on the planet, see Volition.com or check out JobSlinger.com. It costs nothing. (And be sure to read up on the latest mystery-shopping scams—I have never, ever, ever been asked to cash checks in my six years of shopping. Ever.)

After some time, I gave up on mystery shopping. The $8–10 an hour wasn't worth the work (especially as my family grew). For some, this could still be a really good deal. Just be aware of the facts, and decide what's right for you. — **Linsey Knerl**

Sweeping 101: Secrets of Sweepstakes Winners

Hi, my name is Linsey, and I'm a sweeper. It is sometimes difficult to admit, but I belong to that persistent group of individuals who go to considerable lengths to enter sweepstakes. I also win fairly regularly. My recent winnings include a bicycle, a home automation system, two satellite radios, hotel stays, cell phones, gift cards, cash, DVDs, spa visits, clothing, baby items, video games, gaming systems, office supplies, a digital camera and printer, a trip to San Francisco, and so much more! Winning is more about knowing than anything else, so I'm going to give you the basics to get started. You can't win if you don't enter!

WHAT IS A SWEEPSTAKES?

Simply put, a sweepstakes is a random drawing of entries for a prize. Generally sponsored or paid for by companies wishing to promote their products or services, sweepstakes are a billion-dollar marketing tactic used by thousands of companies a year. You should never have to purchase anything to enter. If a sweepstakes requires a UPC code, special form from a product, or a "winning game piece," there will always be an alternate means of entry, or it is not a legal sweepstakes. If entry into a sweepstakes requires an entry fee or raffle ticket purchase, it is not a true sweepstakes.

WHERE DO I FIND SWEEPSTAKES?

While sweepstakes are simply hard to avoid these days, there are some very good resources for finding all the good ones in one place. The top sites that sweepers use are Online-Sweepstakes.com and SweepsAdvantage.com. Both are very good resources with different formats. Other places to find sweepstakes are in magazines, e-mail newsletters, grocery stores (the liquor aisles usually have many), and local radio stations.

HOW DO I GET STARTED?

While all you really need to get started is a computer and some extra time, there are some tricks of the trade that you should know. First, get a separate e-mail for your sweepstakes entries. While the chances of spam aren't too much greater (assuming you are only entering legitimate sweepstakes), you will receive some sponsor newsletters as a condition for entry into some of the better sweepstakes. You really don't want that cluttering up your work or personal in-box. Also, make sure you have a physical mailing address set up for your entries. Some prize fulfillment companies do not ship to P.O. boxes, as they want to enforce "one prize per household" rules.

WHAT TOOLS WILL I NEED?

I'm a big fan of the Firefox Web browser (Firefox.com) with the Fasterfox add-on (fasterfox.mozdev.org). This saves my pages for quick viewing later, and if you are entering some of the same sweepstakes daily, this will save you time. (Just be sure to clear everything weekly or more to avoid PC clutter and security issues.) Also, I have been using the free version of Roboform (RoboForm.com) for filling out all of my forms quickly. This doesn't violate the terms of most sweepstakes regulations which prohibit automated entry, as you are manually entering the contest by loading the page and hitting submit.

HOW DO YOU HAVE TIME TO DO THIS?

I make time. Seriously, like anything else, I maximize time spent entering to get the biggest bang for my buck. I only enter for things I want, need, or can sell for a nice chunk of cash. I spend 30–45 minutes a day during my morning coffee or an afternoon snack entering the sweepstakes that are ending the next day, and I sometimes glance through the instant wins for things I really want. By being selective but persistent, I have a good chance of getting in entries and not ending up with some junky prize that I have to make room for later.

HOW LONG BEFORE I WIN SOMETHING?

I don't know. But I will say that as a general rule, it will take at least six months to really see the fruits of your labor. Or you may be one of those really, really unlucky people that don't ever win anything. But I tend to think that those people just aren't entering all that often, or they give up after a month or two.

WHAT ABOUT TAXES?

Pay them. You should get a 1099 for any prizes valued over $600. You should also be an honest person and figure the value (true fair market value) on your other winnings. Claim it as unearned income on your return, and pay up. It really is no big deal for most people. My trip to San Francisco cost me $120 in taxes on a trip valued at over $2,500. While this will all depend on your tax bracket, it is still a really awesome deal!

I HATE SWEEPERS. THEY'RE JUST GREEDY PEOPLE LOOKING TO GET STUFF FOR FREE.

I'm sorry you feel that way. I love getting stuff for free, and that is my main motivation for entering. But most companies love sweepers. Entering sweepstakes exposes me to thousands of new products and offerings that I may not have otherwise been aware of. By being a part of that marketing effort, I am 10 times more likely to buy something than if I had just seen an ad in a magazine. My opinion of the company is more favorable if they like "giving back" to the consumer. And I can't tell you how many products I have become brand-loyal to because the sponsor sent a small sample or a prize that I went on to love forever. Sweepstakes are marketing genius. And if you figure that the cost of these sweepstakes campaigns are figured into the cost of the product that we all buy anyway, shouldn't you get in on that sweet deal?

Sweeping can be a fun way to win prizes you can't afford to buy. If you're already spending two hours a day on MySpace or playing online games, just pop open that extra browser window and enter a few now and again. Who knows,—you just might be a winner! — **Linsey Knerl**

142 Resources that will Save You Cash

Over the years, we have compiled a terrific list of money-saving resources. We are adding to this list every day. For the latest updates check out WiseBread.com/resources.

TOOLS FROM WISE BREAD

Deals Roundup

(wisebread.com/bestdeals)—Get today's best deals, coupons, and freebies from all the top bargain sites.

Product Reviews and Ratings

(wisebread.com/reviews)—Find the best personal finance products and services ranked by votes from consumers like you.

Community Forums

(wisebread.com/forums)—Saving money is easier when you have a support group. Come join our community and share your story with us, or stick around for our special events featuring appearances by top authors and experts.

Top News & Tips of the Day

(wisebread.com/news)—See the latest personal finance news and tips in a Digg-style news aggregator.

MONEY MANAGEMENT TOOLS

Buxfer

(buxfer.com)—Buxfer makes it easy to track IOUs and shared expenses among friends. It is a fantastic tool for splitting expenses like rent, poker debts, and group dinners. You can even use it to track your own expenses like a traditional money management tool.

JustThrive

(justthrive.com)—Thrive brings all your financial accounts into one place so you can easily see what you have, what you owe, and where you can grow. Thrive's Health Score function, which predicts your financial stability using many of the same tools and indicators that financial planners provide for the affluent, is what really sets it apart from its competitors.

Mint

(mint.com)—The easiest way to keep track of your finances. Take five minutes to set up an account by adding your bank, credit card, and investment account information. After that, Mint will start tracking your spending and generate useful budget reports. It'll even send you notices when your bills are due. Mint can make any lazy man feel like a financial genius.

PearBudget

(pearbudget.com)—The 1% of money management software you actually need. The genius of PearBudget is that it focuses on solving one specific problem and it does it better than any other tool out there; it helps you create a simple budget and stick to it.

Quicken Online

(quicken.intuit.com)—A light version of the popular Quicken money management software, Quicken Online is free and lets you track what you're spending and where. A wonderful tool for those of us who grew up using Quicken.

RateSurfer

(ratesurfer.com)—Get a bird's-eye view of your credit cards. Alerts you when your bills are due or your rate changes (great for tracking promotional APRs). RateSurfer can even automatically transfer your balances to the lowest rate card. It's a download, not a website, so your account information is never on a third-party server. An essential tool if you're balancing several cards.

SmartyPig

(smartypig.com)–You set a goal, choose the amount you want to contribute each month to reach that goal, and SmartyPig automatically pulls that amount from your checking account each month. You can make your goals public to friends and family, and they can contribute to your goal as well. Like a savings account at your local bank, SmartyPig pays an interest on deposits and all deposits are FDIC insured. You can withdraw your money at any time via a debit card or electronic transfer. SmartyPig provides the instant willpower many of us need to reach our financial goals.

TurboTax

(turbotax.intuit.com)–It's fast, cheap, and easy to file your taxes online. Made by Intuit (of Quicken fame), TurboTax is one of the most trusted names in tax preparation.

Wesabe

(wesabe.com)–Wesabe tracks your spending information and provides customized tips for you to save money based on your spending habits and the community's spending habits. You must check out Wesabe's wonderful community of smart and helpful forum users. It is one of the best personal finance communities around.

RATE COMPARISON AND SEARCH TOOLS

BankRate

(bankrate.com)–The best comparison site for financial products like mortgage rates, home equity loans, CDs, car loans, credit cards, and money market accounts. BankRate provides several helpful financial calculators including a refinance calculator, mortgage payment calculator, auto loan monthly payments, CD earnings, FICO score estimator, 401K savings calculator, and more. Check out BankRate before signing up for a new financial account to make sure you're getting the best deal available.

BillShrink

(billshrink.com)–Get a list of cell phone plans or credit cards that are better than what you have in less than five minutes. Answer a few questions about your current credit card or cell phone plan (or have BillShrink do it automatically by up-

loading your last statement), and BillShrink will recommend better phone plans or credit cards that fit your needs.

CheckingFinder

(checkingfinder.com)–The easiest way to find the best checking account in your area. Just enter your zip code and compare the checking accounts offered by your local banks and credit unions.

Credit Karma

(creditkarma.com) –Track your credit score for free and save money by getting customized offers (credit cards, loans, savings accounts, etc.) based on your score. This is one of my favorite financial services.

FiLife

(filife.com)–You select the options that are important to you, set ranges for your personal habits, and get a recommended list of financial products that caters to your specific needs. Perfect for people who are constantly looking for the best deals.

Insure.com

(insure.com)–Instantly get quotes from over 200 trusted insurance companies online. When you customize your search by entering pre-existing conditions, you are doing so anonymously, so you can get accurate quotes without divulging personal information.

MoneyAisle

(moneyaisle.com)–Find the highest interest rate you can collect on your savings or CD deposit right now. You enter the amount you're looking to deposit into a high-yield savings account or CD, then member banks (all FDIC insured) bid on the interest rate they're willing to pay you. The bidding is fast and furious, and you'll see the winning rate in a matter of minutes. Finally, a bank service that puts **you** in the driver seat.

Smart Hippo

(smarthippo.com)–Smart Hippo is a community of people who share their reviews of mortgages, banks, and lenders. This is one of the best places to go for honest reviews.

Zillow

(zillow.com)—The most comprehensive and easy-to-use tracker of real estate prices. Get historical prices for a house and compare home prices around the neighborhood. A must-have resource for home owners, buyers, and sellers.

BORROWING, LENDING, AND INVEST-MENTS

Covestor

(covestor.com)–Covestor lets you follow the trades of top performing investors. Piggyback on proven winners to grow your wealth. If you're one of those proven winners, Covestor will pay you for every person who follows your stock trades. Finally, a Web 2.0 company that rewards its best users with real money.

Cake Financial

(cakefinancial.com)–Get a complete picture of your investment portfolio, plus customized tips based on your goals. You can follow the trades of the top investors on the site and talk to people who have similar goals and portfolios as you. Cake Financial is as addictive as it is useful.

Folio Investing

(folioinvesting.com)–Provides knowledgeable investors a flexible way to customize their own portfolios. This is perfect for the personal finance geek who is tired of letting the Bernie Madoffs of the world mismanage their money.

Lending Club

(lendingclub.com)–A peer-to-peer lending network. As a borrower with good credit, you can borrow cash at more favorable rates than offered by banks. As a lender, you can help a family or fund entrepreneurial projects, while getting a good rate of return on your investment. Lenders can choose which loans to fund. This is one of the most innovative ideas we've seen in a long time.

Prosper

(prosper.com)–Get lenders to bid for your loan by outdoing each on the interest rate. You, as a borrower, can set a maximum interest rate you're willing to pay, and lenders will bid down the interest rate to win the right to service your loan.

By forcing lenders to compete for your business, you will walk away a winner every time.

GREAT FOR STUDENTS

STATravel

(statravel.com)–Largest full-service travel agency dedicated to serving students. If you're a college student looking for a break, STATravel is your first stop for the best packages, flight deals, hotel discounts, and tips.

SimpleTuition

(simpletuition.com)–Search for, compare, and apply for student loans. Enter the amount you need, answer a few questions about where the loan will be used (location, university, year graduating, etc.), and SimpleTuition will search for and show you the best student loan offers available. A great way to navigate through the confusing student loans process.

UPromise

(upromise.com)–What could be better than saving money and building a college fund at the same time? You get 125% back from shopping online through upromise.com, or by shopping at over 30,000 offline restaurants, drug stores, and supermarkets. Your discounted savings can be automatically deposited into a 529 college savings plan.

GreenNote

(greennote.com)–A peer-lending network focused on student loans. We really like the idea that you're funding someone's future with your money. Talk about building karma.

DEALS, COUPONS & FREEBIES

AbleShoppers

(ableshoppers.com)–A straightforward, no-fuss site that lists the deals without the unnecessary bells and whistles. Want to know what the deals are without having to scroll through pages of photos and ads? Here's the perfect place for the simple, low-maintenance bargain shopper.

Baby Cheapskate

(babycheapskate.blogspot.com)–An essential destination for the busy parent and homemaker. The site has the best baby, kid, and maternity bargains available, as well as the weekly circulars for grocery and drug stores. Another awesome feature is their Monthly Deal Forecast where they predict upcoming bargains, so you don't miss out by buying too early!

Bargainist

(bargainist.com)–Deals are handpicked and updated several times a day here. This popular site gets on all the "top lists" for good reason. They've also got a fantastic tips section that offers valuable bargain hunting advice.

BargainJack

(bargainjack.com) and **BargainJill** (bargainjill. com)–A husband and wife team passionate about shopping for insane discounts. Jack posts deals for tech, tools, and sports. Jill finds the best discounts on clothing and accessories, home and garden, and health and beauty. Between the two of them, deals can be had for everyone in the family.

BeatThat!

(beatthat.com)–100% community driven, this site rewards members for finding the lowest price with cold, hard cash. It's the perfect shortcut for deal hunters who don't want to run through multiple sites to verify the best price on a product.

Ben's Bargains

(bensbargains.net)–One of the longest running bargain sites around and still going strong, Ben has a loyal following because of his carefully selected deals, which include advance notice of upcoming deals and exclusive offers (not to mention fantastic giveaways) for his readers. There are also special tracker tools that track down hot and hard to find items, so you don't have to run all over town yourself.

BradsDeals

(bradsdeals.com)–One of the few non-tech oriented deals sites, this one covers an array of deals that tackles the shopping lists for everyone in the family. Brad's been interviewed by many news and talk shows and is recognized as an expert bargain hunter. You can't go wrong following his picks.

Buxr

(buxr.com)–A fun and innovative site that gives deal-hounds another thing to be excited about. Not only do users vote deals up or down, but they get money and prizes for doing what they do best—finding the best deals and telling others about it.

Cheap Stingy Bargains

(cheapstingybargains.com)–A top resource for Dell and HP coupons and an indispensable site for anyone considering a computer purchase. Of course, there are coupons and deals for all sorts of products, too. The site is updated hourly, often posting more than a hundred deals and coupons a day.

Coupon Album

(couponalbum.com)–If you have a favorite store or don't like the idea of ordering from a place you've never heard of, stop by Coupon Album where the deals are listed by store. They've got coupons and deals for hundreds of the most popular stores.

CouponCabin

(couponcabin.com)–A popular coupon site that updates their directory three times a day to keep their coupons fresh. Their straightforward navigation allows you to find coupons based on features like "most used," "printable," and "free samples."

Coupon Code

(couponcode.com)–A clean and simple coupon site that offers discounts for over 1,000 stores. You'll have no problems finding just the right discount for you.

Coupon Mom

(couponmom.com)–A favorite site for the busy mom, Coupon Mom breaks up the offerings into easy-to-manage-and-digest sections. Find printable grocery deals by state, restaurant coupons, free offers and samples, and a daily roundup of the best coupons on the site.

CouponMountain

(couponmountain.com)–Updated several times a day, the site offers exclusive online coupon codes, link-based coupons, product discount news and sale announcements. Follow their blog for the most up-to-date announcements, and their forums for all kinds of hot deals, like travel, online auctions, rebates, and sweepstakes.

Coupons

(coupons.com)–A super user-friendly site for the most current grocery coupons. You can enter your zip code for area specific deals, then select the coupons you want and print them out. It's a great alternative to going through the Sunday paper and clipping your own.

CurrentCodes

(currentcodes.com)–A veritable clearinghouse for coupons, the site has a full-time staff whose only job is to find coupon and discount codes and verify their accuracy. The site doesn't try to do several things at once—they just focus on creating the best coupon code database on the Web. No hype, just current codes.

DealCatcher

(dealcatcher.com)–A top site that offers a full staff of editors to ensure the quality of the deals, along with a large forums community that contributes shopping advice and reviews. Their Sunday Ads section allows you to look at discounts from over 200 stores. Stop buying the Sunday paper just for the ads.

Dealhack

(dealhack.com)–A well-organized and nicely styled site that provides a ton of information without overwhelming. They also have loads of additional cool stuff like buyer's guides, gift guides, a Firefox add-on, and a podcast.

Dealigg

(dealigg.com)–A terrific community site which features the best deals found by regular shoppers like you. No editors. No filters. If you like getting unbiased and timely bargain information provided by like-minded deal hunters, this is the site for you.

Dealighted

(dealighted.com)–Aggregates deal discussions among the most popular and largest communities. You no longer have to visit several forums to find the best deal—Dealighted does all that work for you. You won't find anything featured but the very best and most current deals.

Dealio

(dealio.com)–Members vote for the best coupons and sales and never miss a deal again with their Comparison Shopping toolbar. Get instant price comparisons and related coupons and deals without leaving the site to scour the multitude of deals sites to confirm the bargain.

Deal Locker

(deallocker.com)–This clean and simple site makes searching for coupons a breeze. They have an amazing tool called the Amazon Discount Finder which searches for items currently at 10%–99% off. You'll also find great free sample coupons in the Coupon Blog.

Dealnews

(dealnews.com)–The writers at dealnews do the very hard work of scouring the Web every day for only the best deals on the hottest items. Users can be assured that every deal has been verified and the retailers are reputable (they ban any store with a history of poor customer service). Unlike many other deals sites, their site is easy to navigate and use, which is a godsend for any deal-hound trying to get in and out quickly so they can catch the deal they want.

Deals

(deals.com)–With a slogan like "because paying retail is a crime," you can be sure that they take their deals seriously. A vibrant community votes for the hottest deals and their Quick Submit tool makes submitting deals just one click away.

Deals2buy

(deals2buy.com)–A clean and simple deals site that packs a punch without the clutter. If you are looking for a site with great deals but won't overwhelm you with hundreds of deals and links at once, Deals2buy is the place to go.

Deals of America

(dealsofamerica.com)–Presenting only hand-picked bargains from the most reputable American retailers, the staff is committed to providing every resource to help shoppers save money. They understand the uncertain credibility of many unknown online retailers, so they try to search bargains from big online retailers or stores with nationwide presence, so shoppers can feel safe and secure with their purchases.

DealsPlus
(dealspl.us)—A site that uses the power of social media to determine the best deals to feature. Members submit and vote for the best deals. You can be sure that only deals with member consensus show up on the homepage. Along with coupons, store specials, and freebies, you'll also find the Sunday circulars from any store that has one—an extremely useful feature to prepare for seasonal sales like Black Friday.

DealTaker
(dealtaker.com)—A deals site that doesn't just focus on tech bargains. Find discounts for clothes, toys, jewelry, and more. Their simple design makes the forums easy to navigate—no small favor for the rookie deal hound.

Ebates
(ebates.com)—A site that gives you money back for shopping. Most coupon and deals sites make money through commission. Ebates does, too, but they like to pass some of that back to you—the actual shopper. What better bargain can you get than that?

eCoupons
(ecoupons.com)—One of the largest online coupon Web sites that list more than 5,000 stores and tens of thousands of active coupons and deals. Members can earn cash back when making purchases with participating partner stores.

Entertainment Book
(entertainment.com)—Buy a book of coupons for your area for less than twenty bucks, and get coupons for restaurants, movie theaters, and shopping. You can get exclusive discounts on stuff you buy every week like movie rentals, pet supplies, books, office supplies, lunch, clothes, and a lot more. Get an Entertainment Book every year and make your money back in the first two months.

FatWallet
(fatwallet.com)—A robust forums community (fatwallet.com/forums) of dedicated bargain hunters. In addition to hot deals and coupons, FatWallet offers a variety of tools for reviews, price comparisons, and instant alerts. Their greatest unique feature is their cashback rewards program for shopping with hundreds of partner stores. Get money back for cashing in on a huge deal? It doesn't get any better than that.

Freecycle
(freecycle.org)—One man's trash is another man's treasure. Find your location and see if anyone is giving away something you need, and vice versa. What a great way to be green and frugal at the same time.

FreeShipping
(freeshipping.org)—One of the few drawbacks of online shopping—and the bane of a bargain hunter's existence—is to have a great deal spoiled by a shipping charge. FreeShipping saves the day by providing free shipping codes for over 800 vendors on the Internet.

Free Shipping On
(freeshippingon.com)—Get free shipping codes for hundreds of online stores. Their best tool is a rocking search engine to help you find items with free shipping on Amazon.com and eBay.com.

Got | Apex
(gotapex.com)—Not only do they have the latest deals on all the hot computers and accessories, they also have hardware and software reviews, how-to tutorials, and the latest industry news. It is a one-stop shop for computer fanatics.

GottaDeal
(gottadeal.com)—A very well-rounded site that offers deals for a variety of items (as opposed to mainly tech-focused). Their annual coverage of Black Friday deals is truly spectacular and an essential destination for any bargain shopper.

Hey, It's Free!
(heyitsfree.net)—Run by a team of eccentric characters, HIF lists only the best freebies on the Web. Who doesn't love getting something for nothing?

iStorez

(istorez.com)–Browse sales and deals from only the biggest brand names and retailers. Design your own mall so you only see offers from the stores and brands you like. It's the most efficient way to keep tabs on your favorite stores and window shop right from your desk.

Mpire

(mpire.com)–An innovative site that not only provides price comparisons for products sold at the largest retailers (including eBay), Mpire also has charts that show pricing trends. Maybe a product is in its "off-season" and many places are marking it down at a steal. Maybe it's still a hard-to-find item that a prudent shopper should hold off on purchasing right away. Mpire is an invaluable tool for any shopper.

MyGroceryDeals

(mygrocerydeals.com)–An extensive site that provides a comprehensive listing of the grocery deals in your area. The filter settings in your profile allow you to specify things like food allergies, preferred stores, and dietary considerations, so you'll get a customized list of only the most relevant items for you and your family.

NexTag

(nextag.com)–One of the top names in the industry, NexTag offers a comprehensive price comparison engine. There's a very useful Price History tool that shows a product's price and number-of-sellers history. Along with consumer products, NexTag also compares mortgage rates and travel deals.

Online-Sweepstakes

(online-sweepstakes.com)-Lists thousands of available sweepstakes and contests with an easy to navigate design, useful sorting options, and a robust forums community. They also offer a very affordable premium membership which allows access to exclusive listings and tools that make entering easier and winning more likely.

PriceGrabber

(pricegrabber.com)–An extremely popular site, and for good reason. This place has it all: a superb comparison shopping engine, comprehensive product reviews, the hottest deals, and even "storefronts" to sell your own items.

Prices and Coupons

(pricesandcoupons.com)–A relatively new site that is attempting to bridge the gap between price comparison and coupon codes. Most price comparison engines don't take into account separate store coupons that can be applied to a product. The search engine on Prices and Coupons does exactly that. Bargain hunting just got one step easier.

Prizey

(prizey.net)–A site that features great giveaways from small sites and companies that get lost in the larger sweepstakes directories. The giveaways listed here are typically run by blogs and small businesses, mostly targeting parents and families.

ResellerRatings

(resellerratings.com)–The Internet is full of small and obscure vendors. Some of them have terrific customer service and high quality products. Others are less scrupulous. ResellerRatings is *the* place to go before placing that order with Boondocks, Inc.

RetailMeNot

(retailmenot.com)–A leading consumer destination for online coupons, discounts, and promotional codes for merchandise, travel, and services, RetailMeNot is committed to helping consumers enjoy a hassle-free shopping experience. Members rank coupons based on their reliability. Tools, widgets, and a Firefox extension are available for quick and easy access to your coupons. Their people-powered price comparison engine, Beat My Price (beatmyprice.com), allows you to enter the deal you've found to see whether it truly is the best available.

Shop It To Me

(shopittome.com)–Rather than scour through all the deals on the Web, create your own wish list of items and wait for a bargain to appear. Select your size, brand, and other preferences, and you'll get notified if there's a relevant sale. It's like having your own personal shopper!

Shopping

(shopping.com)–A pioneer of online comparison shopping, shopping.com has become one of the largest shopping destinations on the Web. Shopping.com offers price comparison for thousands of merchants on the world's largest product catalog, plus millions of unbiased product and merchant reviews, all in one place. There's no simpler way to find the right product at the right price and from the right merchant.

Shopzilla

(shopzilla.com)–A leading comparison shopping service that allows users to compare prices offered by different stores on one screen. Any serious bargain hunter should stop here to check for the best possible price on the product they are looking to buy.

SlickDeals

(slickdeals.net)–One of the more popular deal sites around today. The homepage displays only the hottest deals, but the true action happens in their forums (forums.slickdeals.net), where the community reigns. You won't be wading through an ocean of not-so-slick deals because the community takes care of those for you. You can always get the inside scoop on the most current deals. In addition, their shopping tools, feeds, and alerts ensure that you won't miss a single sale.

Spoofee

(spoofee.com)–A fun, quirky site that features a wide range of deals across different categories. Deals are ranked by the community and you can follow the wild antics of the owner in the blog section.

Sweepstakes Advantage

(sweepsadvantage.com)–Their extensive sweepstakes listing includes cash sweepstakes, free giveaways, online freebies, instant win sweepstakes, writing and photo contests, and much more. Browse the sweepstakes listings by category, prize, or destination and track the sweepstakes you've entered with their free My Sweepstakes feature.

Techbargains

(techbargains.com)–An essential stop for any technology purchase, they not only provide deals, coupons, and the latest bargain news, but they also have a variety of helpful shopping tools. Their search engine includes eBay sales—a useful feature. Read their "Hot Tip" articles for important shopping advice. Review their recommended products database for items you should consider buying. Get rebate and vendor information for no-fuss execution.

Trezr

(trezr.com)–Their motto is "share the wealth," and they certainly follow through. Not only are the deals and coupons submitted by users great finds, but advertising and affiliate revenue generated by the site are also shared with users. Innovative, fun, and profitable, their groundbreaking model is sure to be a crowd pleaser.

Valpak

(valpak.com)–Everyone is familiar with the thick Valpak envelope of coupons that arrive in the mail. Now you can get instant access to all coupons currently available for your area. This is hands down the best place to get coupons for local services like dry cleaning, auto repair, and restaurants.

JOB & CAREER RESOURCES

Elance

(elance.com)–By far the largest marketplace of freelancers and freelance employers. You can get freelance gigs ranging from programming, design, writing, virtual assistant, Internet research, and more. Elance's success as a marketplace is due to its escrow service, provider rating system, and global reach.

Indeed

(indeed.com)–Most comprehensive job listings aggregator and search engine. Indeed.com grabs job listings from all over the Internet and puts them in one place. You can search by job title and location.

Problogger Job Board

(jobs.problogger.net)–Premier job board for professional blogging gigs run by uber-problogger, Darren Rowse. If you want to find a blogging job, this is the only stop you need.

Sparkplugging

(sparkplugging.com)–Resources for and community of entrepreneurs, freelancers, consultants, authors, work-at-home moms and dads, and other independent workers. Founder Wendy Piersall's passion for helping work-at-home folks and solo business owners really shines through on the site.

Work at Home Success

(workathomesuccess.com)–The most comprehensive site for people looking to work at home. WAHS has getting-started guides, where to find work-at-home job listings, and a community of other work-at-home folks sharing tips and tricks. WAHS gives you the tools and know-how to earn a side income from home or to start your new work-at-home career.

PERSONAL FINANCE AUTHORS

Leo Babauta

(zenhabits.net)–Leo is the author of Zen Habits, one of the top 100 blogs in the world and one of the best resources for useful articles on productivity, simplicity, and personal finances. Leo's new book, *The Power of Less*, is a powerful tool that will help you strip away the petty distractions so you can enjoy a happier, simpler life. You can download a free copy of Leo's ebook, *Thriving On Less*, at tinyurl.com/thriving-on-less.

Tim Ferriss

(fourhourworkweek.com)–The first time I finished reading *The 4-Hour Workweek* I immediately bought a bunch of copies for my closest friends. Although I haven't cut down my workweek to four hours just yet, many of Tim's best ideas—sticking to your strengths, outsourcing mindless work, and exploring cheaper living arrangements—have made a tremendously positive impact on my life.

Jonathan Fields

(jonathanfields.com)–Jonathan made a seemingly impossible career transformation from a tired attorney to a happy entrepreneur who can't wait to get out of bed every morning. In his book *Career Renegade*, Jonathan shares his secret of how

you can escape an unhappy career. Filled with actionable advice, *Career Renegade* is as helpful as it is inspiring. If you're not 100% happy with your job, you'd be crazy not to read this book.

Trent Hamm

(thesimpledollar.com)–Trent Hamm is the author of *365 Ways to Live Cheap* and editor of *1001 Ways to Make Money If You Dare*. His book is filled with great DIY and frugality tips, such as using cold water to wash most clothes to save $63 a year, minimizing your carload to reduce your gas mileage by 5%, and buying a deep freezer to save 30% off meat. Trent's blog, The Simple Dollar is the most respected personal finance voice in the blogosphere.

Ellie Kay

(tinyurl.com/ellie-kay)–Ellie went from having a $40,000 consumer debt to being completely debt-free in less than three years. She did this as a mother of seven, living off one military income. Her latest book, *Living Rich for Less,* shows readers how to put more than $30,000 into their pockets per year. Easily one of the most likable financial experts, Ellie is destined to be a superstar in the financial field.

Carrie McCarthy and Danielle LaPorte

(carrieanddanielle.com)–Carrie & Danielle's book, *Style Statement: Live By Your Own Design,* will help you make authentic choices, from your personal style to your relationships. While it is not a personal finance book in the traditional sense, by helping you get in touch with your authentic self, Carrie and Danielle's advice will guide you to a more honest life filled with growth and happiness instead of mindless consumerism.

David Loeper

(tinyurl.com/david-loeper)–David is the most popular guest contributor we've ever had on Wise Bread. His latest book, *Stop the Retirement Rip-off: How to Avoid Hidden Fees and Keep More of Your Money*, is a must-read for anyone who is serious about saving for their retirement. With over twenty-three years of experience as an investment adviser, David knows all the traps his less scrupulous colleagues use to siphon money away from your precious retirement accounts. By following his advice, you may be able to add more than $100,000 to your nest egg.

Suze Orman

(suzeorman.com)–Suze is like that tough teacher you once hated in high school but now remember with fondness because of how much you learned from her. Wise Bread readers constantly share how Suze changes lives for the better. If we can ask only one personal finance expert for help, we'd use our final lifeline on Suze.

Sharon Harvey Rosenberg

(frugalduchess.com)–An award-winning journalist, Sharon writes a popular frugal living column for the *Miami Herald* called "The Frugal Duchess" and a blog by the same name. Her book, *The Frugal Duchess: How to Live Well and Save Money,* is a treasure trove of tips on how to live the high life without paying the high price. Engaging and humorous, Sharon's book is worth buying for the entertainment value alone.

Gretchen Rubin

(happiness-project.com)–Can money buy happiness? No one has given this question more thought than Gretchen, who spent an entire year of her life contemplating the nature of happiness. *The Happiness Project* chronicles the year she spent test-driving every principle, tip, theory, and scientific study she could find, whether from Aristotle or St. Therese, Martin Seligman or Oprah. She explains these rules for living and reports on what works and what doesn't in a series of profound and fascinating articles that will blow you away.

Ramit Sethi

(iwillteachyoutoberich.com)–One of the first personal finance bloggers to become a media superstar, Ramit Sethi's new book, *I Will Teach You To Be Rich,* offers twenty to thirty-five-year-olds a completely practical approach to personal finance delivered with a nonjudgmental style. Smart, witty, and completely approachable, Ramit is considered by many as one of the best financial voices of his generation.

Carolyn Wilman

(contestqueen.com)–Canada's self-proclaimed contest queen, Carolyn fills out 50,000 contest ballots a year and has won more than $100,000 worth of prizes over the past five years. Her self-published book, *You Can't Win If You Don't Enter,* **is** the first Internet-focused contest resource book in Canada, and includes time saving tips and tools of the trade that is indispensable for any would-be contest queen (or king).

Jeff Yeager

(ultimatecheapskate.com)–Jeff writes at a homemade desk in an office furnished with thrift store treasures. When he goes on a book tour, he couchsurfs with friends and lives off supermarket samples. He is by far the funniest (and craziest) frugal guru out there. His book, *Ultimate Cheapskate's Road Map To True Riches,* elevates frugal living to an art form. You'll be so busy laughing out loud at Jeff's exploits that you'll barely notice how much money he is dropping into your wallet.

BEST PERSONAL FINANCE BLOGS

All Financial Matters

(allfinancialmatters.com)–Named by *Money Magazine* as the "most sensible" personal finance blog online, All Financial Matters features the prudent advice of Jeffrey Pritchard, a financial planner from Beaumont, Texas. He doesn't chase trends or offer sensational headlines—just comforting, solid advice that has withstood the test of time.

Alpha Consumer

(usnews.com/alpha)–Kimberly Palmer's Alpha Consumer delivers expert consumer advice in an engaging and entertaining format. Not only does she offer useful tips on how to be a savvy shopper, but Kimberly's posts are also bursting with fun facts you can use to entertain people at cocktail parties. If you've been avoiding personal finance blogs because you think they are dry and boring, Kimberly will change your mind.

Bargain Babe

(bargainbabe.com)–What do you get when you combine an award-winning journalist and a cheapskate? The most informative and dogged bargain hunter, of course! Julia Scott promises to bring you the best bargains without ever accepting money from businesses to blog about their products. While Julia is great at tracking deals all over the world, she has a special knack for finding terrific bargains in Southern California.

Bargaineering

(bargaineering.com)–Jim's a twenty-something recent university grad who entered the "real world" and found that college life was a lot more fun and a lot less stressful. Jim claims he is only a "personal finance novice struggling to understand some pretty complex and confusing topics." But he is just being modest, as Jim is one of the nicest and most informative personal finance bloggers. After reading a couple of his posts you can't help but root for him to succeed.

Consumerism Commentary

(consumerismcommentary.com)–This informative group blog was honored by Kiplinger as a "must-read" blog and named as one of Yahoo!'s "Ten Money Blogs Everyone Should Read." Flexo created Consumerism Commentary in 2003 to hold himself accountable for his finances: "My plan was to regularly publish my account balances and spending information so I could publicly track them over time and perhaps gain support from readers."

Consumerist

(consumerist.com)–*The Consumerist* empowers consumers to fight back by informing them about the top consumer issues of the day. Editor Ben Popken and his crack team of reporters have exposed countless corporate scams. These guys are not afraid to jump into the fray to browbeat and ridicule corporations until they make things right for the little guys. This is one of the few Web sites I check several times a day, and its great content usually leaves me pumping my fist in the air or laughing my head off.

Dumb Little Man

(dumblittleman.com)–There's nothing dumb or exclusively male about Jay White's ultra-helpful productivity blog. Possibly the best-named blog in the world, Jay's success is the result of his mer-

ciless focus on his core mission: to provide you with tips that will save you money, increase your productivity, or simply keep you sane. And boy, does he deliver. There are no filler posts, product placements, or political grandstanding. Just all great tips, all the time.

Elevenmoms

(walmart.com/elevenmoms) Elevenmoms is a tight-knit community of talented bloggers assembled by Wal-Mart. Think of them as superheroines with a license to help you defeat wasteful spending and unhealthy lifestyles. The members include Heather Batts of TheDomesticDiva.org, Amy Clark of MomAdvice.com, Jenn Fowler of FrugalUpstate.blogspot.com, Alyssa Francis of KingdomFirstMom.com, Tara Kuczykowski of DealSeekingMom.com, Erin Gifford of CouponCravings.com, Lynnae McCoy of BeingFrugal.net, Colleen Padilla of ClassyMommy.com, Lucretia Pruitt of GeekMommy.net, Denise Sawyer of TheCentsibleWawyer.blogspot.com, Christine Young of FromDatesToDiapers.com, Jennae Petersen of GreenYourDecor.com, Katja Presnal of SkimbacoLifestyle.com, Monica Brady of MommyBrainReports.com, Lori Falcon of ACowboysWife.com, Mercedes Levy of CommonsenseWithMoney.com, Linsey Knerl of WiseBread.com, Melissa Garcia of ConsumerQueen.com, Arianne Segerman of ToThinkistoCreate.com, Merlene Paynter of Frugalous.com, and Sheena Williams of MommyDaddyblog.com.

Finance for a Freelance Life

(mrsmicah.com)–Mrs. Micah is the unofficial welcome wagon of the personal finance blogosphere. Generous with her praise and good humor, Mrs. Micah leaves a positive impact on every blog or forum she visits.

Five Cent Nickel

(fivecentnickel.com)–Written by a man who has been meticulously recording his finances since 1997 (stored in Quicken), Five Cent Nickel is one of the oldest and most respected blogs around. This blog often provides great commentary on—and summaries of—useful financial tips featured by other publications. If you're too lazy to read every little money article out there, just stop by Five Cent Nickel and get the cream of the crop.

Free Money Finance

(freemoneyfinance.com)–This blog has one of the best background stories ever: "Through the years, I've done the things I've talked about here at Free Money Finance—spent less than I've earned, paid off all my debt, managed my career, invested regularly and the like. During that time, my net worth has grown and grown, allowing my family to be in the upper percentages of wealth in the U.S. I'm not writing about topics I've read about one time and regurgitated with opinions based on nothing—I have lived these topics, applied these principles, and know what works and what doesn't." Can you resist following this blog after reading that description?

Gen X Finance

(genxfinance.com)–No blogger has better credentials than Jeremy of Gen X Finance. A licensed retirement planning specialist, Jeremy is also the financial planning guide for About.com—a site that gets 38 million unique visitors a month. Thorough and intelligent, Jeremy is one of the best assets you can add to your RSS reader.

Get Rich Slowly

(getrichslowly.org)–Named most inspiring money blog by *Money Magazine*, JD Roth's Get Rich Slowly is by far one of the best personal finance blogs we've ever read. True to its name, this blog provides detailed and methodical step-by-step guides to every personal finance problem you face in your life. When JD reviews a product or service, it is usually the most comprehensive and helpful review you'll find anywhere.

Lazy Man and Money

(lazymanandmoney.com)–If you're a fan of getting the maximum return for a minimum amount of effort, this is the blog for you. While targeted at lazy people (we prefer "motivationally challenged," thank you), the blogger himself is anything but lazy. His writing is crisp and his advice superb.

Lifehack

(lifehack.org)–The list of Lifehack's writers is a virtual who's who of the best productivity bloggers in the world. Almost every popular blogger has featured an article or two on this great blog. Of course, I'm especially partial to articles by Thursday Bram and Torley Wong, who also write for Wise Bread.

Lifehacker

(lifehacker.com)–Simply the best productivity blog. Period. This award-winning blog features tips, shortcuts, and downloads that help you get things done smarter and more efficiently. While Lifehacker has a slight tech slant, it provides incredible tips from all over the Web on almost every topic. If there's a great tip out there about how to simplify your life, you'll find it on Lifehacker. I love how the amazing writers of Lifehacker always give their tips in plain English without any unnecessary tech babble. This is truly a productivity blog anyone can benefit from.

LifeRemix

(liferemix.net)–The brainchild of Brett Kelly and Glen Stansberry, the LifeRemix blog network is an exceptional resource for self-improvement. You will find an incredible amount of useful tips here, including how to be a man in the modern age (artofmanliness.com), productivity advice for creative people (behance.com), insanely helpful freelancing resources (freelanceswitch.com), inspired ideas for hacking IKEA furniture (ikeahacker.blogspot.com), brilliant tips for living smarter (pickthebrain.com), industrial strength productivity advice (crankingwidgets.com), how to design a better life (lifeclever.com), advice for home-based entrepreneurs (successfromthenest.com), spectacular tech reviews (productivity501.com), advice for living a more creative life (thinksimplenow.com), and, of course, how to get things done (lifedev.net).

Mighty Bargain Hunter

(mightybargainhunter.com)–Written by a father in his mid-thirties with a wonderful wife and a beautiful daughter, the Mighty Bargain Hunter provides solid tips about saving money and finding deals. He analyzes complex financial deals in layman's terms and often brings a fresh perspective that other experts fail to consider.

Money Blue Book

(moneybluebook.com)–Ray from Money Blue Book is probably one of the most talented bloggers out there. Not only does he have a bachelor's degree in finance and a law degree, Ray is also quite knowledgeable about everything related to computers and the Internet. I consider Money Blue Book the "thinking man's guide" to personal finance.

MyMoneyBlog

(mymoneyblog.com)–Named by *Money Magazine* as the most voyeuristic financial blog, MyMoneyBlog is written by a thirty-year-old IT engineer who is brutally honest about his financial successes and failures. One of the most analytical and informative blogs, MyMoneyBlog is where I go for the most technically sound personal finance tips.

No Credit Needed

(ncnblog.com)–Check out the Debt Reduction E-Book section to get a great step-by-step guide on how to pay off your debt and live debt-free. If you'd like to share your own financial journey, try the No Credit Needed Network widget (ncnnetwork.com), which allows you to publish a snapshot of your latest financial standings. It's the perfect tool for bloggers who want to be held publicly accountable for their debt reduction.

No Impact Man

(noimpactman.typepad.com)–No Impact Man chronicles Colin Beavan's daring experiment of getting his family to live in the heart of New York City for one year without causing any net environmental impact. In other words: no electricity, cars, or even toilet paper! It is an incredible story that will keep you entertained and inspired to make a few green choices in your own life.

Smart Spending

(blogs.moneycentral.msn.com/smartspending)–Karen Datko and Donna Freedman are two of the warmest and most talented frugal living bloggers you'll ever encounter online. When reading their articles, you feel like you're sharing a conversation with a couple of old friends. The Smart Spending blog is also famous for frequently featuring talented new bloggers. If you are new to personal finance blogs, this is the first place you should visit.

Stop Buying Crap

(stopbuyingcrap.com)–This is one of the funniest finance blogs out there. Here's a sample: "One morning I woke up and realized I've amassed over $10,000 in credit cards debt—and I wasn't even of legal drinking age yet. Not cool. Thankfully, I got rid of the debt after a year of being less of a moron. If you can handle poorly written post with equally poor grammar, then I implore you to subscribe to the blog. Doing so guarantees you to two worthwhile post per year."

Unclutterer

(unclutterer.com)–The Unclutterer is a godsend for anyone who desperately needs more organization, efficiency, and Zen in their lives. Fully stocked with simple yet exceptional tips, The Unclutterer (and the book by the same name) is a life-changing resource.

MORE GREAT RESOURCES

1-800-Free411

(free411.com)–There is zero reason for you to pay for 411 services when Free411 is around. The voice recognition is snappy and the information is just as accurate as your phone company's.

360 Financial Literacy

(360financialliteracy.org)–Get free, unparalleled expert guidance for every stage of your financial life from the prestigious American Institute of Certified Public Accountants.

Angel Food Ministries

(angelfoodministries.com)–A non-profit co-op that sells prepackaged groceries at unbeatable prices. You can feed a family of four for one week on $30! A wonderful idea for busy families and starving students.

Certified Financial Planner Board of Standards

(cfp.net)–The Certified Financial Planner (CFP) is the gold standard of financial planning certifications. The C.F.P designation ensures that you're getting an expert with the highest ethical and professional standards.

Gazelle

(gazelle.com)–Sell your old or unwanted electronics for cold hard cash. Gazelle will buy your cell phones, digital cameras, gaming systems, and other gadgets. Avoid the hassle of selling it yourself and make sure you get a fair price for your old gear.

Lease Trader

(leasetrader.com)–The biggest marketplace for dumping or taking over a car lease. You save money by getting cheaper and shorter leases than what dealerships offer. On the flip side, you can get out of your lease without paying hefty fines.

National Foundation for Credit Counseling

(nfcc.org)–The NFCC is the largest and longest serving nonprofit credit counseling organization. NFCC certification is one of the first things you should look for in a credit counselor. Recently, the NFCC partnered up with MSN Money to provide an invaluable online Q&A service, which you can find at tinyurl.com/nfcc-msn.

Springpad

(springpadit.com)–This awesome app is like Google Notebook on steroids. It helps simplify your life with free online notebooks to organize, share, and tackle life's tasks and projects. Springpad automates access to the Web's most popular transactional services and makes it easy to interact and personalize useful advice from bloggers and online publishers. Think of it as the ultimate cheat sheet and to-do list all rolled into one.

Trusted ID

(trustedid.com)–I started following this company after reading the high praise it received from Tech Crunch's Michael Arrington: "I recommend everyone in the U.S. [to] strongly consider using this service". No wonder; the company's co-founder was formerly the vice president at Fair Isaac, creator of the FICO score. Who better to help you protect your credit score than a FICO expert?

Use Credit Wisely

(usecreditwisely.com)–This educational program sponsored by Visa offers a wide range of useful tools that will help you use credit wisely. There are several helpful sections dedicated to specific groups, such as women (womenandco.com), college students (students.usecreditwisely.com), Spanish-speaking consumers (cuidatucredito.com), and small business owners (business.usecreditwisely.com).

Zilok

(zilok.com)–Weird name but incredibly cool concept, Zilok is a marketplace to rent your stuff out (or rent someone else's stuff for a day). For owners, get more out of your purchases by renting them out. Just a few rentals could pay for the item! For renters, you can save money by renting, instead of buying, seldom used items. Everything from canoes, laptops, cameras, cars, books, baby strollers, and everything in between is available for rent from someone near you.

— **Greg Go, Lynn Truong, and Will Chen**

This is just the tip of the iceberg. The list continues on WiseBread.com—our huge treasure trove of ideas on how to live large on a small budget. Our writers are adding great new tips here everyday. Join the fun and watch your savings add up. Enjoy!

$$$$

Acknowl-edgements

We've always suspected that authors use the acknowledgements section as a frugal way to thank people without actually buying them any gifts.

Now that we've actually put together our first book, we realize authors love shouting their appreciation because no book is possible without the generous support of so many incredible people.

Our editor Ann Treistman has earned our undying gratitude for believing in our book from the very beginning and providing us with unwavering support throughout the entire process. We absolutely loved working with the talented folks at Skyhorse Publishing—Tony Lyons,

Bill Wolfsthal, Abigail Gehring, Kathleen Go, and LeAnna Weller Smith—let's do another dozen books together! A huge thanks goes to our wonderful agent Stacey Glick and her crew at Dystel & Goderich. Your patience, intelligence, and guidance helped make this book possible.

First-time authors need lots of handholding, and we received plenty of it from veteran writers such as Jonathan Fields, Jeff Yeager, Leo Babauta, Scott Fox, Trent Hamm, Ramit Sethi, Darren

Rowse, Sharon "The Frugal Duchess" Rosenberg, David Loeper, and Mary Webber. If you ever need an excuse to buy a new book instead of using the library, these authors are worth every penny.

Our online community owes much of its modest success to the early exposure we received from top bloggers like Donna Freedman and Karen Datko of MSN Money Central; J.D. Roth from Get Rich Slowly; Kimberly Palmer of U.S. News & World Report; Jeremy Vohwinkle of About.com; Ben Popken, Meghann Marco, Chris Walters, Carey Greenberg-Berger, Alex Jarvis and their team of savvy curmudgeons at the Consumerist; Gina Trapani, Wendy Boswell, Adam Pash, Kevin Purdy, Jason Fitzpatrick, Asian Angel, Infmom, and their team of busy beavers at Lifehacker; Glen Stansberry, Brett Kelly, and the LifeRemix Network; John Nardini and the Money Blog Network; and John Wesley and the Positive Blog Network.

Attending Rita Arens's inspiring "Blog to Book" session at the BlogHer08 conference gave us the confidence to pursue a book deal. Thank you Rita, Elisa Camahort Page, Jenny Lauck, Elana Centor, and all the great ladies of BlogH-

er, for giving us the confidence to transform our dreams into reality.

We are deeply grateful for the wonderful support from the Elevenmoms family. Every email, chat, and meetup we share reminds us of your enormous talent and unlimited generosity. Special thanks go to John Andrews of Wal-Mart for bringing us together, and to Melinda Osborn, Melanie Hartman, and Jessica Simmons from Rockfish Interactive for showing us so many unique ways to spread our frugal living message.

We tip our hats to Muhammad Saleem for sharing his awesome marketing tips. Along the same lines, we also thank Nicole Glor and Megan Esteves from Regan Communications for showering us with brilliant ideas. Much appreciation goes to legal beagles Cyndi Wong, Howard Zaharoff, Schuyler Moore, and Lee Roudnicki for saving us from our stupid ideas. And we can't forget to salute Heather Tang, because we promised we would

This book wouldn't exist without the tireless editing efforts of Linsey Knerl and Myscha Theriault. Thank you for giving up so many nights and weekends to make this book a success.

Author Bios

Leo Babauta

Leo is the author of *The Power of Less* and the productivity blog zenhabits.net, one of the top 100 most popular blogs in the world. He is considered by many as one of the leading experts on simple living and productivity. A former journalist and freelance writer for eighteen years, Leo is a husband and father of six children and lives on the island of Guam where he leads a very simple life.

. . . .

Thursday Bram

Thursday's freelance writing career led her directly to frugality: managing a less than stable income has given her plenty of chances to learn about managing her money. She also writes about personal finance and small business topics all over the web, including investopedia.com, lifehack.org, and more. Thursday blogs about the business of freelance writing at thursdaybram.com.

. . . .

Will Chen

Will is the marketing director for wisebread.com, a thriving community of talented writers and savvy consumers. A well-respected social media consultant, Will is a top-ten Digg contributor and an active member of several popular blog networks. His writings and insight have been featured on CNN, Forbes, *USA Today*, Fox News, *Newsweek*, *Houston Chronicle*, and about. Com, among others.

. . . .

David DeFranza

David is the producer of the Discovery channel's planetgreen.com. He has spent months at a time wandering around remote corners of the world, living off paltry savings extended by a dedication to frugality. When he is not traveling, David spends his time in Washington, D.C., hoarding his pennies and dreaming of his next adventure. He writes about travel and frugal living, sharing tips and

experiences that help make the dream a reality.

. . . .

Andrea Dickson

Andrea is a writer based in Seattle, Washington. Andrea graduated from Mount Holyoke College with a Bachelor of Arts in Chinese Studies, so becoming a writer was sort of an accident. She *should* be working in import/export (according to her father). Andrea enjoys discovering and writing about little-known facts about everyday things. Her general laziness provides her with the impetus to seek out money-saving tips that require minimal effort.

. . . .

Nora Dunn

Nora is a professional

hobo and international freelance writer, having traveled the world full-time since 2007, and continuing to enjoy life with no fixed address. With a background as a certified financial planner, she enjoys preparing for tomorrow, but not at the expense of realizing her dreams today. You can learn more about her whereabouts and latest adventures at theprofessionalhobo.com.

·········

Margaret Garcia-Couoh

Margaret is a writer/ mother/ professor who lives in the northern Sierra Mountains with her husband, two kids, and cats. A dedicated telecommuter, she comes off the mountain only for Thai food, thrift stores, and Japanese stationary. You can follow her exploits at her blog, Tales of a Sierra Madre (writerchick-mama.blogspot.com).

·········

Greg Go

Greg quit his cushy corporate job to pursue his entrepreneurial dreams full-time in 2006. As technology director of wisebread. com he uses the site daily to keep his financial house in order. Greg also helps others make a living off the internet as the about. com guide to online business (onlinebusiness.about.com). He loves to work in pajamas from his home in Los Angeles.

·········

Trent Hamm

Trent is the author of the book *365 Ways to Live Cheap* and editor of *1001*

Ways to Make Money if You Dare. He writes daily articles about frugality and money management at thesimpledollar.com. Trent lives in rural Iowa with his wife and two children.

·········

Carrie Kirby

Carrie embraced the frugal life when she left her job as a reporter at the *San Francisco Chronicle* to become a stay-at-home mother and freelance writer. She specializes in jaw-dropping grocery deals and working drugstore rewards programs, and writes about her exploits at shopliftingwith permission.com. Her work has also appeared in *Cookie*, *Parenting*, and *Wired*.

·········

J.D. Roth

J.D. is an average guy who found himself with over $35,000 in consumer debt. Using the timeless principles of smart money management, he turned his life around. Three years later, he was debt-free and writing one of the most popular personal-finance sites on the internet:

getrichslowly.org, which was named "most inspiring money blog" by *Money* magazine.

·········

The Digerati Life

The Digerati Life is a mom of two with a background in software engineering and development, who is currently self-employed in the realm of web publishing. She runs several popular websites, including thedigeratilife. com and thesmarterwallet. com, which focus on general personal finance, investing, small business, debt management, and consumer issues.

·········

Xin Lu

Xin graduated from the University of California, Berkeley in 2005 with a Bachelor of Science in electrical engineering and computer science. She works as a software release engineer in the Silicon Valley and writes about personal finance and the world in her spare time. She lives with her husband in Redwood City, California.

·········

Paul Michael

Born and raised in England, and now living in Colorado, Paul is a professional advertising copywriter with a degree in visual communication. His inside knowledge of marketing has helped him create a better life for his wife Nicole and their two girls. If there are deals around, he'll find them.

. . . .

Sarah Winfrey

Sarah winfrey comes to freelance writing with a background in spiritual formation. She loves playing with words and writes about everything, though she prefers spirituality, relationships, and personal finance. You can find her in her cheap, fabulous apartment with her husband in Whittier, California or on the web at sarahwinfrey.com.

. . . .

Sharon Harvey Rosenberg

Sharon, an award-winning journalist and blogger, writes the *Miami Herald's* weekly "frugal duchess" column, and regularly in other newspapers. She also writes the daily Frugal duchess blog (sharonhr.blogspot.com), which is one of the top-ranked frugal-living, personal finance blogs. Her work has been mentioned in *People*, *Black Enterprise* and the

Wall Street Journal online. In 2008, she published *The Frugal Duchess: How to Live Well and Save Money*.

. . . .

Lynn Truong

Lynn Truong is the managing editor of wisebread.com and dedicated to its motto of "living large on a small budget." Her passion for writing and her entrepreneurial spirit inspired her to leave her job at CBS/King World to make her mark in the blogosphere. Lynn has spoken at Blogher and Blog World Expo conventions to share her expertise in online publishing.

. . . .

Linsey Knerl

Born and raised in a small Nebraska town, Linsey has experienced firsthand just how complicated the "simple life" can be. Staying within budget isn't just a desire for her rural family, it is a survival skill that she acquired early on and loves sharing with her readers. Linsey's savvy tips can be found on Wal-Mart's Elevenmoms community, Wise Bread's official radio show, and in various publications like the *New York Times*, *Christian Science Monitor*, and the *Seattle Times*.

. . . .

Myscha Theriault

Born and raised in Maine, Myscha has a bachelor's degree in elementary education and spent much of her teaching career overseas before launching the education web site, thelessonmachine.com. She and her husband used savvy personal finance strategies to start their own business, live debt-free, and travel the world. Myscha writes extensively about travel, education, personal finance, food, spirits, and wine. Her articles and advice have been featured by wall street journal online, *USA Today*, and the *Miami Herald*.

. . . .

Julie Rains

Julie holds a Bachelor of Science in business administration and a certificate in technology and communication from the University of North Carolina at Chapel Hill. She is an experienced business writer and a certified professional résumé writer. Her work appears in the career-services books *Expert Résumés for Military-to-Civilian Transitions*, *No-nonsense Cover Letters*, and *Résumés for the Rest of Us: Secrets From the Pros for Jobseekers with Unconventional Career Paths*.

. . . .

$$$$

Index